Contents

01	Inside or outside?	4
Revision Unit 1		12
02	Making it happen	14
Revision Unit 2		22
03	True story?	24
Revision Unit 3		32
04	Things they don't teach you	34
Revision Unit 4		42
05	Green world	44
Revision Unit 5		52
06	Before time	54
Revision Unit 6		62
07	The feel-good factor	64
Revision Unit 7		72
08	Magic numbers	74
Revision Unit 8		82
09	All change	84
Revision Unit 9		92
10	Inspiration	94
Revision Unit 10		102
11	The art of make-believe	104
Revision Unit 11		112
12	Find your voice	114
Revision Unit 12		122

Gold
EXPERIENCE

B1+

Pre-First for Schools

Workbook

Sheila Dignen

Inside or outside?

READING

1 Read the article about four young people. Choose the correct answer, A, B or C.

1 Marta is studying to become a vet.
 A True
 B False (circled)
 C Not given

2 Marta has her own horses.
 A True
 B False
 C Not given

3 Connor likes the same work as his father.
 A True
 B False
 C Not given

4 A landscape gardener does lots of different jobs in a garden.
 A True
 B False
 C Not given

5 Marie doesn't like the litter in the streets of the town.
 A True
 B False
 C Not given

6 Marie cleans up rubbish at weekends all through the year.
 A True
 B False
 C Not given

7 Leo gets up later when it's cold or rainy.
 A True
 B False
 C Not given

8 Old trees sometimes fall during bad storms.
 A True
 B False
 C Not given

2 Read the article again. Choose the correct person, A, B, C or D.

Who:
1 gets paid while learning about a job? _B_
2 is interested in a job that is not well-known? ____
3 plans to do a job connected with where he/she lives? ____
4 doesn't like the results of bad weather? ____
5 does a job that is physically demanding? ____
6 doesn't worry about irregular working hours? ____
7 does work that is not organised by someone else? ____
8 enjoys things about life in the town and the countryside? ____

3 Find words or phrases in the article with the following meanings.

1 a strong liking for something
 (a) passion
2 worth doing
 ____
3 concentrate on a particular area of work
 ____
4 being free
 ____
5 strong and able to deal with difficult situations
 ____
6 making you feel pleased and happy
 ____
7 someone who looks after a forest
 ____
8 existing only in small numbers
 ____

Inside or outside?

OUT AND ABOUT

A MARTA Marta Reed has a passion. She adores animals and wants to spend her working life looking after them. She lives on a farm with her parents and two sisters and already knows nearly everything there is to know about horses, cows, pigs and sheep! However, Marta is only fifteen so she has to wait for a while before she can start studying to be an animal doctor – a vet. But she's getting some practice. Every weekend she helps out at the local animal hospital as an assistant. Sometimes she goes with the vet to visit sick animals on farms too. 'I love it,' says Marta. 'I know it's hard work. Vets have lots of early starts and sometimes work long hours, but it's a rewarding job. I want to specialise in big animals like horses and cows.' We think Marta would be a perfect vet. She's caring and reliable and she loves animals. What else do you need?

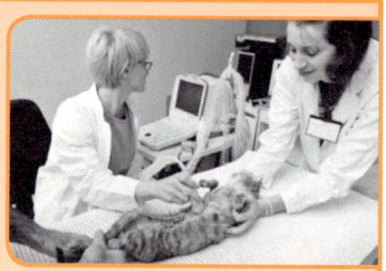

B CONNOR Connor can't stand being inside! 'I like the freedom of being out in the fresh air. Wind and rain, that's OK with me, but four walls make me feel like I'm in prison,' he says. Connor is making plans to have a career like his father. He wants to be a landscape gardener. 'That's not just someone who plants flowers and cuts the grass,' he laughs. 'I want to design beautiful gardens for people. They might be big or they might be small – it doesn't matter.' In his holidays, Connor works with his dad and he earns some money too. He can already build walls and fences and is learning more about growing plants and trees every day. It's often dirty work because he does a lot of digging. Also he needs to be tough as his dad gives him all the heavy jobs! But it's good preparation for the future.

C MARIE Marie lives in the town centre. She enjoys living there because there's a lot for her and her friends to do, but every weekend she escapes to the countryside on her bike. She goes on long rides through the forest and along the nearby beaches. She loves these rides, but something makes her very angry: it's the rubbish that visitors to the beach and the countryside leave behind them. 'Every Saturday and Sunday in the summer, the beach is covered with plastic bags and empty bottles. It's horrible,' she says. So, Marie started a group to help clear up the rubbish. During the summer holidays, she and some friends pick up rubbish and put it in big bags for collection. They don't get paid but it's satisfying work. And now Marie knows what she wants to do in the future. She wants to learn about the problems that affect the countryside and help to solve them. That's certainly a good start!

D LEO It's a very cold Saturday morning but teenager Leo is not warm in bed, he's out in the forest near his home. He's with a group of girls and boys who want to be foresters in the future. So, what is a forester? 'Well,' says Leo. 'We all go for walks in the forest but many of us don't know that there are people whose job is to look after the trees and the animals that live there. That's what I want to do.' Foresters control the forests and protect rare plants and animals. It's important and Leo thinks it's the best job in the world. On Saturday mornings, he and his group watch foresters at work so that they can learn about the job. Leo doesn't mind getting up early and going to the forest even when it's raining hard! 'The worst time,' says Leo, 'is after a big storm with strong winds. We see a lot of lovely old trees lying on the ground. Sometimes they're hundreds of years old.' But that's part of forest life, as Leo is finding out.

VOCABULARY
Work and work skills

1 Unscramble and write the adjectives related to work and skills.

1. _part-time_ (trap-mite)
2. _____ (erlaxngi)
3. _____ (lelw-daip)
4. _____ (eassnoal)
5. _____ (lulf-mite)
6. _____ (ewraridng)
7. _____ (isatsfygni)
8. _____ (sessrtluf)

2 Complete the sentences with adjectives related to work and skills.

1. Working in a busy restaurant can be very s_tressful_ sometimes.
2. My mum only works in the mornings, so she doesn't work f_____ .
3. A lot of work on farms is s_____ , because there isn't much to do in the winter.
4. My brother loves money, so he definitely wants a w_____ job in the future.
5. I enjoy tidying my room – it's very s_____ to see it looking nice.
6. He's looking for a p_____ job, just two or three days a week.
7. Babysitting is quite a r_____ job when the children are asleep!
8. I guess teaching is a r_____ job when you can see that the children are learning.

3 Choose the correct answers.

1. We're *making/doing/getting* plans for our summer holidays.
2. Our boss *puts/keeps/has* an eye on us all the time.
3. Sam couldn't be a builder. He hates *getting/making/having* his hands dirty!
4. You need to wear warm clothes when you're working *out/outdoor/outdoors*.
5. I don't think I could cope *for/with/to* being the boss.
6. I'd like to *make/prove/give* to myself that I can do this job.

4 Complete the adjectives with the missing vowels.

1. f_a_ sh _i_ _o_ n _a_ bl _e_
2. _ n c r _ d _ bl _
3. c _ m f _ rt _ bl _
4. t _ rr _ bl _
5. s _ ns _ bl _
6. _ nd _ rst _ nd _ bl _
7. r _ l _ bl _

5 Complete the job advert with these words.

flexible   organised   practical   punctual
reliable   ~~responsible~~   suitable

Assistant Zoo Keeper

We are looking for a part-time helper at the zoo. You must have the following qualities:
You must be 1) _responsible_ , and take your work seriously.
You must be 2) _____ and arrive on time for work.
You must be 3) _____ and able to keep your workplace tidy.
You must be a 4) _____ person, who's good at dealing with problems and deciding what is possible in different situations.
You must be 5) _____ , as the working hours change each week.
You must be a 6) _____ person, because we need someone that we can trust.
If you think you are 7) _____ for this job, please email us at the address above.

01 Inside or outside?

GRAMMAR
Present tenses

1 Choose the correct answers.

1. My brother *always is*/*is always*/*is always being* late for school!
2. Jamie *doesn't wear*/*isn't wearing*/*isn't wear* a hoodie today.
3. The price of clothes *is getting*/*gets*/*are getting* higher and higher.
4. I *don't often see*/*don't see often*/*am not often seeing* my friends at the weekend.
5. I'm sorry, I *am not understand*/*don't understand*/*am not understanding* this.
6. My dad *tells always*/*always tells*/*is always telling* me I should study more. It's so annoying!
7. We can't play tennis, because it *rains*/*is rain*/*is raining* at the moment.
8. I *enjoy always*/*am always enjoying*/*always enjoy* music lessons at school.

2 Write sentences in the present simple or the present continuous.

1. Sam / play / tennis / at the moment
   Sam is playing tennis at the moment.
2. my brother / always / borrow / my things
3. I / usually / do / my homework / after dinner
4. they / live / in London / ?
5. my friends / wait / for me / right now
6. where / you / go / ?
7. it / often / sunny / in July
8. the hero / jump / out of the aeroplane
9. have / you / a / evening / job / ?
10. Who / she / talk to / ?

3 Complete the sentences with the present simple or present continuous form of these verbs. Include the adverbs where they are given.

always / be   always / use   live   look after
make   ~~never / get up~~   not study   watch

1. I ___*never get up*___ before nine o'clock on Saturday mornings.
2. I don't want to come out at the moment. I _____ a movie on TV.
3. Joe _____ happy when his team wins!
4. (you) _____ in New York?
5. My sister _____ my phone. It really annoys me!
6. We _____ German this year.
7. (you) _____ your baby sister today?
8. This week we _____ plans for our summer holidays.

4 Complete the email with one word in each space.

| mailbox | Today | Mail | Calendar | Contacts |

Reply | Reply All | Forward | Delete

To: **Jenna**   Subject: **I'm bored!**

Hi Jenna,
What 1) ___*are*___ you doing? 2) _____ you want to come round to my house? I'm 3) _____ doing anything interesting 4) _____ the moment, and there isn't anything interesting on TV, 5) _____ usual! If you 6) _____ free now, maybe we can get together tomorrow or 7) _____ the weekend? I 8) _____ have any plans yet. My cousin is 9) _____ telling me I should go to the new cinema in town. Maybe we should do that.
See you soon,
Anja

VOCABULARY
Describing clothes

1 Look at the pictures and write the words.

1 _hoodie_
2 _____
3 _____
4 _____
5 _____
6 _____
7 _____
8 _____

2 Find eight words for clothes and accessories. The words go across, down or diagonally. The first letter of each word is highlighted.

w	c	a	j	k	i	p	l	u	r	o
e	a	o	e	p	i	a	f	r	n	u
a	s	t	w	l	y	t	l	a	r	t
t	u	g	e	f	l	e	a	b	s	f
t	a	r	l	r	v	o	t	a	c	i
y	l	o	l	a	p	i	s	t	o	t
h	y	h	e	m	i	r	h	e	a	l
j	s	t	r	i	p	y	o	r	t	p
w	o	r	y	y	i	b	e	o	r	t
b	a	g	g	y	m	l	s	a	f	e

3 Match the adjectives for describing clothes (1–7) with the definitions (a–g).

1 stripy
2 baggy
3 tight
4 spotty
5 plain
6 casual
7 patterned

a with any kind of pattern
b fitting close to your body
c with no pattern
d with a pattern of lines
e not fitting close to your body
f with a pattern of small circles
g not formal

4 Unscramble and write the words for clothes and accessories.

1 She wears a lot of _jewellery_ (ejewrlley), like rings and necklaces.
2 Your new _____ (ahriystle) really suits you.
3 I think you worry about your _____ (migea) too much!
4 At school, we wear a jumper with the school _____ (gool) on it.
5 I sometimes wear a _____ (itwrsabdn) on my arm when I play tennis.
6 I like your new hat and _____ (csraf).
7 He often wears a hoodie and some _____ (rtacktuis tombots).
8 I never buy expensive _____ (neresdig bella) clothes.

5 Read the article and choose the correct answer, A, B, C or D.

The best job!

I think my job is the most 1) _satisfying_ job in the world! I'm a water-slide tester! Of course, this job isn't for everyone. It's 2) ____, so you can't work all-year round. And you have to cope 3) ____ getting wet all the time! But I think it's great. It's never 4) ____, because you feel as if you're on holiday all the time! And you don't have to worry about what to wear to work, because there's only one possible 5) ____ – your swimming costume! I must admit that it isn't a very 6) ____ job, but then money isn't everything. Although it's fun, you do have to be 7) ____ and concentrate on what you're doing. And you need to 8) ____ an eye on your speed, because it can be dangerous if you go too fast!

1 A satisfy   B satisfying
  C satisfied   D satisfies
2 A monthly   B annual
  C seasonal   D partial
3 A for   B of
  C to   D with
4 A stress   B stressful
  C stressed   D stressfully
5 A outfit   B clothes
  C logo   D suit
6 A generous   B rich
  C well-paid   D wealthy
7 A sensitive   B right
  C carefully   D sensible
8 A keep   B have
  C get   D put

01 Inside or outside?

GRAMMAR
Articles

1 Choose the correct answers.
1. My cousin lives in *USA/the USA*.
2. *Money/The money* isn't very important to me.
3. Did you watch that documentary on *the TV/TV*?
4. Do you want to go to *cinema/the cinema* today?
5. *Life/The life* can be difficult sometimes.
6. He wants to climb *Mount Everest/the Mount Everest*.
7. We swam in *Pacific Ocean/the Pacific Ocean*.
8. My brother doesn't have a job, so he's looking for *work/the work*.

2 Complete the conversations with *a*, *an* or *the*.

A Do you want to go to 1) _the_ theatre tonight?
B Yes, and why don't we go to 2) _____ restaurant first, for 3) _____ meal?
A Good idea. We can go to 4) _____ Italian restaurant I went to last week. It's very nice.

A Can I borrow 5) _____ pen, please?
B Where's 6) _____ pen I lent you last week?

A Excuse me, is there 7) _____ bank near here?
B Yes. There's one next to 8) _____ police station.

A Have you got 9) _____ new phone?
B Yeah. It was 10) _____ birthday present.

3 Choose the correct answer, A, B or C.
1. There were more than _a thousand_ people at the concert.
   A thousand   B thousands   **C** a thousand
2. Trains are a very popular form of _____.
   A transport   B a transport   C the transport
3. I usually see my friends three _____ week.
   A times   B times a   C times the
4. There's a really good shoe shop on _____.
   A the North Street   B a North Street   C North Street
5. My brother's at _____.
   A Bristol University   B a Bristol University   C the Bristol University
6. We waited for three and _____ hours!
   A half   B a half   C the half
7. My mum always reads _____ magazine.
   A *Vogue*   B the *Vogue*   C a *Vogue*
8. We visited _____ in London last week.
   A National Gallery   B the National Gallery   C a National Gallery

4 Underline the mistake in each sentence.
1. I'd love to visit <u>the</u> South America.
2. I love music, but I'm not very interested in the art.
3. I'm reading the very interesting book right now.
4. We go out for a meal once the week.
5. Paris is the capital city of a France.
6. The plane leaves from a Heathrow Airport.
7. They climbed the Mount Kilimanjaro with a guide last summer.
8. Do you prefer watching TV or going to theatre?

5 Complete the article with *a*, *an*, *the* or *–*.

No hoodies?

A lot of young people wear hoodies, but there's 1) _a_ shopping centre in Kent, in 2) _____ UK, where hoodies aren't allowed. 3) _____ shopping centre decided to stop teenagers wearing hoodies from coming in because some older customers found them frightening. Jack, 4) _____ teenager from the town, is angry. 'It's not fair. I always met my friends here before,' he says. 'There's 5) _____ nice café where we met and we went to 6) _____ cinema here once or twice 7) _____ week. Now we can't do that.' Now Jack and his friends are taking 8) _____ advice from a lawyer and hope that they can make 9) _____ shopping centre think again!

LISTENING

1 1.1 Listen to people talking about six different topics. Match the speakers (1–6) with the topics (a–f).

Speaker 1 — a a wedding
Speaker 2   b an essay
Speaker 3   c choosing subjects
Speaker 4   d a writer
Speaker 5   e a summer job
Speaker 6   f buying clothes

2 1.2 Listen again and choose the correct answer, A, B or C.

1 You hear two people talking about work. Why didn't the boy apply for the job?
   A It wasn't part-time.
   B It wasn't well-paid.
   C It wasn't rewarding.
2 You hear two people talking about a problem. What prevented the girl from doing what she wanted?
   A She couldn't find the right information.
   B She didn't have enough time.
   C She made a mistake on her computer.
3 You hear a girl leaving a voicemail message. What did she buy online?
   A some jewellery
   B a coat
   C some jeans
4 You hear two students talking about making a decision. How does the boy feel about making the decision?
   A worried
   B confused
   C confident
5 You hear two people talking about an event. What influences the girl's decision about what to wear?
   A comfort
   B the weather
   C the cost
6 You hear a person talking about her job. What is she doing?
   A correcting people's ideas about what being a writer involves
   B explaining how to become a successful writer
   C giving advice about getting ideas

SPEAKING SKILLS

1 Complete these sentences from a personal profile. Choose the correct words.

1 I'm definitely *in/into* music and I'm a big fan *of/by* bands like the Kaiser Chiefs.
2 I'm not very interested *on/in* science subjects, *especially/actually* biology!
3 In *fact/point* I'm not enjoying school much at all at the moment.
4 I'm keen *at/on* all types of sports and I'm quite good *at/by* running.
5 I like *shopping/shop* but I *don't/can't* stand waiting in queues for ages.
6 *To/For* be honest, I don't watch a lot of TV. *Especially/Actually*, I only watch one or two programmes regularly.

2 Match the questions (1–6) with follow-up questions (a–f).

1 Which language are you studying? e
2 Do you belong to any clubs?
3 What are your favourite sports?
4 Who do you like seeing at the weekend?
5 Do you know what job you want to do?
6 Do you ever go to concerts?

a How often do you go to them?
b Is it well-paid in your country?
c What type of music was it?
d Do you practise them in the evenings?
e How long have you been learning it?
f Does she speak English?

3 Prepare a one-minute talk about your own personal profile. Include some of these topics.

1 where you're from
2 what you like or don't like at school
3 your free time interests
4 friends and family
5 if you have a part-time job
6 if you belong to any clubs

01 Inside or outside?

WRITING

1 Match the phrases (1–5) with the functions (a–e).

1 In my view
2 On balance
3 In spite of that
4 In addition
5 This is because

a summarising
b giving opinions
c giving reasons
d adding more points
e contrasting opinions

2 Complete the paragraph with these words.

however   in addition   in spite of
on balance   ~~personally~~

People often say that it's boring in the country but 1) _personally_ I don't agree at all. It's true that there aren't many cinemas and cafés. 2) _____, many people enjoy the peace and quiet and 3) _____, you learn a lot from greater contact with your natural environment. 4) _____, I suppose that there are benefits and downsides to life in both the country and the city but 5) _____ that, I know where I prefer to live!

3 Read the essay question. With reference to small village schools, do the sentences give a benefit (B), a downside (D) or a conclusion (C)?

The Students' Voice!

Would you like to see your essay in our magazine? Write your answer to the question below and send it to us at studentsvoice.com

It's better for children to go to a small village school than a big city one. Do you agree?

1 All the children and teachers know each other well. _B_
2 Usually the class sizes are smaller and the children get more attention. ___
3 You can study more subjects in big schools because there's more space and equipment. ___
4 In big classes it's sometimes noisy and difficult to concentrate. ___
5 For me, there's not a lot to do after school and it's easy to get bored. ___
6 I think it depends on the person, but I'd prefer to send my children to a city school. ___
7 From a health point of view, there can be a lot of air pollution in a city. ___
8 If children have problems the teachers know about them quickly and can help. ___
9 Getting to school can be quite dangerous with all the busy traffic. ___
10 On balance I think going to a village school is better for shy students. ___

4 Read the essay question again. Write your essay in 140–190 words.

Revision Unit 1

1 Complete the table with the correct form of the word given.

Verb	Noun	Adjective
relax	–	1) *relaxing*
suit	–	2)
satisfy	–	3)
–	sense	4)
–	stress	5)

2 Choose the correct answer, A, B or C.

1 Mark doesn't like *getting* his hands dirty.
   A having   **B getting**   C making
2 I don't think Jo will ___ with this job.
   A cope   B enjoy   C achieve
3 I want to prove ___ myself that I can do it!
   A for   B with   C to
4 He asked me to keep ___ on the young animals.
   A eyes   B my eyes   C an eye
5 We're busy ___ plans for next year.
   A making   B doing   C getting
6 You're going to be in a movie? That's ___!
   A terrible   B incredible   C suitable
7 Mia isn't ___ enough to do that job.
   A comfortable   B suitable   C responsible
8 We had a great holiday but the weather was ___.
   A terrible   B flexible   C incredible

3 Complete the sentences with one word in each space.

1 You wear w*aterproo*f clothes to protect you from the rain.
2 You wear an a_____n to keep your clothes clean when you're cooking.
3 A h_____e is a top that has a part to cover your head.
4 Wearing g_____s keeps your hands warm.
5 You wear g_____s to protect your eyes when you are skiing or swimming.
6 Your h_____e is the way your hair is cut and shaped.
7 A s_____-s_____ shirt has sleeves that only cover the top part of your arms.
8 You wear a s_____f around your neck to keep you warm.

4 Complete the sentences with these words.

baggy   designer label   flip-flops   ~~image~~
kit   necklace   outfit   plain

1 I'm careful about choosing clothes because my *image* is quite important to me.
2 I prefer _____ clothes. I hate clothes that are too tight!
3 I bought a smart new _____ for my job interview.
4 Do you like Manchester United's new _____?
5 Do you prefer _____ T-shirts or patterned ones?
6 Oh, what a lovely gold _____!
7 I've got a pair of _____ to wear at the beach.
8 I can't afford to buy _____ clothes!

5 Complete the sentences with the correct form of the words in capitals.

1 I wear *comfortable* shoes when I'm working, because I'm on my feet a lot.   **COMFORT**
2 I think that teaching is a very _____ job.   **REWARD**
3 Rob was wearing a _____ shirt and a plain tie.   **STRIPE**
4 I bought a _____ summer dress.   **SPOT**
5 I think it's _____ that Paula was upset.   **UNDERSTAND**
6 You have to be very _____ to do this job.   **ORGANISE**
7 He wants to pass his exams so that he can get a well-_____ job when he leaves school.   **PAY**
8 You must work _____ hours in this job.   **FLEX**
9 You must prove to _____ that you can succeed with this project.   **YOUR**
10 Sam is a very _____ worker. You can always depend on him.   **RELY**

Revision Unit 1

6 Complete the sentences with the present simple or present continuous form of the verbs in brackets.

1. I _usually get_ (usually / get) home from school at 4.30.
2. I _____ (not see / often) my cousins because they live in Canada.
3. My dad is very busy. He _____ (work) really hard at the moment.
4. In the film, Oliver _____ (go) to New York to find work.
5. I think it _____ (become) more and more difficult for young people to find work.
6. My sister _____ (always / wear) a uniform to work.
7. I _____ (try) to be more careful with my money at the moment.
8. My mum is really annoying. She _____ (always / tell) me I don't work hard enough!
9. I'm sorry, I _____ (not agree) with you.
10. This is a great party! I _____ (enjoy) it!

7 Rewrite the sentences correctly.

1. Jack always is late!
   Jack is always late!
2. We buy usually our lunch in the canteen.
3. What do you do at the moment?
4. I play tennis most weekend.
5. I'm watching TV at moment.
6. I often don't cycle to school.
7. My sister always is borrowing my things!
8. I'm sorry, I'm not understanding you.
9. They are not often visiting their grandparents.
10. Karl applies for a job in a local supermarket because he needs some money.

8 Complete the sentences with *a*, *an*, *the* or *–*.

1. Would you like _a_ biscuit?
2. _____ work doesn't have to be boring – it can be fun!
3. I saw _____ really good film last night.
4. My uncle lives in _____ Australia.
5. Look, there's _____ boy I told you about.
6. We usually go on holiday once _____ year.
7. I'd love to go to _____ Bahamas!
8. They sailed down _____ Amazon in a small boat.
9. My brother wants to go to _____ Harvard University.
10. I bought this dress in _____ Harrods.

9 Complete the email with one word in each space.

mailbox Today | Mail | Calendar | Contacts
Reply | Reply All | Forward | Delete
To: **Sara**   Subject: **My new job!**

Hi Sara,
How are you? I started 1) _a_ part-time job last week. I'm working in 2) _____ café in York. I only work for about six and 3) _____ half hours a week, but it's good to have some money! 4) _____ you still looking for a job? I 5) _____ think they want any more waiters here 6) _____ the moment, but I can let you know if anyone leaves. 7) _____ café here is really nice. It 8) _____ serve main meals – just drinks and snacks. You could come in and see me at work. It's OK, you 9) _____ have to buy anything!
Hope to see you soon,
Georgia

02 Making it happen

READING

1 Read the posts and choose the correct answer, true or false.

1 Bailey's mum used a computer to keep him occupied.
   True   **False**
2 Bailey's young sister isn't good with a touch screen.
   True   False
3 Emma played outside a lot as a child.
   True   False
4 Emma often takes her cousin's computer away from him.
   True   False
5 Emma thinks computers have no benefits for young children.
   True   False
6 David's young friend plays quietly on his computer.
   True   False
7 David's mum didn't like him eating a lot of chocolate.
   True   False
8 Dean often babysits for young children.
   True   False

2 Read the posts again and choose the correct answer, A, B, C or D.

Which person:
1 worries about children being alone too much? **B**
2 compares two similar reactions to different things? ___
3 believes children need more time with their parents? ___
4 mentions the problem of depending too much on computers? ___
5 thinks using computers is good preparation for formal education? ___
6 believes there is an alternative way to develop computer skills? ___
7 is concerned about the effects of computers on a child's mood? ___
8 appreciated an activity in the past because it was unusual? ___
9 talks about the types of toys he/she liked as a child? ___
10 points out what children need to learn from their parents? ___

A BAILEY

B EMMA

C DAVID

D DEAN

VOCABULARY
Technology

1 Complete the crossword with technology words.

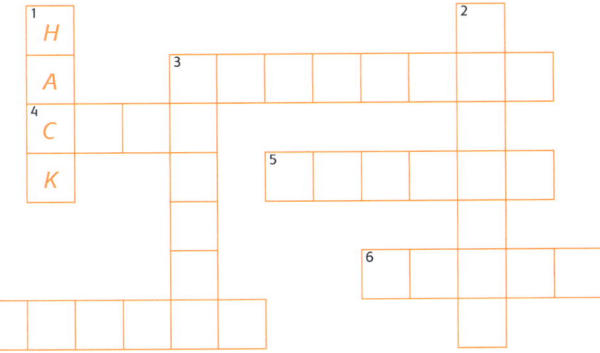

Across
3 to move information from the Internet onto a computer or smartphone
4 a set of instructions that tell a computer what to do
5 to add more information to something
6 a set of instructions that can damage a computer
7 a group of documents that you store together on a computer

Down
1 to get information from someone's computer secretly
2 an object that provides a supply of electricity for a device such as a smartphone
3 to remove something that is stored on a computer

2 Choose the correct answers.
1 Did you read Sara's *tweet/signal* about her party?
2 It's a very useful application and you can download the *connection/software* free this month.
3 I've just got a new *touch screen/virtual* phone.
4 I couldn't call you earlier, because I couldn't get a *signal/connection* for my phone.
5 John plays lots of *online/click* computer games.
6 My sister spent £5 on food for the animals in her *program/virtual* zoo!
7 It takes ages to download things because the Internet *website/connection* is so slow!
8 Allgames.com is a great *online/website* for games.

3 Complete the sentences with the correct form of these verbs.

> access   charge   click   ~~delete~~   download
> hack   scroll   update

1 I was so annoyed! I accidentally _deleted_ my essay from my computer, so I had to write it again!
2 I forgot to _____ my phone last night, and now it's out of battery!
3 If you _____ down the page, you'll see more information at the bottom.
4 These files are protected, so you need a password to _____ them.
5 If you _____ on that icon, the program will open.
6 Listen to this song – I _____ it onto my phone yesterday. Do you like it?
7 The school website hasn't got any information about this term's events yet. They need to _____ it.
8 Someone _____ into the bank's computer last night and stole information about customers' accounts.

4 Match the sentence beginnings (1–6) with the endings (a–f).
1 I'm going to follow up   _c_
2 I'm still trying to work out   ____
3 You need a password to log on   ____
4 You have to key in   ____
5 Can you zoom in   ____
6 You'll save energy if you turn off   ____

a to the website.
b your name and then press 'Enter'.
c your idea of trying to get a summer job.
d on that picture, so we can see it better?
e your computer at night.
f the answer to this maths problem.

GRAMMAR
Past tenses

1 Write sentences. Use the past simple, the past continuous or both.

1 Martha / show / me / her new tablet
   Martha showed me her new tablet.
2 I / not enjoy / the exhibition
3 we / watch / a movie / when / you / phone
4 you / read / that article / about computers / ?
5 I'm sorry, / you / sleep / ?
6 where / you / go / when / I / see/ you / ?
7 I / not pay / for / the software
8 she / work / on her laptop / at the time

2 Complete the text with the correct past simple or past continuous form of these verbs.

decide   form   get   leave   live   return
spend   ~~start~~   study   work

Steve Jobs

Steve Jobs was an American inventor and businessman. He was always interested in technology and 1) *started* building computers while he 2) _____ at college. He 3) _____ with his parents at the time. He 4) _____ college after only six months and 5) _____ some time travelling around India. When he 6) _____ to the US, he 7) _____ a job with the technology company Atari. While he 8) _____ there, he 9) _____ to set up his own company. Jobs 10) _____ the Apple company in 1976 with his friend Steve Wozniak, and together they changed the world of phones and personal computing for ever.

3 Choose the correct answers.

1 *Did you use to/You use to/Would you* play football games on the computer when you were younger?
2 We *used watch/would watch/would watching* TV every evening when I was young.
3 I *used to love/would love/use to love* taking photos on my dad's old camera.
4 My grandparents *didn't use to/didn't used to/not use to* have a music player.
5 I *used text/would to text/used to text* my friends every day.
6 My best friend *used to live/would live/use to live* in New York.
7 *Did you used to/You use to/Did you use to* buy things online fifteen years ago?
8 I *wouldn't have/didn't use to have/not use to have* a mobile phone.
9 When my parents were young, *they used to/they would/they use to* play in a band together.
10 A friend of mine *taught herself/would teach herself/use to teach herself* Russian.

4 Choose the correct answer, A, B or C. Sometimes more than one answer is possible.

1 I ____ in London when I was younger.
   A used to live   **B** would live   **(C)** lived
2 I ____ my grandparents every weekend.
   A was visiting   **B** used to visit   **C** would visit
3 Who ____ the mobile phone?
   A invented   **B** used to invent
   C was inventing
4 My grandma ____ scared of technology.
   A was being   **B** used to be   **C** would be
5 It ____ when we left home this morning.
   A used to rain   **B** was raining   **C** raining
6 I ____ my first tablet two years ago.
   A got   **B** was getting   **C** would get
7 I didn't hear my phone last night because I ____ .
   A slept   **B** was sleeping
   C used to sleep
8 In the 1980s, most people ____ computers at home.
   A didn't have   **B** didn't use to have
   C wouldn't have
9 ____ cycle to school when you were young?
   A Were you   **B** Did you use to
   C You used to
10 In my teens, I ____ spend hours writing adventure stories.
    A did   **B** would   **C** was

VOCABULARY
Inventors and inventions

1 Read the definitions and write the words.

1. a machine that prints documents — *printer*
2. a device that transmits a signal _____
3. a machine that scans documents _____
4. someone who collects things _____
5. someone who competes _____
6. someone who invents things _____
7. someone who plays a game _____
8. someone who employs someone to do something _____

2 Complete the table with the correct noun forms.

Verb	Noun
receive	1) *receiver*
amplify	2) _____
generate	3) _____
photocopy	4) _____
advise	5) _____
refrigerate	6) _____
program	7) _____
narrate	8) _____

3 Complete the sentences with nouns formed from these verbs.

> amplify   calculate   ~~refrigerate~~   play
> generate   instruct   invent   photocopy

1. The meat is all stored in a *refrigerator* to keep it cool and fresh.
2. Jo dreams of being a professional football _____ one day.
3. The music isn't loud enough for this big hall. We need an _____ to make it louder.
4. We had a really good ski _____ who taught us a lot about skiing.
5. I can't do this maths in my head. Can I borrow your _____?
6. The school has its own _____ to produce electricity if there's a power cut.
7. Who was the _____ of the first computer?
8. Can I use your _____? I need to make a copy of my passport.

4 Complete the sentences with the correct form of the verbs in brackets. Use *re-* or *dis-*.

1. Jack was here a few minutes ago, but he's *disappeared* (appear) now!
2. I spilled water on my homework, so I had to _____ (do) it!
3. I'm sorry, but I _____ (agree) with you. I think you're wrong!
4. Can you _____ (play) that song? I love it.
5. I didn't understand the text about technology. I had to _____ (read) it several times.
6. My grandad _____ (approve) of new technology, and he refuses to go near a computer!
7. The band couldn't get the song right, so they decided to _____ (record) it the next day.
8. I wouldn't dare to _____ (obey) my parents! They would be furious!
9. Sara's really nice – I can't understand why you _____ (like) her!

5 Complete the fact sheet with the correct form of the words in brackets.

Music, TV and Radio
Did you know…?

- The first electric 1) *amplifier* (amplify) was invented in 1909 by Lee De Forest. Without him, there would be no rock concerts!
- The first portable music 2) _____ (play) went on sale in the 1960s. It used small cassettes, with recorded music on.
- Alan Blumlein was the 3) _____ (invent) of stereo sound, the system that directs different sounds through different speakers. He invented it in 1931.
- The first radio 4) _____ (receive) was designed by Alexander Popov in 1896, but people didn't start having radios in their homes until the early 20th century.
- The first TV 5) _____ (transmit) was developed by John Logie Baird in London in the 1920s.
- The song *Yesterday* by the Beatles was first recorded in 1965, and since then it has been 6) _____ (record) over 2,000 times by different singers.
- Some rock bands and singers are difficult to please. The band Van Halen used to demand packets of coloured sweets, but with all the brown ones removed because they 7) _____ (like) these ones!

GRAMMAR
Pronouns

1 Complete the sentences with these reflexive pronouns.

> herself   himself   ~~myself~~   ourselves   itself
> themselves x2   yourself   yourselves

1 I really enjoyed _myself_ at the party.
2 My brother designed the app all by _____ .
3 We paid for the tickets _____ .
4 Did you make this cake _____ , Tom?
5 Mum bought a new computer for _____ .
6 Make sure you all behave _____ while you're out!
7 Dan and Jacob organised the trip _____ .
8 This light switches _____ on when you enter the room.
9 I prefer cats to dogs because they almost look after _____ .

2 Complete the conversations with a reflexive pronoun or *each other*.

A Are you going to the cinema by 1) _yourself_ tonight?
B No, Sam's coming with me. We often go to the cinema with 2) _____ .

A Do George and Milly help 3) _____ with their homework?
B Yes, of course they do! George wouldn't get such good marks if he did all his homework 4) _____ !

A Anna is so selfish! She only thinks about 5) _____ !
B I know. And it's really strange that she and her sister never buy birthday presents for 6) _____ !

A Jack and Fiona are both sitting by 7) _____ on opposite sides of the room.
B Yes, but they keep looking at 8) _____ across the room!

A If I need a drink, can I help 9) _____ ?
B Yes. Everyone can help 10) _____ to water but you have to pay for other drinks.

3 Choose the correct answers.

1 Jane is a friend of *me/my/mine*.
2 I love that computer game of *yours/your/you*.
3 Dan showed me a new app of *he's/his/him*.
4 Anna introduced me to a cousin of *her/she/hers*.
5 Are Beth and Sam still working on that project of *their/theirs/they*?
6 We can lend you some books of *our/us/ours*.
7 Have you still got that DVD of *me/mine/my*?

4 Complete the email with one word in each space.

mailbox   Today | Mail | Calendar | Contacts
Reply | Reply All | Forward | Delete
To: **Tania**   Subject: **New game!**

Hi Tania,
I wanted to tell you about this new computer game of 1) _mine_ . It's called *Alien Attack*. I bought it for 2) _____ with my birthday money. It's a game that you can play by 3) _____ , but I think it's more fun if you play with someone else. It was Paul who told me about it. He and his brother play this game with 4) _____ other a lot. He says they can amuse 5) _____ for hours with it.

Why don't you come round this evening? We could order a pizza for 6) _____ , too. I've only got one games controller, but perhaps you could bring one of 7) _____ with you? Let me know what time you can come!

Stella

LISTENING

1 2.1 Listen to a teacher talking about a famous inventor, Rachel Zimmerman. Choose which topics (a–g) she mentions.

The teacher talks about:
a communicating online
b a good teacher
c science tests
d international prizes
e speaking a foreign language
f a competition
g computer problems

2 2.2 Listen again and complete the sentences. Use one word in each space.
1 Some people have problems communicating because the _keyboard_ is difficult for them to use.
2 Blissymbols are a set of _____ that people can use for communication.
3 In the past the disabled person had to have an _____ with them to help.
4 Rachel Zimmerman designed her invention at the age of _____ .
5 She developed some new _____ to use on computers.
6 The disabled person's message appeared as _____ on the screen.
7 The name of Rachel's invention was a Blissymbol _____ .
8 Rachel has a job today with _____ .

Rachel Zimmerman in 1985

SPEAKING SKILLS

1 Match the questions (1–8) with the answers (a–h).
1 What kind of music are you into? _e_
2 That's an interesting T-shirt. ___
3 Where are you from? ___
4 Hi, nice to meet you! ___
5 Do you like sport? I'm a big football fan. ___
6 How often do you go to the cinema? ___
7 Who do you spend your free time with at the weekends? ___
8 Are you going to Olga's party next weekend? ___

a Southampton. That's in the south of England.
b I enjoy watching it and playing it.
c My best mate Tony and sometimes my older sister Carole.
d I'd like to, but to be honest I need some early nights!
e I love rock and I go to lots of concerts, too.
f You too. I'm Julio.
g A couple of times a month. I like romantic comedies!
h Thanks. I got it in Madrid.

2 What do these comments show? Choose the correct answer, A, B or C.
1 It would be much better to have a talk about space exploration than have to read about it.
   A speculation   **B preference**   C agreement
2 The speaker might be able to answer questions about living on a space station.
   A speculation   B preference   C agreement
3 That's exactly what I think. It's not an interesting topic at all.
   A speculation   B preference   C agreement
4 I'd definitely choose to learn more about robots because they're fascinating.
   A speculation   B preference   C agreement
5 You're right there. We learned a lot about inventions last term.
   A speculation   B preference   C agreement
6 It would be a bit difficult I think.
   A speculation   B preference   C agreement
7 The speaker in the second workshop is a lot more interesting than in the first.
   A speculation   B preference   C agreement

02 Making it happen

WRITING

1 Complete the sentences from an essay with these words.

> balance   benefit   downside   fact
> ~~main~~   opinion   personally   spite

1 The _main_ reason I use computers is to communicate with friends.
2 One _____ of having a tablet computer is that I can carry it everywhere.
3 _____, I don't think it's a good idea to use computers in exams.
4 The _____ of depending on computers is that they sometimes go wrong.
5 In my _____, children should learn to use computers when they're very young.
6 On _____, I disagree with this statement about computers.
7 Computers are important in schools. In _____, I think every classroom should have a computer for each student.
8 Computers can give you a headache. In _____ of that, people still work at them for too long.

2 Number the sentences (a–h) in the correct order (1–8).

a Most people say that they make life easier for us. ____
b After all, they quite frequently go wrong. ____
c What do you think about all the new gadgets available today? _1_
d In spite of those points I'm sure people won't ever get tired of having new gadgets. ____
e In addition to that, they cost us a lot of money. There's always some pressure to have the latest one. ____
f So I suppose we'd better accept that they are here to stay. ____
g But personally I'm not so sure. ____
h My main reason is that we spend so much time looking after our gadgets. ____

3 Read the essay task and write your essay in 140–190 words.

> Some people say we rely too much on computers today. What's your opinion?
>
> Write about:
> • necessity
> • losing our skills
> • your own idea

Revision Unit 2

1 Complete the sentences with these words.

> access battery charge delete download
> hack program tweet

1 This torch doesn't work. It must need a new _battery_.
2 The singer sent a _____ about her next concert.
3 Be careful you don't _____ the file by accident.
4 Only students at the school can _____ this part of the website.
5 I'd love to learn how to _____ a computer to do what I want it to do.
6 Don't forget to _____ your tablet overnight, or you won't be able to use it tomorrow.
7 It only takes a few minutes to _____ a film, and then you can watch it!
8 Someone managed to _____ into my account and steal all my passwords.

2 Choose the correct answer, A, B, C or D.

1 Click ___ the 'Go' button to start your search.
   A on   B to   C for   D in
2 Key ___ your password and then press 'Enter'.
   A on   B in   C into   D to
3 My computer isn't working. I think it's got a ___.
   A software   B code   C website   D virus
4 I can't look at the website now because I haven't got an Internet ___.
   A program   B software   C connection   D online
5 I think you spend too much time in the ___ world of computer games!
   A program   B touch screen
   C virtual   D website
6 Don't forget to turn ___ your computer before you go to bed.
   A off   B down   C out   D over
7 My brother came up ___ a great idea for a new game.
   A for   B in   C in   D with
8 I keep all my important files in one ___.
   A code   B tweet   C folder   D website

3 Complete the sentences with one word in each space.

1 I can't work _out_ the answer to this question.
2 I'll log _____ to my computer and then we can look on the website.
3 Can you zoom _____ and look at our house?
4 It's a really good suggestion, and I'm going to follow it _____.
5 Scroll _____ to the bottom of the page.

4 Read the definitions and write the words. Use nouns formed from these verbs.

> amplify calculate generate instruct
> invent narrate photocopy transmit

1 a machine that can make copies of documents or pictures   _photocopier_
2 a machine that makes sounds louder   _____
3 a machine that helps you do maths   _____
4 a machine that sends out radio signals   _____
5 a machine that produces electricity   _____
6 someone who tells a story   _____
7 someone who teaches you a skill   _____
8 someone who thinks of ideas and makes new things   _____

5 Complete the sentences with the correct form of the words in capitals.

1 My sister wants to be a computer _programmer_ when she leaves school.   **PROGRAM**
2 I _____ that man – I really don't think he's honest!   **TRUST**
3 She beat all the other _____ in the race.   **COMPETE**
4 If you _____ the music player from the speakers, you won't be able to hear any sound.   **CONNECT**
5 If the game is still 0-0 at the end, they will have to _____ it next week.   **PLAY**
6 IBM is a major _____ in this area. Over 2,000 people work for the company.   **EMPLOY**
7 I can use my _____ to send a photo of the document to your computer.   **SCAN**
8 I really _____ of young people who behave badly!   **APPROVE**

Revision Unit 2

6 Complete the sentences with the correct past simple or past continuous form of these verbs.

> buy   design   do   rain   not try on   ~~walk~~
> watch

1 I met Gary while I *was walking* home from school.
2 We decided not to play tennis because it _____ .
3 I _____ a film when I heard a noise outside.
4 She _____ the shoes before she bought them.
5 My brother _____ an app while he was studying at university.
6 I _____ my homework when my computer crashed.
7 My parents _____ me a new phone because I did very well in my exams last term.

7 Choose the correct answers.

1 My dad *used to live*/used live/would live on a farm.
2 I *used to get/getting/was getting* very nervous before exams, but I'm OK now.
3 Jack *would win/used to winning/won* the drama prize last term.
4 My sister *would go/used go/was going* horse-riding every day when she was younger.
5 I *used to have/was having/would have* a desktop computer, but I have a tablet now.
6 *Did you use to see/Did you used to see/Were you seeing* your cousins every weekend?
7 I *wasn't/wouldn't/didn't use to* like swimming in the sea.

8 Choose the correct answer, A, B or C.

1 I bought ___ a new camera yesterday.
  A me   **B myself**   C mine
2 James lent me an interesting book of ___ .
  A he   B his   C himself
3 I'm going on holiday with a cousin of ___ .
  A me   B mine   C myself
4 My phone is more modern than ___ .
  A your   B yourself   C yours
5 Be careful you don't cut ___ on that knife.
  A you   B yourself   C yours
6 The lights switch ___ on and off while we're out.
  A them   B each other   C themselves
7 Tom's always looking at ___ in the mirror – he's so vain!
  A his   B himself   C each other
8 Toby and Rob often help ___ with homework.
  A theirs   B themselves   C each other

9 Rewrite the sentences using the word given. Use between two and five words, including the word given.

1 No one helped me make this cake.   **ALL**
  I made this cake *all by myself* .
2 My sister learned to swim by herself.   **TAUGHT**
  My sister _____ swim.
3 They had a good time at the party.   **THEMSELVES**
  They _____ at the party.
4 Sam writes to Kim and Kim writes to Sam.   **EACH**
  Sam and Kim _____ .
5 George is my friend.   **OF**
  George is a _____ .
6 Computers were slower in the past.   **USE**
  Computers didn't _____ fast in the past.
7 I started to eat my lunch and then the phone rang.   **WHILE**
  The phone rang _____ my lunch.
8 Our old flat wasn't as big as this one.   **USED**
  We _____ in a smaller flat.

10 Complete the blog post with one word in each space.

> 🗨 View previous comments   Cancel   Share   Post
>
> I 1) *was* talking to my dad about computer games yesterday and he told me about this game – *Pong*. It was one of the first ever computer games. It was a kind of sports game, I think. My dad says it 2) _____ to be quite slow. I don't think it was very exciting! You could play by 3) _____ or two people could play against 4) _____ other. My dad says he and his brother loved it. They 5) _____ play for hours. I'm amazed that they 6) _____ get bored with it!
> Anyway, it got me thinking. What other computer games did people 7) _____ to play in the 1970s and 80s? If there are any relatives of 8) _____ who played computer games at this time, I'd love to hear about it!

Write a comment   Support

23

True story?

READING

1 Read the blog and choose the correct answer, true or false.

1 The writer hates spiders.
   True   False
2 She thinks she has got her mother's singing talent.
   True   False
3 She has been in several music shows at school.
   True   False
4 She decided to write to *The Voice* because she liked this type of competition.
   True   False
5 Her family watched her from the studio audience.
   True   False
6 The presenter of the show gave her some good advice.
   True   False
7 The writer has won the competition.
   True   False

2 Read the blog again. Match the sentences (a–i) to the spaces (1–8) in the blog. You do not need one of the sentences.

a   I was so shocked, but I couldn't refuse, could I? ____
b   It made me laugh and then I was OK. ____
c   The second time was last week. *1*
d   I was dead scared that everyone was going to laugh at me. ____
e   The audience was completely silent while I sang. ____
f   Anyway – I think I take after my dad. ____
g   I was so nervous that my body was frozen with fear. ____
h   It was time for them to watch me face the biggest challenge of my life. ____
i   But that didn't mean that I wanted to go on the programme. ____

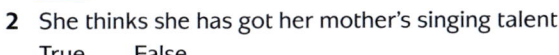

View previous comments   Cancel   Share   Post

Mandy's blog

Have you ever been so scared that you couldn't move? It's happened to me a couple of times in my life. Once when I was about five and I woke up to see the biggest spider in the world, sitting on the end of my bed! I couldn't stop screaming! 1) *The second time was last week* - something much more terrifying happened. And my nightmare hasn't finished yet. Let me tell you what's been happening.

As you know, I love singing. My mum says I've been singing since I was born – but I think that's a slight exaggeration! 2) _____ He was always singing when I was a kid. He adores singers like Madonna and I used to copy him. But I did all my singing in my bedroom or in the bathroom – never on a stage. He and mum tried to persuade me to audition for school shows but I was way too nervous for anything like that. 3) _____

However, my darling sister recently did something that I'm either going to love her or hate her for forever! She secretly recorded me singing a Madonna song in the bath and she sent it off to *The Voice* – you know, that big singing competition on TV. I actually like that show, because the judges have their backs to you while you're singing so they concentrate only on your voice. 4) _____

The first thing I knew about it was a phone call. 'We love your voice and we'd like you to be on the show,' said this television person! 5) _____ I decided that for once in my life I was going to be brave and I agreed to go for the audition.

Well, I went up to London with the whole family (they had special tickets for the show) on the day of the first auditions. We had a brilliant day, looking round the studios and meeting some really interesting people. Then they went to sit in the audience. 6) _____ I waited backstage for the performer before me to finish his song and then suddenly it was my turn. I heard my name and I put on a smile and put one foot on the steps that led to the stage. But that was it. One foot only. My other leg refused to move! 7) _____

The presenter realised that something was wrong and she came over to me and gave me a hug. Then she told me a joke about one of the judges. 8) _____ I could move! Then she said, 'The judges aren't looking at you, so you don't have to look at them. Why don't you shut your eyes and pretend you're on your own?'

So, I went on that stage, I shut my eyes and I sang my song. Guess what. The judges liked it! The problem is I have to go back next week for the next stage of the competition. And this time I can't shut my eyes. My nightmare continues ...

Write a comment   Support

VOCABULARY
A personal story

1 Complete the text with nouns formed from these verbs.

achieve experience feel grin hope
offer recognise vote

Do contestants really enjoy the 1) *experience* of taking part in TV talent shows? It doesn't always look like it. I guess they feel it's an 2) _____ to get through the auditions to the TV performances, but each week seems to be more painful than the last. You can see the 3) _____ of nervousness that they have before they perform each week. And then, as their 4) _____ of winning the competition fades, you see their desperate appeals to the audience because they know that every 5) _____ counts. What is it that drives them? Is it the desire for 6) _____ of their talents, or perhaps it's that tempting 7) _____ of a recording contract for the winner that encourages them to continue? Whatever it is, surely it can't be worth it, as for every contestant that leaves with a 8) _____ on their face, there are fifty who leave in tears.

2 Choose the correct answer, A, B or C.

1 Tom ____ to help me move flat.
   A felt   B recognised   **C offered**
2 I didn't ____ Sam when I saw him with a beard!
   A recognise   B stare   C experience
3 He finally ____ his goal of becoming a rock singer.
   A felt   B achieved   C voted
4 My hands were ____ because I was so nervous.
   A shaking   B staring   C grinning
5 I really ____ I can get into the final!
   A achieve   B share   C hope
6 People now ____ him by his stage name.
   A experience   B refer to   C vote
7 Thousands of people ____ for her.
   A shared   B experienced   C voted
8 He hates it when people ____ at him.
   A feel   B stare   C share
9 She said she would ____ the prize money with her family.
   A stare   B share   C offer
10 She was ____ because she was so happy.
   A grinning   B achieving   C hoping

3 Unscramble and write the words.

1 Leaving the show was a *massive* (sismave) disappointment.
2 I have a real _____ (eessawnk) for chocolate!
3 Her voice is her biggest _____ (trsegthn).
4 It was a great _____ (rliefe) when we knew that everyone was safe.
5 I got an attack of _____ (ernves) before the show.
6 He performed some amazing _____ (fatse) of balance.
7 I felt very _____ (seent) before the final, but my performance went well.
8 Everyone was hot and _____ (wsatye) after the dance routine.
9 It's important to stay _____ (osptivie) when things go wrong.
10 The show had some _____ (nteiagve) reviews.

GRAMMAR
Present perfect tenses

1 Put the words in the correct order to make sentences.

1 never / read / book / I / that / have
   I have never read that book.
2 been / on TV / has / a few times / She
3 been / all morning / have / practising / I
4 well / feeling / hasn't / recently / She / been
5 a celebrity / met / you / ever / Have / ?
6 you / been / What / doing / have / ?
7 have / book / I / the worst / ever / It's / read
8 first / performed / It's / she / time / the / on stage / has
9 won / have / a competition / I / never

2 Choose the correct answers.

1 I've been playing the guitar *for/since/still* ten years.
2 I've called her three times, but she *already/never/still* hasn't called me back.
3 I haven't finished doing my homework *yet/already/just*.
4 She has wanted to be a singer *for/since/already* she was four years old.
5 Have you *ever/still/yet* sung with a band?
6 Hurry up! The film has *still/already/ever* started!
7 I've known Sara *since/for/yet* about two years.
8 He's applied to be on a few TV shows, but he's *yet/ever/never* been successful.
9 He's *just/still/ever* finished singing, so let's hear what the judges say now.
10 She's the funniest comedian I've *never/ever/still* seen.

3 Complete the article with the present perfect simple or present perfect continuous form of these verbs.

already/start   ever/happen   ~~just/have~~
reject   send   tell   think   try   write

Success for young writer

Dale Bradbury is feeling excited. He 1) *has just had* a letter from a publisher, offering to publish his first novel, *Snowstorm*. Dale, who is only seventeen, 2) _____ to get the novel published for over two years now. He 3) _____ the story to more than ten publishers, but until now, all of them 4) _____ it. Now he's feeling very positive. 'This is the best thing that 5) _____ to me,' he says. 'I 6) _____ stories since I was about six years old, but this is the first time that anyone 7) _____ me that one of my stories was good enough to publish.' Dale now has plans for the future. He 8) _____ his next novel and he 9) _____ about how he can turn his first story into a film, although he doesn't have any firm plans for that yet.

4 Rewrite the sentences using the word given. Use between two and five words, including the word given.

1 I haven't acted in a play before.   **ACTED**
   It's the first *time I've acted* in a play.
2 I started writing poems two years ago.   **WRITING**
   I _____ two years.
3 Mike left a few moments ago.   **JUST**
   Mike _____ .
4 I last saw Sam on Tuesday.   **SEEN**
   I _____ Tuesday.
5 It started raining five hours ago!   **RAINING**
   It _____ five hours!
6 It's been three months since I ate meat.   **EATEN**
   I _____ three months.
7 I've never read such a good book before.   **BEST**
   This is the _____ read.

VOCABULARY
Describing actions

1 Complete the sentences with these verbs.

> crept remained spotted ~~stared~~
> vanished waved yelled

1 I couldn't believe what I was seeing, and I just _stared_ in disbelief at the creature.
2 I _____ quietly out of the door while no one was looking.
3 The animal looked at me for a few minutes, and then _____ completely!
4 When was the last time someone _____ the Loch Ness Monster?
5 I called to her, but she _____, 'Go away!'
6 We sat down by the lake and _____ there quietly for over two hours.
7 He stood up and _____ goodbye.

2 Complete the tables with these adverbs.

> ~~carefully~~ eventually frequently happily
> here immediately never often outside
> quietly there yesterday

Manner	Frequency
1) _carefully_	4)
2)	5)
3)	6)

Time	Place
7)	10)
8)	11)
9)	12)

3 Put the words in the correct order to make sentences.

1 wait / I'll / you / outside / for
  I'll wait for you outside.
2 shouted / us / angrily / at / The man

3 on TV / never / watch / talent shows / We

4 call me / immediately / You / if / must / happens / anything

5 Sally / cheerful / always / is

6 waiting / They / by / were / the bus stop / for us

4 Choose the correct answers.

1 The family vanished *mystery/mysterious/mysteriously* overnight.
2 Are you lying or are you being *truth/truthful/truthfully*?
3 She walked out onto the stage *nerves/nervous/nervously*.
4 I can't hear anything because of all the *noise/noisy/noisily*.
5 He still felt quite *hope/hopeful/hopefully* that his team could win.
6 The two boys were behaving *suspicion/suspicious/suspiciously*.
7 Jack was feeling really *happiness/happy/happily* that day.
8 He would love to play tennis *profession/professional/professionally* one day.

5 Complete the text with the correct form of the words in brackets.

Teenage heroes steer school bus to safety

Tom Dalton and his friends were chatting 1) _happily_ (happy) on the school bus on their way home from school last night. Then one of them 2) _____ (sudden) noticed that the driver had become ill. He had fallen over the wheel and wasn't steering the bus. Tom and his friends 3) _____ (immediate) ran to the front of the bus. Using all their 4) _____ (strong) they pulled the driver away from the controls. Tom sat down in the driver's seat and 5) _____ (calm) brought the bus to a stop. At the same time, Tom's friends looked after the driver and called an ambulance. Tom says, 'I didn't feel 6) _____ (nerve) at all. I just did what I had to do. It was a great 7) _____ (feel) when the bus 8) _____ (eventual) stopped moving.' The driver is still 9) _____ (serious) ill in hospital, but 10) _____ (hope) will make a full recovery. Meanwhile, Tom and his friends are celebrating being heroes!

GRAMMAR
Verbs with direct and indirect objects

1 Choose the correct answer, A, B or C.
1. I've bought some flowers ____ .
   A for you   **B** you   **C** to you
2. Emma made ____ a cake for my birthday.
   A for me   **B** me   **C** to me
3. He sent an email ____ .
   A for me   **B** me   **C** to me
4. Mrs Adams teaches ____ maths.
   A for us   **B** us   **C** to us
5. I lent ____ some books.
   A for Sara   **B** Sara   **C** to Sara
6. I sold my old bike ____ .
   A for Paul   **B** Paul   **C** to Paul
7. She promised ____ an answer by Monday.
   A for him   **B** him   **C** to him
8. Dan couldn't go to the show, so he offered his ticket ____ .
   A for me   **B** me   **C** to me
9. My grandfather told ____ that story.
   A for me   **B** to me   **C** me
10. Why did you lend your phone ____ ?
    A for him   **B** to him   **C** him

2 Rewrite the sentences changing the order of the objects (direct or indirect).
1. I've written a letter to the school.
   I've written the school a letter.
2. Don't tell this secret to anyone!
   _____
3. She read us the letter.
   _____
4. They brought some warm clothes for us.
   _____
5. My uncle has found me a part-time job.
   _____
6. He showed the photos to all his friends.
   _____
7. I've bought you a present.
   _____
8. I can send the concert details to you.
   _____

3 Complete the email with one word in each space.

mailbox   Today | Mail | Calendar | Contacts
Reply | Reply All | Forward | Delete
To: Grandma   Subject: Thanks!

Hi Grandma,
Thanks so much for the camera you gave 1) *me* for my birthday. I've already taken loads of photos with it. I'll show them 2) _____ you when I see you. Mum and Dad bought some clothes 3) _____ me, which was great, because I never have enough clothes! I got a book from Aunt Sally. I've promised 4) _____ that I'll read it! My cards were all lovely. The card from my cousins was really funny – I must send 5) _____ an email to thank them. I had a really nice day on my birthday. Some of my friends came round and Mum made some food 6) _____ us all. Then I found 7) _____ a DVD to watch, which we all enjoyed. I'll write again soon and I'll send some more photos 8) _____ you.
Love,
Laura

4 Rewrite the sentences using the word given. Use between two and five words, including the word given.
1. Where did you learn how to ski?   **TAUGHT**
   Who _*taught you how*_ to ski?
2. I borrowed this camera from Matt.   **ME**
   Matt _____ camera.
3. Who is that text from?   **SENT**
   Who _____ you?
4. I bought this book from George.   **SOLD**
   George _____ book.
5. Mike let me see his new tablet.   **SHOWED**
   Mike _____ tablet.
6. Paul said I could have his old phone.   **OFFERED**
   Paul _____ me.
7. I got this DVD from my aunt.   **GAVE**
   My aunt _____ DVD.

LISTENING

1 **3.1 Listen to five people talking and match the speakers (1–5) with the photos (A–E). Then choose the correct answer, A, B or C.**

Speaker 1: *E*
Speaker 2: ....
Speaker 3: ....
Speaker 4: ....
Speaker 5: ....

A They are all talking about events when they were young children.
B They are all talking about things that used to annoy them.
C They are all talking about lies they've told.

2 **3.2 Choose the correct answer, true or false. Listen again and check.**

1 Speaker 1 wanted to learn the piano.
　True　False
2 Speaker 2 didn't tell many lies when she was young.
　True　False
3 Speaker 3 couldn't find her laptop.
　True　False
4 Speaker 4 broke her guitar.
　True　False
5 Speaker 5 likes crime drama.
　True　False

3 **3.3 Listen again and match the speakers (1–5) with the questions (a–f). You do not need one of the questions.**

Which speaker:
a regretted telling a lie?　........
b told a lie to get good marks?　........
c lied to keep a secret?　........
d wanted to impress people?　*1*
e tried to hide something she'd done?　........
f lied to hurt someone?　........

SPEAKING SKILLS

1 Complete the sentences with the correct form of these verbs.

> be   have   just start   ~~never read~~
> not   see   play

1 I'_ve never read_ a novel in English, but I'm going to try one soon!
2 My sister _____ to sing in a choir and she loves it. I don't because she practises a lot at home!
3 My friend and I _____ to lots of open air pop concerts this year. They're good fun.
4 My brother _____ the new Star Wars movie yet, but I'm going to go with him soon.
5 Our sports teacher _____ football matches in important competitions in the last few years.
6 My friend _____ lots of barbecues at his house recently because the weather has been so fantastic.

2 Complete the sentences with these words.

> another   both   ~~first~~   looks
> main   though   whereas

1 The people in the _first_ photo have probably been running.
2 The children look as _____ they're at a party.
3 The man _____ as if he's angry.
4 _____ photos show people doing leisure activities.
5 The _____ similarity is that both groups of people are doing an outdoor sport.
6 In one photo a girl is reading on her own _____ in the other she's with a group of class mates.
7 _____ difference is that the weather isn't very good in the second photo.

3 Match these follow-up sentences (a–g) with sentences (1–7) from Exercise 2.

a In one they're running in the park and in the other they're playing football. ____
b They're things you can do at home in your free time. ____
c They wearing smart clothes. ____
d They look a bit hot and tired. _1_
e But in the first one it's a bright sunny day. ____
f However, it's clear that they are all interested in the books. ____
g Perhaps he has had an argument with someone. ____

4 Read the task and a student's answer. Complete the answer with one word in each space.

Your photos show people at different events. Compare the photos and say how you think the people are feeling.

The photos 1) _show_ people at different events. 2) _____ the first photo the people are at a football match and in the second they are probably at a party. The people at the match 3) _____ shouting and waving their scarves and the people at the party are dancing and laughing. The 4) _____ similarity is that they all look 5) _____ . though they are having a good time! 6) _____, I think this is for different reasons. In the first photo the people are probably happy because their team is winning 7) _____ in the second photo they're happy because they like dancing and maybe the music is good. 8) _____ similarity is that all the people are in groups. They're enjoying an activity with their friends. They are obviously 9) _____ happy but that might change if their team loses 10) _____ the party finishes!

03 True story?

WRITING

1 Match the sentences (1–6) from a story with the comments (a–f) about how to make a good story.

1 The day that changed my life started in a very ordinary way. _d_
2 The man spoke loudly and clearly. ___
3 I felt as though the whole world was against me. ___
4 It was a disastrous decision. ___
5 It was my sister who had sent the letter. I couldn't believe it! ___
6 My heart jumped when the man spoke. ___

a Use a simile.
b Give the story an unexpected or happy ending.
c Use a range of adverbs.
d Get the readers' attention.
e Use some interesting verbs.
f Use interesting adjectives.

2 Match the adjectives, adverbs and verbs (1–6) with those with similar meanings (a–f).

1 nervous   a incredible
2 smile   b spot
3 at last   c tense
4 take   d grab
5 extremely good   e eventually
6 notice   f grin

3 Read the story task and the sentences (a–f) that a student has written for an opening paragraph. Number the sentences in the correct order (1–6).

Write a story finishing with the words:

I wanted some adventure in my life and that day I certainly got it!

a I sighed deeply as I set off for the station. ___
b It started as just another ordinary day. _1_
c My life was like a prison and I wasn't going to escape – ever! ___
d Where was the adventure in my life? I wondered as I walked along the road. ___
e It was another Monday morning, another boring journey to school by train. ___
f I felt as though I were a mouse running around in a cage. ___

4 Which two sentences in Exercise 3 have a simile in them?

5 Read the task again and write your story in 140–190 words.

31

Revision Unit 3

1 Complete the words with the missing letters.
1. Going on stage with the band was a great ex_p_e_r_i_e_n_c_e.
2. She's hoping that lots of people will v__t__ for her so she wins the show.
3. The men performed some amazing f_____s of strength.
4. I felt horribly hot and s w____y after the race.
5. I didn't realise that it was Sophie, because she's changed beyond r__c__g n_____n.
6. I always suffer from n____v__s before important exams.
7. I was upset because my teacher made some n__g_____e comments about my essay.
8. I could tell she was happy because of the massive g____n on her face!
9. We've won the Cup – what an a_____v__m____t!
10. His w____k_____s as a performer is that he can't dance very well.

2 Choose the correct answer, A, B or C.
1. We went home ___after___ an hour.
   A later B then **C after**
2. At last ___ big day had arrived!
   A the B on C a
3. It only took a ___ of seconds to make my decision.
   A couple B few C lot
4. I knew ___ the outset that the trip would be a disaster!
   A in B on C at
5. I saw him on TV for ___ first time last night.
   A a B the C some
6. Sam called me a few minutes ___.
   A late B lately C later
7. She's been busy filming in Europe for the ___ few months.
   A latest B last C recent

3 Match the verbs in the box with the definitions (1–7).

creep   remain   spot   ~~stare~~   vanish
wave   yell

1. to look at someone for a long time — _stare_
2. to notice something or someone _____
3. to stay in a place _____
4. to disappear _____
5. to move your hand or arm around so that someone will notice you _____
6. to shout loudly _____
7. to move in a quiet, careful way _____

4 Complete the sentences with the correct form of the words in capitals.
1. It took all my ___strength___ to open the door. — **STRONG**
2. There was no _____ to the accident in the newspaper. — **REFER**
3. It was a really great _____ to win the game! — **FEEL**
4. The book gives details of all his _____. — **ACHIEVE**
5. It was such a _____ when we finally got home! — **RELIEVE**
6. The children were playing _____ outside. — **NOISE**
7. Jack was injured in the accident, but _____ he will be OK. — **HOPE**
8. The money vanished _____. — **MYSTERY**
9. The police arrested her for driving _____. — **DANGER**
10. I'm going to ask you some questions and you must answer _____. — **TRUTH**

Revision Unit 3

5 Complete the sentences with the present perfect simple or present perfect continuous form of these verbs.

> call   look   rain   read   sell   train
> not try   ~~wait~~

1. Why are you so late? We _have been waiting_ for hours!
2. *The Hunger Games* is a great novel. I _____ it three times!
3. I _____ for my passport all afternoon, but I still can't find it!
4. I love Chinese food, but I _____ Japanese food yet.
5. I'm really looking forward to running a marathon. I _____ for three months now.
6. We _____ our car, so now we have to use public transport.
7. Is there something wrong with your phone? I _____ you all day and you haven't answered.
8. This weather's so depressing! It _____ for five hours!

6 Choose the correct answer, A, B or C.

1. I _have never been_ to the United States.
   A have been never
   B have never been ✓
   C have ever been
2. Have you _____ a unicycle?
   A ever ridden
   B ever been riding
   C ridden already
3. It's OK. I _____ the bill.
   A have already been paying
   B have paid already
   C have already paid
4. Have you _____ ?
   A yet finished eating
   B still finished eating
   C finished eating yet
5. I posted the letter three days ago, but it _____ .
   A still hasn't arrived
   B hasn't already arrived
   C yet hasn't arrived
6. I'm sorry, John isn't here. He _____ .
   A already has left
   B has just left
   C has still left
7. We've been living in London _____ ten years.
   A since   B for   C already

7 Complete the article with one word in each space.

Is this the longest gap year ever?

When Martin Stokes and his girlfriend Anna left university, they decided to take a gap year and go travelling. That was five years ago, and they've 1) _been_ travelling ever since! They have 2) _____ been to over twenty countries and they have plans to visit at least ten more before they stop. 'We haven't visited India 3) _____,' says Anna. 'I really want to go there.' So far, they 4) _____ funded their trip by doing casual work when they can. 'Sometimes we work,' says Martin, 'and sometimes people give 5) _____ food and shelter free. People are incredibly kind. Once in the United States we didn't have enough money to buy our train tickets, so someone bought them 6) _____ us!' They both agree that this is the best experience they have 7) _____ had. 'I know some of our friends 8) _____ been working since they left college, but we think this experience is just as valuable as working. Maybe our friends have been earning money 9) _____ the last five years, but we've been living!'

8 Rewrite the sentences using the word given. Use between two and five words, including the word given.

1. He started studying English in 2012.   **BEEN**
   He _has been studying_ English since 2012.
2. I haven't been to New York before.   **FIRST**
   This is the _____ to New York.
3. We moved here six months ago.   **LIVING**
   We _____ six months.
4. I haven't eaten nicer food than this.   **EVER**
   This is the _____ eaten.
5. Paul bought my old bike from me.   **TO**
   I _____ Paul.
6. I received a letter from my aunt.   **SENT**
   My aunt _____ letter.
7. My dad said I could have a lift to the station.   **OFFERED**
   My dad _____ to the station.
8. Can I borrow your pen?   **LEND**
   Can _____ your pen?

33

04 Things they don't teach you

READING

1 Read the website article and choose the best title.
1 Goodbye to a lovely teacher
2 French made easy!
3 More than just a teacher

2 Choose the correct answer, A, B or C.
1 The writer has always called this teacher Anne.
   A True   B False   C Not given
2 He thinks her students today call her Miss Smith.
   A True   B False   C Not given
3 Anne Smith didn't worry about rules at school.
   A True   B False   C Not given
4 The writer was often punished at school.
   A True   B False   C Not given
5 Anne Smith didn't often give good grades.
   A True   B False   C Not given
6 The writer now speaks three foreign languages.
   A True   B False   C Not given
7 The writer was one of Anne's favourite students.
   A True   B False   C Not given
8 The writer has a job as an interpreter.
   A True   B False   C Not given

3 Read the article and choose the correct answer, A, B, C or D.
1 What does the writer need to make clear?
   A the teacher's name
   B the teacher's nationality
   C the teacher's age
   D the teacher's attitude
2 What does *got suspended* in line 20 mean?
   A had to stay after school
   B had to talk to the headteacher
   C had to do more homework
   D couldn't go to school for a certain period
3 The writer had problems at school because
   A he didn't live with his parents.
   B he wanted to do art all the time.
   C he didn't want advice from anyone.
   D he wasn't interested in school subjects.
4 What is true about Miss Smith's teaching methods?
   A She took her students to see films in French.
   B She asked them to write letters to French newspapers.
   C She introduced them to French friends.
   D She only spoke French in class.
5 *It* in line 40 refers to
   A meeting the French au pairs.
   B Miss Smith's methods.
   C the French language.
   D his career decision.
6 What is the result of Anne Smith's influence on the writer?
   A He doesn't argue with his parents.
   B He is more confident than before.
   C He isn't worried about changing career.
   D He has time to fit in his artistic activities too.

04 Things they don't teach you

Some people have an important effect on us and we remember them for the rest of our lives. Things they've said come back to us again and again and continue to influence our decisions long after we've said goodbye to them. One of these people in my life was a French teacher I had at secondary school. When I say French teacher, I mean she taught French – she was as English as you could be with the name Miss Smith! And her first name was Anne, but I only used that when I met her again years after leaving school. She was a fair but strict teacher and never allowed her students to call her by her first name. She was a traditionalist. I often wonder whether she's changed, but somehow I doubt it.

Before I had Anne Smith as my teacher, I wasn't a very hard-working student. In fact, I was a bit of a rebel. I skipped school pretty often and was naughty in class. I had loads of detentions and once I got suspended for a month because I painted graffiti on the school wall. I'd thought it was pretty artistic but the headteacher didn't agree. Looking back I think it was because I was bored and I had no real direction. My parents didn't have a lot of time for me and my teachers were too busy to see that I needed some good advice. Then Anne Smith became our French teacher and she practically turned my life round within a few weeks.

To begin with her influence is easy to explain. Her teaching style brought the language alive for us. We began to see that French was not just a boring subject in a book, but a way of talking to people. She never spoke English to us. That was hard but we got used to it! We watched films, listened to French singers, looked at French newspapers and she even brought in some French au pair girls to talk to us about life in France. It was a turning point for me. I'd found a subject that I loved and that, surprise, surprise, I was good at! I shall always be grateful to Anne for pointing me in the right direction. I went on to study two more languages at college and now I'm training to be an interpreter.

However, Anne gave me a lot more than a career direction. She was kind and concerned about her students. We all knew that if we needed to talk to someone she would be there for us. And her advice was good. In particular she taught me about different study methods and how to discipline myself to get through my work well. My parents were amazed. From a kid who couldn't care less about homework I was now discussing things like time management with them! She also taught me to believe in myself and that if I put my mind to it, I could do anything I wanted. That advice still helps me today and because of Anne Smith, I am sure that I'm going to finish this course, get good grades and work as an international reporter. A long way from painting graffiti on walls!

VOCABULARY
Money

1 Complete the crossword with words related to money.

Across
1. a piece of paper that shows an amount of money you have to pay
5. coins and banknotes
7. someone who buys things in a shop
8. a reduction in the usual price of something
9. a line of people who are waiting for something
10. the whole amount of money that you pay for something (5, 4)
11. a small cart on wheels in which you put things you want to buy in a supermarket

Down
1. something that is good value for money
2. a passage between rows of shelves in a supermarket
3. the place where you pay in a supermarket
4. a piece of paper with a special offer
6. someone who helps you or serves you in a shop

1 Down: BARGAIN

2 Complete the sentences with the correct form of these verbs.

> borrow   cost   economise   ~~lend~~   pay   save
> spend   be worth

1. I _lent_ John £10 yesterday, and he promised to pay me back today.
2. How much do you _____ on snacks every week?
3. Can I _____ some money to buy a drink?
4. Those shoes look expensive. How much did they _____ ?
5. Some old books _____ a lot of money.
6. I can't come to the cinema with you because I'm trying to _____ .
7. How much does your aunt _____ you for babysitting?
8. You can _____ a lot of money if you buy things online.

3 Choose the correct answer, A, B or C.

1. Contact us if you need some ….. about money.
   A knowledge   B education   **C advice**
2. I'd like to study …. at university.
   A economics   B economic   C economy
3. Toby's doing some work ….. in a bank.
   A knowledge   B finance   C experience
4. Visit their website for more …….
   A sense   B knowledge   C information

4 Choose the correct answers.

1. Jake has got no *common*/personal sense at all!
2. Her uncle offered to teach her about money/personal finance.
3. If you've got a good level of common/general knowledge, why don't you enter our quiz?
4. I'm absolutely hopeless at money/practical management – I spend far too much!
5. Are you interested in higher/common education after you leave school?
6. It's good to get some higher/practical experience of a job while you're still at school.

GRAMMAR
Relative clauses

1 Decide if the sentences contain defining (D) or non-defining (N) relative clauses.

1 That restaurant, which opened last year, is very expensive. **N**
2 That's the café where we often have lunch. ____
3 I usually sit next to Tara, who's my best friend. ____
4 Tom, whose father runs his own business, always has loads of money to spend! ____
5 Can you give me back the book that you borrowed last week? ____

2 Choose the correct answers.

1 Jenna was the only person *who/which* did well in the test.
2 At school, I want to learn about things *who/which* are important.
3 The library is a quiet place *when/where* you can read and study.
4 The weekend is a time *when/where* I relax.
5 Tim is a boy *who/whose* marks are always good.
6 The programme *where/that* I watched last night was very interesting.
7 Mia, *who/that* lives near me, is really interested in cooking.
8 History, *that/which* is my favourite subject, is easy.

3 Choose the correct answer, A, B or C.

1 Mike, ____ in London, is my best friend.
 A who lives **B** he lives **C** who he lives
2 The field ____ we play football is quite close to my home.
 A which **B** where **C** that
3 Maria is so spoiled! Her parents buy her everything ____!
 A who she wants
 B she wants
 C that she wants it
4 That's the girl ____ sister won the lottery!
 A who **B** who her **C** whose
5 The Internet is a very useful tool ____ help you with your studies.
 A which it can **B** can **C** that can
6 First Aid, ____ about last year, is a useful skill.
 A I learned **B** that I learned
 C which I learned

4 Join the sentences using the correct relative pronoun in brackets. Use commas only where necessary.

1 This voucher is worth £15. I found it in a magazine. (which / who)
 This voucher, which I found in a magazine, is worth £15.
2 I have an aunt. She loves hunting for bargains. (which / who)
3 My friend wants to start an online business. Her name is Tina. (who / whose)
4 I'll take you to the park. I usually meet my friends there. (that / where)
5 This old radio is now worth £500. I bought it for £20! (which / that)
6 The shoes are lovely. She bought them yesterday. (who / that)

5 Rewrite the sentences correctly.

1 Simon who wants to be an engineer loves maths.
 Simon, who wants to be an engineer, loves maths.
2 The girl who he met her last week is very nice.
3 Money management, that is a very useful subject, is not taught in schools.
4 That's the discount store who I told you about.
5 This book, I read last year, has lots of interesting information in it.
6 I met someone who brother plays football for Manchester United!

VOCABULARY
Learning skills

1 Choose the correct answers.

1 I find it difficult to concentrate *on/for/to* my homework if the TV's on.
2 Sara finds it difficult to cope *in/for/with* the stress of exams.
3 Tom has a really good memory *in/for/with* dates.
4 Please pay attention *in/for/to* what I am saying.
5 I've learned the words to the song *at/by/in* heart.
6 You should focus *in/on/to* one thing at a time.

2 Complete the study tips with one word from each box.

learning   spider   ~~study~~   study

diagram   methods   ~~space~~   style

Tips for successful study

- It's important to have a quiet 1) __study space__ where you can really concentrate on learning.
- Get to know your own individual 2) _____. For example, do you need to see things visually or do you learn better by doing practical things?
- Try out different 3) _____, for example making lists or highlighting words to help you remember them.
- If you're finding it difficult to understand something, it can be useful to draw a 4) _____, to help you understand all the different facts and ideas.

3 Complete the sentences with one word in each space.

1 I hate it when other students mess __about__ in class.
2 If I don't understand a word, I usually _____ it up in an online dictionary.
3 I try to get on _____ my homework as soon as I get home from school.
4 If you don't write _____ what you have to do for homework, you'll forget!
5 We're trying to _____ up a chess club at school.
6 The Internet is a great place to find _____ about all kinds of things.
7 I'll be so happy next year, because I can _____ up all the subjects I hate!
8 It's a good idea to look _____ your notes after the lesson, to make sure you understand them all.
9 It's great if you can get _____ by reading about a subject before the lesson.
10 Sometimes when we have to take notes, it can be difficult to _____ up with the teacher, because she talks so fast.

4 Read the blog post and choose the correct answer, A, B or C.

View previous comments   Cancel   Share   Post

My school diary

Today was a bad day! I got a really bad mark in my history test! I tried to revise, of course, but when I 1) _looked through_ my notes they didn't seem to make any sense! Then in maths the teacher told me off for 2) _____ in class. It really wasn't my fault – honestly! Still, I'm not going to 3) _____ and stop trying. I'm sure I can do better in history if I try to 4) _____ with the teacher in class better and pay more attention to what I 5) _____. I'm going to make more of an effort in other subjects, too. We're studying volcanoes in geography tomorrow, so I'm going to 6) _____ by trying to 7) _____ about them before the lesson. I'm also trying to 8) _____ a homework club at school. I think I'd find it easier to 9) _____ with my homework if I was in a classroom with no computer games or TV to distract me. Right, I'd better go now and 10) _____ 'volcanoes' online. Should be interesting!

Write a comment   Support

1 A looked up   **B looked through**   C looked at
2 A finding out   B messing about   C looking up
3 A give out   B give off   C give up
4 A keep up   B set up   C get ahead
5 A set up   B write down   C give up
6 A set up   B get ahead   C give up
7 A find out   B keep up   C write down
8 A keep up   B set up   C give up
9 A mess about   B find out   C get on
10 A look through   B get on with   C look up

38 GOLD EXPERIENCE

04 Things they don't teach you

GRAMMAR
Reduced relative clauses

1 Choose the correct answers.
1. Students *studying/studied* philosophy will read works by Aristotle.
2. A lot of the things *sold/selling* in that shop are made in China.
3. This is a teaching method *using/used* in many parts of the world.
4. Students *living/lived* in London find it easier to visit museums and art galleries.
5. The World Cup is a sports competition *watching/watched* all over the world.
6. The people *taking/took* part in the race come from all over the country.
7. You should take notice of advice *giving/given* to you by your teachers.
8. Students *learning/learned* languages are often shy about speaking in class.

2 Rewrite the sentences using reduced relative clauses.
1. Italy is a country which is known for its good food.
   Italy is a country known for its good food.
2. Students who are taking the exam should be at school by 8.45.
3. The law which was introduced last year has made no difference.
4. Students who have breakfast before they come to school get better grades.
5. Confucius is a philosopher who is admired all over the world.
6. Supermarkets which offer big discounts are becoming more popular.
7. The subject which was discussed in last week's programme was 'different learning styles'.
8. This is the latest film which features James Bond.

3 Read the article and choose the correct answer, A, B or C.

Maria Montessori

Maria Montessori was an Italian educator 1) *who developed* a new approach to the education of young children. She grew up in the late nineteenth century, when most of the methods 2) ____ by teachers were very traditional. Teachers stood in front of the class and explained things to children 3) ____ at their desks in rows. Montessori believed that children 4) ____ to discover and learn things on their own, through play, would actually learn more. She opened her first school for young children in 1907. Children 5) ____ the new school were allowed to spend a lot of their time in free play or creative activities. The new kind of education 6) ____ by the school proved extremely popular. Teachers 7) ____ in the school noticed that the children seemed happier and more relaxed than in traditional schools, and they also seemed to learn more. Now there are thousands of Montessori Schools all over the world 8) ____ children according to Maria Montessori's principles.

1. A developing B developed **C who developed**
2. A using B they use C used
3. A sitting B which were sitting C sat
4. A were left B left C who left
5. A attended B who attending C attending
6. A providing B provided C which provided
7. A worked B who working C working
8. A taught B who taught C teaching

LISTENING

1 **4.1 Listen to a radio interview about memory. Choose the correct words from the interview to complete the sentences.**

1 Elizabeth Smallwood is a *psychologist/novelist/memory champion*.
2 Her book entered the best seller charts in *January/February/June*.
3 She spent her childhood in *Colombia/Namibia/Venezuela*.
4 Elizabeth thinks the interviewer's problem is *normal/irritating/unusual*.
5 She uses *keys/faces/names* as an example of something we forget.
6 She suggests thinking of a *funny/simple/well-known* picture to remember things.
7 The interviewer doesn't need *sugar/cheese/lemonade* from the supermarket.
8 Elizabeth advises students not to get *stressed/angry/bored* before exams.

2 **4.2 Listen again and choose the correct answer, A, B or C.**

1 The interviewer makes a mistake with
  (A) Elizabeth's surname.
  B the name of Elizabeth's book.
  C the country Elizabeth lives in.
2 The interviewer admits that he has a problem
  A remembering where he met people before.
  B remembering the reason for going to a place.
  C remembering where he puts things.
3 Elizabeth advises using
  A a camera.
  B your imagination.
  C a written record.
4 She gives the example of
  A a person who wins a competition.
  B a person who does tricks.
  C a person who designs rooms.
5 What does the interviewer put in his mental picture?
  A a chicken with a glass of lemonade
  B a painting of some flowers
  C a book with an animal on the front
6 In Elizabeth's opinion, to prepare for an exam students should
  A do some study at night.
  B practise different memory techniques.
  C get a lot of rest.

SPEAKING SKILLS

1 Match the phrases (1–7) with the functions (a–g).

1 Some people say it's better to learn things from books than computers. _c_
2 It's good because you remember things more easily. ___
3 I think so too. You're right. ___
4 But I feel it's quicker on computer. ___
5 Not necessarily. It depends on the topic. ___
6 I use books, for example, when I need to check a lot of things. ___
7 You can look quickly through the chapters so you get the information faster. ___

a agreeing
b disagreeing
c giving an opinion
d giving an example
e giving a reason
f showing a result
g giving an opposite opinion

2 Put the words in the correct order.

1 you / thought / going / of / have / on a course
  Have you thought of going on a course ?
2 but / point / can / I / your / see / I'm afraid I don't agree
  _____ .
3 too / so / think / but / I / not everyone has enough money
  _____ .
4 what / people / can't / who / about / but / use computers very well
  _____ ?
5 depends / my / it / opinion, / on / in / your situation.
  _____ .

3 Complete the conversation with these words.

because   example   opinion   point   so   ~~think~~

A: What do you 1) _think_ about the advantages of learning on your own rather than in a group?
B: Well, in my 2) _____ it depends on what you're learning. For 3) _____, if you're learning a new language, sometimes it's good to have a private teacher. It's better 4) _____ they can help you with all your problems.
A: I can see your 5) _____ but I think that learning a language in a group is good. There are lots of people 6) _____ you can practise speaking with them.

04 Things they don't teach you

WRITING

1 Read the writing task and choose the correct words in the sentences (1–6).

1 You need to write *a notice/an email*.
2 You have to choose *one/two* idea(s).
3 You should explain your reasons for *this choice/sending money to Africa*.
4 You are asked to suggest a *date and a time/some ideas* for the event.
5 Your reply is to the *headteacher/your class teacher*.
6 You should use *informal/semi-formal* language.

You see this notice in your classroom.

We are planning to organise an event to raise money to help build a school in a village in Africa. Here are some of our ideas. Please write and let me know which idea you prefer and why. In addition to this, please give your own ideas about how we should run the event.

1 a talent show
2 a fashion show
3 a quiz show

Thank you.
Roger Peters
Headteacher

2 Match the incorrect sentences from a student's email (1–6) with the types of mistakes (a–f).

1 I write to tell you my ideas. *b*
2 Firstly of all I think this is an excellent idea. ___
3 I think be good to have a talent show. ___
4 In adition there could be some good music. ___
5 Hi Mr Peters, ___
6 In reply at your request, here are my ideas: ___

a wrong spelling
b wrong tense
c wrong preposition
d wrong formality
e wrong word
f missing word(s)

3 Read the writing task again and write your answer in 140–190 words.

Revision Unit 4

1 Complete the words with the missing letters.

1 These shoes only cost £15. They were a real b **a r g a i** n!
2 We finished eating and asked for the b _____ l.
3 There were only a few c ___ s _____ s in the shop.
4 The shop a _____ s t _____ t helped me find the right size.
5 You can pay in c _____ h or by credit card.
6 There's a 10 per cent d ___ s _____ t on all clothes this week.
7 You'll find tinned foods in the next a ___ s ___ e.
8 Take everything to the c _____ t where you can pay for it.
9 My t _____ e y was full of food!
10 There was a long q _____ e of people outside the shop.
11 This v _____ r allows you 20 per cent off fresh fruit and vegetables.
12 The t _____ l c _____ t of the weekly grocery shop keeps going up.

2 Choose the correct answers.

1 I'll *pay/spend* you £5 if you mend my bike for me.
2 I like your phone. How much did it *cost/worth*?
3 I'm *saving/economising* money for my holiday.
4 Can I *lend/borrow* your pen, please?
5 My mum's ring is *cost/worth* nearly £1,000!
6 Could you *lend/borrow* me £1 to buy a drink?

3 Complete the sentences with these words.

by   for   ~~on~~   on   to   with

1 I want to focus _on_ improving my maths.
2 Have we got to learn all these verbs _____ heart?
3 She never pays attention _____ what the teacher is saying!
4 I don't think I can cope _____ all this homework!
5 I can't concentrate _____ my essay when everyone's talking!
6 I haven't got a very good memory _____ names.

4 Unscramble and write the words.

1 The answer's obvious – it's just _common sense_! (mmoonc snsee)
2 You should read more if you want to improve your _____. (gealern nokwedlge)
3 He wants to get a job, rather than go into _____. (herghi euciondat)
4 Have you got any _____ of working? (talpaccir perexceien)
5 My _____ is very visual, so I need to see things to learn them well. (lingarne stely)
6 I always draw a _____ to help me organise my ideas for an essay. (dipser dramiga)
7 I've got a really nice _____ in my bedroom. (sudty pasce)
8 I use a lot of different _____ when I'm revising for exams. (syutd mthedso)

5 Complete the text messages with one word in each space.

Messages   **Lia**

Hi Anna,
How are you getting 1) _on_ with your geography homework on fuels? I've looked 2) _____ my notes, but I can't understand anything! I give 3) _____!

Hi Lia,
I'm finding it difficult to concentrate 4) _____ homework, too, as it's so warm and sunny outside. And my little brother's messing 5) _____ with his friends in the next room – that makes it difficult, to focus 6) _____ work, too!

Well, why don't you come round to my house? We can see if we can find 7) _____ anything by looking online, and write 8) _____ the key points in our books.

Good idea. It's much easier to cope 9) _____ difficult homework when you do it together. See you soon!

Revision Unit 4

6 Complete the sentences with the correct relative pronouns. Sometimes more than one answer is possible.

1. Here's the DVD _that_ I was looking for!
2. That's the place _____ I usually sit to have my lunch.
3. The books _____ my grandma used at school were really boring!
4. Mrs Giddings, _____ teaches us French, lived in Paris for three years.
5. 1966 was the year _____ England won the World Cup.
6. Physics, _____ is taught in most schools, is quite a difficult subject.
7. Children _____ parents give them a lot of support tend to do better at school.
8. My friend Matt is someone _____ always does well in exams.

7 Choose the correct answer, A, B or C.

1. Sam _, who lives near me,_ is very good at tennis.
   - **A** , who lives near me,
   - **B** that lives near me,
   - **C** , which lives near me,
2. I've got some photos of the house _____ in France.
   - **A** , where we stay
   - **B** where we stay
   - **C** that we stay
3. The book _____ is about two teenagers from New York.
   - **A** , which I'm reading at the moment,
   - **B** who I'm reading at the moment
   - **C** I'm reading at the moment
4. Sara _____ decided to go home.
   - **A** who was feeling tired
   - **B** was feeling tired
   - **C** , who was feeling tired,
5. My friend Michael _____ has always wanted to study medicine.
   - **A** , who mother is a doctor,
   - **B** , whose mother she is a doctor,
   - **C** , whose mother is a doctor,
6. Mr Simpson is a teacher _____ a lot.
   - **A** , who I admire,
   - **B** that I admire,
   - **C** I admire him
7. Her first album _____ sold over a million copies.
   - **A** , it was called *Love alone*,
   - **B** , which was called *Love alone*,
   - **C** , that was called *Love alone*,

8 Complete the reduced relative clauses using the present or past participles of these verbs.

collect   give   know   ~~study~~   teach   wait
watch   write

1. Students _studying_ German next year will get the chance to go on a school trip to Germany.
2. The people _____ the film were shocked by some of the violent scenes.
3. The test _____ to the students last term was very difficult.
4. All the money _____ at the charity event will go to help poor children in India.
5. Stephen Hawking is a scientist _____ for his books on the origins of the universe.
6. The books _____ by Charles Dickens in the nineteenth century are still popular today.
7. The people _____ outside the shop are keen to find bargains when the sale starts.
8. The person _____ you history next term will be Mr Sharpe.

9 Rewrite the sentences using the word given. Use between two and five words, including the word given.

1. It's a festival celebrated all over the world. **WHICH**
   It's a festival _which is celebrated_ all over the world.
2. Can you give me back the pen you borrowed last week? **WHICH**
   Can you give me back the pen _____ you last week?
3. Children taught to read before they go to school usually do well. **LEARN**
   Children _____ before they go to school usually do well.
4. Students wanting to come on the trip should add their names to the list. **WANT**
   Students _____ on the trip should add their names to the list.
5. Is there a shop selling souvenirs? **BUY**
   Is there a shop _____ souvenirs?
6. The information you can get on the website isn't always accurate. **GIVEN**
   The information _____ isn't always accurate.

43

05 Green world

READING

1 Read the comments on page 45 quickly and match the photos (1–4) with the people (A–D).

1 _B_
2 _____
3 _____
4 _____

2 Choose the best heading (1–5) for each online comment (A–D). You do not need one of the headings.

1 Thin is good — _D_
2 A tasty thought — _____
3 Help those in power — _____
4 A tall solution — _____
5 A loss for the world — _____

3 Read the online comments again. Match the statements (1–8) with the texts (A–D).

Which comments mention:
1 the importance of using others' experience? — _B_
2 the unpopularity of one solution? — _____
3 a problem created by people's greed? — _____
4 a clever way of dealing with two problems? — _____
5 the difficulty for individuals to influence change? — _____
6 an unexpected solution based on recycling? — _____
7 the need to accept a different way of life? — _____
8 an expensive but effective solution? — _____

4 Complete the campaign slogans with these words from the comments.

alternative   endangered   habitats   solar   ~~spaces~~   waste

1 Kids need a place to play. Save our public _spaces_!
2 Save the whale and other _____ species!
3 No toxic _____ here!
4 Stop destroying wildlife _____!
5 NO MORE NUCLEAR POWER STATIONS. WE NEED MORE _____ ENERGY!
6 Use _____ panels for green electricity!

05 Green world

💬 View previous comments   Cancel   Share   Post

Are you worried about the environment? Tell us your thoughts!

A MAGDA

Read More >

B MARTIN

Read More >

C MAGNUS

Read More >

D ELVIRA

Read More >

Write a comment   Support

VOCABULARY
The environment

1 Complete the sentences with one word in each space.

1 The country doesn't grow much food, so it is d_ependent_ on food from abroad.
2 I prefer to buy o_____ fruit and vegetables because they're grown without chemicals.
3 I always buy r_____ paper because it's better for the environment.
4 They grow most of their own food – they're practically s_____-s_____ .
5 Would you prefer to live in a city or a r_____ area?
6 Destroying the rainforest has a very serious ec_____ impact.
7 Badgers are a p_____ species, which means people aren't allowed to kill them.
8 Foxes can live equally well in the countryside or in an u_____ environment.

2 Complete the sentences with one word from each box.

> be catch ~~die~~ go pick report
>
> back into on ~~out~~ towards up

1 If we continue to destroy the rainforest, many species will _die_ _out_ .
2 I can't go on the nature walk on Saturday, but Joe's going, and he says he'll _____ _____ and tell me all about it.
3 Our cake sale raised over £150, which will _____ _____ the cost of solar panels.
4 The idea of cycling to school is really starting to _____ _____, so more and more people are doing it.
5 If you join your local environmental group, you can _____ _____ lots of useful tips about things you can do to make a difference.
6 I don't think I'll ever _____ _____ growing my own food, but I really admire people who do it!

3 Match (1–6) with (a–f) to make collocations.

1 an urban   a generations
2 a natural   b garden
3 a concrete   c habitat
4 future   d landscape
5 a bus   e jungle
6 a botanical   f route

4 Read the article and choose the correct answer, A, B, C or D.

Green City

Hamburg in the north of Germany is known for its many factories and 1) _industries_ . But now the city plans to change its image of being a concrete 2) ____ and become a truly green city. It wants to ban cars from large parts of the city to cut down on traffic 3) ____ and reduce air 4) ____ . Instead, people will be encouraged to cycle on a new Green Network, hundreds of new cycle 5) ____ that are being built all over the city. There will also be improved public 6) ____ to help people move around the city easily. In addition, large parts of the city centre will be for 7) ____ only, making shopping a more pleasant experience. Gina Hoffman from Hamburg is a keen environmental activist. She already has a 8) ____ garden at her flat and is trying to persuade others in her 9) ____ to do the same. She has also campaigned for more 10) ____ bins in the city. She hopes that Hamburg can set an example that other cities can follow.

1 **A** industries   **B** industrial
   C business   **D** production
2 **A** forest   **B** jungle
   C desert   **D** wood
3 **A** smoke   **B** dirt
   C steam   **D** fumes
4 **A** dirt   **B** smoke
   C pollution   **D** waste
5 **A** roads   **B** paths
   C pavements   **D** walks
6 **A** transport   **B** travel
   C journey   **D** voyage
7 **A** walker   **B** foot
   C pedestrians   **D** walk
8 **A** ceiling   **B** top
   C roofed   **D** rooftop
9 **A** neighbourhood   **B** neighbours
   C neighbouring   **D** neighbourly
10 **A** remaking   **B** reusing
   C recycling   **D** redoing

GRAMMAR
The future

1 Choose the correct answers.

1 *Are/Do/Will* you meeting Sam this evening?
2 We're *go/going/going to* travel by train.
3 I'm sure you *will/going/going to* have a great time.
4 I can't come to the cinema with you this evening. I'll be *do/doing/going to do* my homework.
5 Where *are/will/do* you going to stay?
6 I'll come and visit as soon *as/that/when* I can.
7 It will be dark by *time/the time/the times* we get home.
8 Where will he be *wait/waits/waiting* for us?

2 Choose the correct answer, A, B or C.

1 I can't talk now, but I _will call_ you later.
 A call
 B will call
 C am call
2 Do you think it ____ later?
 A will rain
 B is raining
 C going to rain
3 Jane won't be here on Saturday. She ____ on holiday on Friday.
 A will go
 B will be go
 C is going
4 This time next week we ____ on the beach. I can't wait!
 A will lie
 B am going to lie
 C will be lying
5 Dan is going shopping this afternoon. He ____ some new boots.
 A is buying
 B will buying
 C is going to buy
6 I'll text you as soon as I ____ home.
 A get
 B will get
 C am going to get
7 ____ you get this letter, I'll be in New York.
 A By time
 B For the time
 C By the time
8 It's a great film. ____ enjoy it.
 A Definitely you'll
 B You'll definitely
 C You definitely

3 Complete the sentences with the future simple or future continuous form of the verbs in brackets.

1 I'm sure you _will like_ (like) Tom. He's so nice.
2 I won't be here next week. I ____ (stay) with my aunt in Berlin.
3 If we don't take action, climate change ____ (get) much worse.
4 In three months' time I ____ (study) at university.
5 Give your computer to Ben. He ____ (mend) it for you.
6 The weather ____ (not be) very nice tomorrow.
7 Come round after eight o'clock. I ____ (not revise) then.
8 Is that bag heavy? I ____ (carry) it for you if you like.

4 Rewrite the sentences putting the adverbs in brackets in the correct place.

1 We're going to visit the Louvre. (definitely)
 We're definitely going to visit the Louvre.
2 I'll be revising this evening. (probably)
3 It will be an interesting experience. (certainly)
4 She's going to train as a nurse. (possibly)
5 The meal won't be very expensive. (probably)

5 Complete the conversation with the correct form of the verbs in brackets.

A What are your plans for the weekend?
B Well, I 1) _'m going_ (go) shopping with Emily on Saturday morning, but I probably 2) ____ (not buy) anything, because I haven't got any money! Then, when I 3) ____ (get) home I've got loads of revision to do, so I 4) ____ (probably / revise) all afternoon. What about you?
A I 5) ____ (call) Rob to ask him if he wants to get together. He's usually free on Saturday, so we 6) ____ (probably / do) something together. I don't know about Sunday. 7) ____ (you / do) anything exciting on Sunday?
B Not really. Some friends of my parents' 8) ____ (come) over for lunch. By the time they 9) ____ (leave) it 10) ____ (probably / be) quite late. Boring!

VOCABULARY
Learning skills

1 Find eight words related to food and water. The words go across, down or diagonally. The first letter of each word is highlighted.

p	r	i	s	t	w	b	u	n	t	e
e	r	t	i	w	h	e	a	t	g	e
s	d	o	f	l	o	v	l	e	t	s
t	b	r	l	h	r	d	e	l	j	u
i	m	p	o	r	t	y	e	x	e	b
c	s	f	o	u	e	w	i	m	x	e
i	n	f	d	r	g	e	l	t	p	s
d	t	r	a	p	o	h	r	e	o	v
e	r	a	i	n	w	a	t	e	r	e
s	a	e	w	p	i	w	l	k	t	t

2 Unscramble and write the words related to food and water.

1. In many rural areas, people's only source of drinking water is the village ____well____ (lelw).
2. People were banned from watering their gardens last summer because there was a _____ (trawe orshaget).
3. After two weeks of rain, there were _____ (fodslo) in many parts of the country.
4. Farmers are being encouraged to use fewer _____ (espictieds) on their crops.
5. No crops will grow in the _____ (dsrtee).
6. There was a _____ (roudght) last summer, with no rain for three months.
7. We collect _____ (anirartew) and use it to water the garden.
8. Organic products are becoming more popular with _____ (csuomenrs).

3 Complete the sentences with one word in each space.

1. I don't understand – it doesn't ____make____ sense!
2. I always have a cup of coffee in the morning – I really can't do _____ it!
3. We should all _____ our bit to help the environment.
4. _____ sure you switch the lights off before you go out.
5. I'm hot – I could do _____ a drink of water.
6. I can't afford a new car, so I'll have to _____ do with this old one!

4 Read the two opinions and choose the correct answer, A, B or C.

do

1	**A** make	**(B)** do	**C** have
2	**A** producer	**B** consumer	**C** buying
3	**A** pesticides	**B** wells	**C** fumes
4	**A** imports	**B** sells	**C** buys
5	**A** value	**B** sense	**C** logic
6	**A** for	**B** without	**C** with
7	**A** sure	**B** effort	**C** try
8	**A** lacks	**B** shortages	**C** absences
9	**A** wells	**B** drills	**C** exports
10	**A** desert	**B** drought	**C** flood

GRAMMAR
so, such, too, enough

1 Put the words in the correct order to make sentences.

1 so / dry / It's / that / here / grows / nothing
   It's so dry here that nothing grows.

2 so / people / There / many / were / that / move / you / couldn't

3 see it / It's / film / such / I / want / a / good / that / to / again

4 box / so / The / was / that / heavy / carry it / I / couldn't

5 cold / It's / sit / too / outside / to

6 eat / food / enough / to / There's / everyone / for

7 too / books / carry / There / were / many / for / me / to

8 homework / too / I've / much / got / do / to

2 Choose the correct answer, A, B or C.

1 I couldn't run ___ keep up with the others.
   A too fast to
   B enough fast to
   C (fast enough to)

2 He's ___ guy that everyone gets on with him.
   A so nice
   B such a nice
   C enough nice

3 She's got ___ money that she doesn't know what to do with it!
   A so much
   B too much
   C so enough

4 There weren't ___ for everyone to sit down.
   A so many seats
   B enough seats
   C too many seats

5 The food was ___ eat.
   A too hot to
   B too much hot to
   C very hot to

6 I was ___ I had to go straight to bed.
   A such tired that
   B tired enough to
   C so tired that

3 Complete the text with one word in each space.

Eco Homes

We all know that we waste too 1) *much* energy at home and we should cut down. But the fact is that most of the homes we live in just aren't energy-efficient 2) _____. They use 3) _____ much energy to keep them warm in winter and cool in summer, and that's without all the lighting and modern electrical appliances we all love. Now, more and more people are looking for an eco-home – a home that is comfortable 4) _____ to live in all year round, without using 5) _____ a lot of energy that it damages the environment. This house has 6) _____ solar panels on the roof 7) _____ generate all its own electricity. In fact, last year it generated 8) _____ much electricity that it sold some to the main electricity supplier. Owner Adam Trilby is delighted with his eco-house. 'It's good to know we're helping the environment,' he says, 'and it's 9) _____ a cheap house to live in that we now have more money to spend on other things.'

4 Rewrite the sentences using the word given. Use between two and five words, including the word given.

1 It was so hot that we couldn't play tennis. **TOO**
   It was _*too hot to play*_ tennis.

2 The water was too cold to swim in. **ENOUGH**
   The water _____ swim in.

3 It rained such a lot that the river flooded. **SO**
   There was _____ the river flooded.

4 There were so many birds that you couldn't count them. **MANY**
   There were _____ count.

5 The dress was so expensive that I decided not to buy it. **SUCH**
   It was _____ I decided not to buy it.

6 He invited so many people that they couldn't all get into the house! **LOT**
   He invited _____ people that they couldn't all get into the house!

LISTENING

1 5.1 Listen to two people talking in six different situations. Choose which situations (1–6) mention the points (a–f):

a statistics
b doctors
c being perfect
d the bus
e a towel   _1_
f a park

2 5.2 Listen again and choose the correct answer, A, B or C.

1 You hear someone leaving a voicemail message. What is she doing?
   A reminding someone about an activity
   B changing an arrangement with someone
   C offering to do something for someone

2 You hear two people talking about cycling to school. Why doesn't the boy cycle?
   A His parents won't get him a bicycle.
   B His home is too far away.
   C He isn't allowed to.

3 You hear a person making an announcement. What does the speaker want the students to do?
   A inform people if they want to go to a talk
   B bring food to a talk by a chef
   C check a list for detailed information

4 You hear two people talking about a possible new road in their town. What do they both agree on?
   A A new road would be a very bad idea.
   B There is too much traffic on the present road.
   C They should encourage people to park outside the town.

5 You hear two people talking about writing an essay. How is the boy feeling?
   A surprised by the question
   B worried about the question
   C confused by the question

6 You hear a book review on the radio. What is true about the book?
   A It's a book written for students learning about climate change.
   B It has photographs of the effects of climate change.
   C It explains how we can all fight climate change.

SPEAKING SKILLS

1 Put these words in the correct column for agreeing with positive or negative statements.

> I'm not either   I will too   Neither have I
> Nor did I   ~~So do I~~   So would I

positive statements	negative statements
So do I	

2 Complete the conversation with these phrases.

> I did   I'm not   Neither am I   Neither have I
> Neither do I   ~~So did I~~   So was I

A: I watched an interesting documentary about sea pollution last night.
B: 1) _So did I_. I thought it was excellent. I've never seen a documentary like that before.
A: 2) _____. I was going to watch the film on Channel 6.
B: 3) _____ but then I saw the advert for the documentary so I switched over. I don't usually watch documentaries.
A: 4) _____ but Mark recommended this one. He saw it last year. I didn't realise plastic bags caused so many problems.
B: 5) _____ because I've read some articles about it. I'm going to a talk about it after school next week.
A: 6) Oh, _____. I've got photography class after school that day. I would really love to know more about the problem. I'm not sure that there's an easy answer to it really.
B: 7) _____, but I'll tell you what they say in the talk.

3 Match the questions (1–5) with the opinions (a–e).
1 Is it a good idea to keep cars out of town centres? _b_
2 Do you think it's important to recycle our rubbish? ___
3 Some people volunteer to clean up beaches. Would you like to do that? ___
4 Is it better to build new roads or more trains? ___
5 How can people save energy in their homes? ___

a Yes, they get very dirty because people don't take their rubbish home with them after a visit.
b If it's possible, I would say yes. So much traffic isn't good for the people who live there because they're breathing in dirty air all the time.
c We can all switch off lights and not leave TVs and computers on. It's not much but if everyone does this, it will help.
d I definitely agree. We throw away much too much these days and where will we put it all when there is no more space?
e In my opinion we should make it easier to use public transport, to travel both long and short distances. It's better for the environment and there are too many cars today.

WRITING

1 Complete the sentences with these words.

> conclusion   first   final   firstly
> lastly   ~~point~~   secondly   start

1 Another _point_ is whether we live near the sea or not.
2 In the _____ place, I am convinced that our houses will change completely.
3 In _____, I have to admit that I think our children will have a lot of problems in the future.
4 To _____ with, we should look at where we might be living.
5 As a _____ point, I must say that I believe our energy supplies will be completely different.
6 _____, I would like to say that I think this is a very interesting question.
7 _____, I should add that recycling is not easy for everyone.
8 And _____, we must finish by looking at the cost of all these changes.

2 Read the essay task carefully and answer the question.

> How can individuals help the environment in the future?
> 1 recycling things
> 2 being careful with energy
> 3 your own idea

Which topic would not be appropriate in this essay?
1 travelling by plane less often
2 saving water
3 agreeing to have wind farms in the area
4 raising the cost of electricity
5 volunteering to clean up beaches
6 planting bright flowers for bees

3 Read the two introductions to the essay, A and B. Which introduction, A or B, do the statements (1–7) refer to?

1 The writer uses a variety of words and phrases to make their point. _B_
2 The writer uses a general statement for an introductory sentence. ___
3 The writer repeats some words and phrases too often. ___
4 The writer uses a short sentence for emphasis. ___
5 The writer makes us think that the rest of the essay will be a list. ___
6 The writer makes a point that he/she will then develop in the rest of the essay. ___
7 This introduction will probably score a higher mark. ___

4 Read the essay task again and write your essay in 140–190 words.

Revision Unit 5

1 Complete the sentences with the correct form of the words in capitals.

1. The oil spill caused an _ecological_ disaster. **ECOLOGY**
2. Many people believe that we are too _____ on oil and fossil fuels. **DEPEND**
3. We should try to preserve the natural world for future _____. **GENERATE**
4. Tigers are an _____ species. **DANGER**
5. There is too much air _____ in our cities. **POLLUTE**
6. We need more _____ bins in the city. **RECYCLE**
7. This is a very pleasant _____ to live in. **NEIGHBOUR**
8. You aren't allowed to camp here, as it's a _____ area. **PROTECT**

2 Complete the sentences with one word in each space.

1. I don't really want a big garden because I'm not _into_ gardening.
2. I would find it very difficult to do _____ my mobile phone.
3. If we don't do more to protect these animals, they will die _____.
4. This money will go _____ providing clean water in rural areas.
5. This is the only food we've got, so we'll have to make do _____ it.
6. Do you think that solar-powered phones will ever catch _____?
7. We went to a green living exhibition to pick _____ some ideas.
8. Mike went to the talk and then reported _____ to us.

3 Complete the sentences with these words.

botanical   concrete   fumes   ~~national~~
natural   rooftop   route   shortage

1. The area is a _national_ park, so it's protected.
2. She's into _____ gardening and has lots of plants up there, as well as a fantastic view!
3. We saw some wonderful plants in the _____ garden.
4. As far as I'm concerned, the city is a _____ jungle and I'd hate to live there!
5. There was a severe water _____ last summer.
6. I can't stand the smell of traffic _____!
7. This woodland area is an important _____ habitat for plants and animals.
8. Which bus _____ is your home on?

4 Complete the sentences with one word in each space.

1. A city is an u_rban_ environment.
2. If people are s_____-s_____, they produce all the food that they need to eat.
3. Public s_____ are areas in a town or city where people can go to spend time or relax.
4. T_____ waste is waste material that is dangerous and harmful to people's health.
5. P_____ are people who are walking in a town or city.
6. If the roads and fields are covered in water, they are f_____.
7. When a country e_____ goods, it sells them to another country.
8. A d_____ is a very dry area where few plants grow.
9. A d_____ is a long period of time without rain.
10. A w_____ is a hole in, the ground from which people get water.

Revision Unit 5

5 Choose the correct answers.

GOING GREEN — WHAT CAN YOU DO?

- Try to become a green 1) *consumer/user/transport* and only buy things that are environmentally-friendly.
- Don't drive places, but use public 2) *export/import/transport* instead, or think about cycling to school or work. There are plenty of cycle 3) *roads/paths/pavements* in most cities.
- Encourage your school or place of work to invest in 4) *alternative/recycling/waste* energy technology such as solar 5) *panels/paths/spaces*.
- Buy 6) *nature/organic/chemical* foods wherever possible, to cut down on the use of 7) *rainwater/pesticides/pollution*.
- Campaign to preserve wildlife 8) *habits/habitats/spaces* to help endangered 9) *species/waste/desert*.

6 Put the words in the correct order to make sentences.

1. tomorrow / time / I'll / This / skiing / be
   This time tomorrow I'll be skiing.
2. going / Where / to have / lunch / we / are / ?
3. definitely / rain / It's / going / to / later
4. next / time / travelling / year / I'll / This / be /
5. probably / late / The train / be / will
6. need / an umbrella / won't / We / definitely

7 Complete the sentences with one word in each space.

1. What are you _going_ to do in the holidays?
2. Do you think that polar bears _____ die out when all the ice melts?
3. I'm quite tired, so I probably _____ go out.
4. What _____ you doing on Sunday?
5. My grandma will _____ sitting by the fire, as usual!
6. Where _____ you be living next year?
7. I'm _____ going to learn to drive yet – it's too expensive!
8. I'll come as soon _____ I can.
9. It will open in three months' _____ .
10. I'll be ready _____ the time you get home.

8 Choose the correct answers.

1. The soup was *so/such* hot that I couldn't eat it.
2. There isn't *enough/so much* land to grow all the food we need.
3. She's *so/such* a popular girl that everyone invites her to their parties.
4. The issue of climate change is *so/too* important to ignore.
5. The weather was *so/such* bad that we couldn't go out.
6. Do you think there's *so much/too much* violence on TV?
7. The bag isn't *enough big/big enough* to take everything.
8. I've got *such a lot/so lots* of books that I need some more shelves.
9. Sara spends *so much/such a lot* time working that she never enjoys herself!
10. You shouldn't eat *too much/too many* sweets.

9 Rewrite the sentences using the word given. Use between two and five words, including the word given.

1. The film was too boring to watch! **SO**
   The film was _so boring that I_ couldn't watch it.
2. My parents think I'm too young to go on holiday alone. **ENOUGH**
   My parents think I _____ go on holiday alone.
3. Mia's got so many clothes that they won't all fit in her wardrobe. **LOT**
   Mia's got _____ that they won't all fit in her wardrobe.
4. I didn't work very hard, so I didn't pass my exam. **ENOUGH**
   I didn't _____ my exam.
5. The book was so good that I recommended it to all my friends. **SUCH**
   It was _____ I recommended it to all my friends.
6. There were such a lot of people that they didn't all fit on the boat. **TOO**
   There were _____ fit on the boat.

06 Before time

READING

1 Read the story and choose the best title, A, B or C.

A A romantic evening
B A ghost story
C A visit to remember

2 Choose the correct answer, true or false. Read and check.

1 Alice drove to meet Jake in Marwood.
   True   False
2 Alice guessed Jake's plan for the evening.
   True   False
3 Jake left his car in the castle car park.
   True   False
4 The castle was brightly lit at night.
   True   False
5 The castle was open to visitors during the day.
   True   False
6 It was a warm evening.
   True   False
7 When they got to the castle it was sunset.
   True   False
8 The tour guide sounds bored with his job.
   True   False
9 Alice was disappointed by the tour.
   True   False

3 Read the story again and choose the correct answer, A, B, C or D.

1 During Alice's first day in Marwood she
   A did lots of shopping in the centre.
   B had a meal near the river.
   C went to the sea for a romantic walk.
   D looked at some historical ruins.
2 *it* in line 7 refers to
   A a reason for dressing warmly.
   B Jake's plan for the evening.
   C his habit of surprising Alice.
   D how Alice feels about Jake.
3 When they arrived at the castle Alice was
   A impressed by the building.
   B scared of the dark.
   C angry with Jake.
   D amused by the situation.
4 *shivering* in line 15 means
   A the people were chatting.
   B the people were shaking.
   C the people were laughing.
   D the people were taking photographs.
5 Ferdinand's story is about a woman who
   A killed herself.
   B was murdered.
   C fell by accident.
   D had killed a family member.
6 What did Alice think of the experience before they saw the body?
   A It was disappointing.
   B It was interesting.
   C It was funny.
   D It was frightening.

54 GOLD EXPERIENCE

Chapter 1

It had been a really interesting day in Marwood. Jake had met Alice from the train and shown her round the town. She loved the historic atmosphere with all the little old shops and houses in the main square and she was surprised to see that parts of the old city wall were still standing and in good enough condition for them to look round and walk on.

Jake had promised her something special for the evening but had kept it a secret. He was always surprising her and Alice liked that about him. All he'd said was: 'Wear something warm!' 'OK, so it must be somewhere outside,' she'd thought. Maybe it would be a walk on the beach or a romantic meal in the garden of the restaurant overlooking the river. That would be nice!

She was wrong. Jake had planned something very different. After parking his car in the town square he pointed to a dark shape on the hill. It was the old castle. 'That's where we're going,' he smiled and put his arm round her shoulders. 'Let's go. We need to be there by 8.30.' Alice still had no idea why they were going to the castle in the evening. It closed to visitors at 5.30. But she felt excited as they walked through the quiet narrow streets and up the hill to the castle.

As they approached the castle entrance she saw a group of people waiting there. It was a cool evening and some of them looked very cold and were shivering. Behind them the massive stone walls of the castle were shining in the late evening sun. Alice thought it was a beautiful sight. They joined the group and suddenly a tall man stepped to the front and addressed them all. 'OK,' he said. 'We're all here now, so we can start. Welcome to Marwood Castle Ghost Walk. My name is Ferdinand and I'm your guide for the evening. I hope we all have a very scary evening! Follow me please.'

'This is a joke, isn't it?' Alice whispered to Jake.

'Not at all!' he smiled. 'I thought you'd love it, I know you read a lot of ghost stories!' Alice punched him on the arm. 'I love stories when I'm safe and warm at home. I'm actually really scared of ghosts!'

'Don't worry! There aren't any real ghosts here! It's just like a tour. You'll enjoy it!'

They followed Ferdinand across a small wooden bridge and into the castle ruins. It was very old and although the outside was undamaged, inside many of the floors and walls had fallen away with time. Alice imagined how it might have been before, full of people and noise. Now, it was empty and silent apart from the low voices of the group.

Ferdinand clearly enjoyed his job. He held an old-fashioned lamp which shone light in a small circle. He gave them a brief history of the castle and then pointed with his stick to a window hole at the top of one wall. 'That, my friends,' he said, 'is where Lord Marwood's first wife, Margaret, jumped to her death. However, that was his story. Other people say that she was pushed. Lord Marwood married a beautiful young cousin shortly afterwards and it was clear why she really died. They say that she walks the castle when the moon is full.'

Alice stared, amazed, at the room, forgetting her earlier fear. It was better than she'd thought it would be. It was almost fun. And then she saw something dark on the wall. 'What's that?' Alice asked. Ferdinand produced a strong torch from his pocket and shone it directly at the ground by the wall.

Alice felt icy cold. The body of a woman was lying there and the dark marks on the wall were blood. This was no ghost.

20

VOCABULARY
Actions and reactions

1 Complete the sentences with these words.

> breath   dry   face   goose-bumps   heart
> lump   nerves   ~~pale~~   shivers   sigh

1 Her face went _pale_ when she saw the huge creature.
2 We all breathed a _____ of relief when we realised that there was nothing there.
3 My mouth went _____ and I could hardly speak.
4 I took a deep _____ and slowly opened the door.
5 We all had _____ on our skin from standing outside in the cold.
6 My _____ began to thump with fear.
7 I suddenly heard a loud roar which sent _____ down my spine.
8 I don't know what I would do if I came face-to-_____ with a wild animal.
9 The noise of the machines was beginning to get on my _____ .
10 It was sad when they left and I had a _____ in my throat as I said goodbye.

2 Look at the picture and write the words.

> back   elbow   knee   neck   shoulder

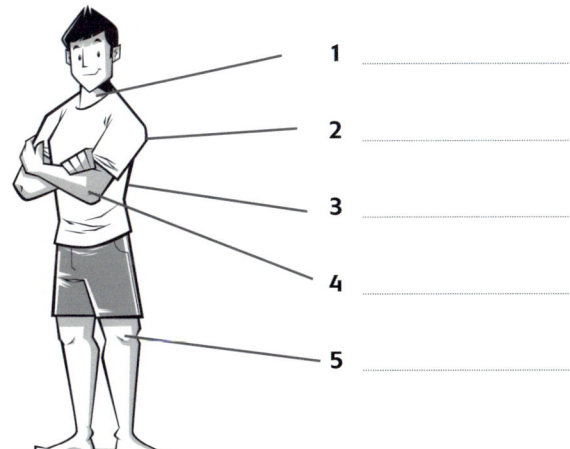

1 _____
2 _____
3 _____
4 _____
5 _____

3 Complete the puzzle and find the mystery word.

1	L	U	N	G	S

1 the part of your body where air goes when you breathe it in
2 the bone around your head
3 the part of your body that pumps blood around your body
4 the strong parts of your body that help you to move your arms and legs
5 the part of your body where food goes when you eat it
6 the hard parts inside your body that give it strength
7 the part of your body in your head that you use for thinking

Mystery word: _____

4 Complete the sentences with these words.

> ~~claws~~   fur   tusks   skin   tail   wings

1 Some animals use their sharp _claws_ to kill other animals.
2 Birds can fly because they have _____ .
3 Cats have very soft _____ .
4 Your _____ covers your whole body.
5 A crocodile has a long _____ .
6 Elephants are killed for their _____ .

GRAMMAR
Past perfect simple

1 Complete the sentences with the past perfect simple form of these verbs.

> forget   give   ~~leave~~   not organise   see
> not tidy   visit

1 I couldn't buy a ticket because I _had left_ my money at home.
2 My mum was angry because I _____ my room.
3 Jenny was upset about losing her watch because her grandmother _____ it to her.
4 I didn't go to the cinema with my friends because I _____ the film before.
5 I went to New York last summer, and that was the first time I _____ the United States.
6 The trip didn't go well because we _____ it carefully enough.
7 My phone ran out of battery because I _____ to charge it the night before.

2 Choose the correct answer, A, B or C.

1 I didn't order any food because I _had already eaten_ .
  A had before eaten
  B had already eaten ✓
  C already eaten
2 The train ___ when I got to the station.
  A had just left
  B already had left
  C had left before
3 They had been friends ___ five years old.
  A since they were
  B since they had been
  C already they were
4 Tom was excited ___ a competition.
  A before he had won
  B because he had won
  C because he already won
5 I realised when I started reading the book that I ___ .
  A read it before
  B had read it before
  C had read it just
6 Scientists had studied the creatures ___ before they made this important discovery.
  A since many years
  B for many years
  C already many years

3 Complete the second sentence with the past simple or the past perfect simple.

1 I ate my lunch and then I called Matt.
  I called Matt when I _had eaten_ my lunch.
2 I lost my purse, so I didn't have any money.
  I didn't have any money because I _____ my purse.
3 Gina arrived and I made some coffee.
  When Gina _____ , I made some coffee.
4 I failed my exam and I felt really upset.
  I felt really upset when I _____ my exam.
5 They paid their bill and then they left the hotel.
  They left the hotel when they _____ their bill.
6 I asked Tom to come with us and he agreed.
  When I _____ Tom to come with us, he agreed.
7 Last summer, scientists found some dinosaur bones here for the first time.
  It was the first time scientists _____ dinosaur bones here.
8 I spent all my money and then I went home.
  I went home when I _____ all my money.

4 Complete the text with the correct form of the verbs in brackets.

What killed the dinosaurs?
In the past, scientists believed that the dinosaurs 1) _died_ (die) out when a giant meteor from outer space 2) _____ (hit) the earth around 66 million years ago. At that time, dinosaurs 3) _____ (live) on the earth for millions of years. According to the theory, the meteor 4) _____ (cause) a massive explosion, which 5) _____ (lead) to a period of darkness. This lack of sunlight 6) _____ (kill) all the plants that dinosaurs 7) _____ (eat) for thousands of years. However, some scientists now believe that when the meteor struck, dinosaurs 8) _____ (already / start) to struggle for survival. It seems that a series of volcanic eruptions 9) _____ (already / cause) problems for these giant creatures, by changing the climate and making it hard for them to find food. Scientists now believe that the explosion caused by the meteor 10) _____ (be) simply the final, fatal blow to these magnificent animals.

VOCABULARY
Describing places and experiences

1 Read the article and choose the correct answer, A, B, C or D.

The oldest humans in Europe

In 2014 scientists came 1) *across* what looked like ancient human footprints in rocks on the east coast of Britain. They weren't able to 2) ___ up any equipment or dig the footprints 3) ___ in order to preserve them, because they knew the tide would come back in and wash them away. But they had time to study them and work 4) ___ their age. It seems the prints date 5) ___ to 850,000 years ago, making them the oldest humans in Europe. Far older prints have been found from Africa, but these prints help scientists to understand when our ancestors first 6) ___ out from Africa for Europe. They have pointed 7) ___ that this discovery leads them to believe this event was earlier than previously thought. No one has yet come up 8) ___ an explanation for why these footprints are there, but scientists will 9) ___ on studying finds such as these in an effort to understand the history of early humans.

1	**A** across	**B** up	**C** with	**D** for
2	**A** get	**B** set	**C** make	**D** let
3	**A** in	**B** away	**C** up	**D** down
4	**A** up	**B** out	**C** away	**D** in
5	**A** away	**B** from	**C** back	**D** up
6	**A** set	**B** got	**C** let	**D** made
7	**A** up	**B** for	**C** to	**D** out
8	**A** to	**B** for	**C** with	**D** at
9	**A** keep	**B** get	**C** make	**D** do

2 Match the adjectives (1–9) with the strong adjectives (a–i) with a similar meaning.

1	tired	a	terrifying
2	bad	b	enormous
3	big	c	marvellous
4	nice	d	deafening
5	dirty	e	exhausted
6	full of people	f	horrified
7	loud	g	dreadful
8	frightening	h	filthy
9	upset	i	packed

3 Complete the adjectives with the missing letters.
1 Lucy is an *a* m *a z i* n g football player.
2 This g ___ n t lizard is the biggest in the world.
3 That was an a ___ s ___ me film – I loved it!
4 We couldn't go out because the weather was so a ___ l.
5 Oh, no. This is t ___ b ___ news!
6 I took a bite of the meat, but it tasted h ___ r ___ b ___ .

4 Complete the sentences with these words.

ancient ~~baking~~ historical musical torrential

1 Our clothes soon dried in the *baking* heat.
2 The piano is quite a modern ___ instrument.
3 Do you think it is important to learn about ___ civilisations?
4 We visited some famous ___ sites from the nineteenth century.
5 There was a terrible storm, with ___ rain.

5 Complete the text with the correct form of the words in brackets.

When European travellers first visited Easter Island in the South Pacific Ocean, they were 1) *amazed* (amaze) to find a collection of large stone statues. At first, no one knew who had made the 2) ___ (mystery) statues. They now know that the 887 statues, called Moai, were made by the Rapa Nui people. The statues were probably carved between 1250 and 1500, but the Rapa Nui have a culture of considerable 3) ___ (sophisticated) which dates back to the first millennium AD.

The statues are carved in quite a plain style, with very little 4) ___ (decorate). Some of the statues have 5) ___ (colour) red headdresses, which experts believe were a sign of power or wealth. Historians believe that creating and moving the statues must have been quite a 6) ___ (complicate) business, involving a large number of people.

Visitors to the island have always been 7) ___ (fascinate) by the statues and in 1995 campaigners were 8) ___ (succeed) in gaining recognition for the statues, as they were declared a world heritage site.

GRAMMAR
Comparatives and superlatives

1 Put the words in the correct order to make sentences.

1 smaller / The room / remembered / than / was / had / I
   The room was smaller than I had remembered.

2 work / didn't / Cara / as / quickly / as me

3 difficult / This exam / more / than / the last one / was

4 the world / oldest / bones / These / in / are / the

5 The exhibition / as popular / expected / wasn't / we / as / had

6 most / This / about / dinosaurs / is / the / surprising thing

7 My sister / less / interested / is / in / history / me / than

8 Jack / run / as me / can't / fast / as

2 Rewrite the sentences using the words in brackets.

1 The tickets don't cost as much as last year. (less)
   The tickets *are less expensive than* last year.
2 The park wasn't as close as we thought. (than)
   The park _____ we thought.
3 Jack did much better than me in the test. (as)
   I didn't _____ Jack in the test.
4 I find French much easier than Spanish. (far)
   I find Spanish _____ French.
5 No other historical site in the world is as important as this one. (the)
   This is _____ site in the world.
6 Lia is a much quicker learner than I am. (quickly)
   Lia _____ I do.
7 The bridge isn't quite as ancient as the tower. (less)
   The bridge _____ the tower.
8 I didn't set off quite as late as the others. (bit)
   I set off _____ the others.

3 Read the article and choose the correct answer, A, B or C.

The ancient Roman city of Pompeii is one of 1) *the most* important historical sites in the world. Although the city wasn't 2) ____ as the capital, Rome, it was still a lively bustling city. But 3) ____ remarkable thing about Pompeii is the way in which it was destroyed. In AD 79 a volcanic eruption, that was 4) ____ powerful than any of more recent times, buried the city within a few days. Because Pompeii was destroyed so quickly, it is one of 5) ____ preserved cities from the time of ancient Rome.
Most historical sites such as palaces and temples tell us a lot about how the rich and powerful lived. Pompeii can tell us about how ordinary people, including 6) ____ people in society, lived. It gives us 7) ____ idea of what everyday life was like than many other sites. For example, food preserved on street stalls can show us that ordinary people had a 8) ____ varied diet than we might expect. Without the destruction of Pompeii in AD 79, we wouldn't be nearly 9) ____ informed about life in the ancient Roman empire as we are.

1 A most   **B the most**   C the more
2 A bigger
   B slightly as big
   C nearly as big
3 A the more   B more   C the most
4 A much more   B lot more   C bit more
5 A the most perfect
   B the most perfectly
   C more perfectly
6 A poorest   B the poorer   C the poorest
7 A the much best
   B the much better
   C a much better
8 A far   B far more   C far most
9 A well   B better   C as well

LISTENING

1 6.1 **Listen to a woman talking about Ayer's Rock. Choose the correct answer, true or false.**

1 The speaker is a scientist.
  True   False
2 Ayer's rock is surrounded by water.
  True   False
3 The Rock is very close to other large rock formations.
  True   False
4 Ayer's Rock is owned by an Aborigine tribe.
  True   False
5 Guests can stay at hotels near the Rock.
  True   False
6 It can sometimes be windy in this area.
  True   False
7 The speaker recommends taking photographs as souvenirs.
  True   False
8 The speaker wants to take a small rock home with her.
  True   False

2 6.2 **Listen again and complete the sentences with one or two words or a number in each space.**

1 The guide's nationality is _Australian_.
2 The alternative name for Ayer's Rock is _____.
3 The height of the Rock is _____.
4 An old Aborigine story says that the Rock was built by two _____.
5 Tourists are warned about the dangers of _____ the Rock.
6 This extra activity will take _____.
7 The visit to Ayer's Rock will finish at _____.
8 Some people believe that it is _____ to take small rocks as souvenirs.

SPEAKING SKILLS

1 Choose the correct words to complete the sentences.

1 The people in the first picture look *as/like* though they're learning together.
2 *However/Unlike* the person in the second picture is on her own. She might even be the teacher.
3 *Both/Two* pictures show people in an educational setting; a school, college or university.
4 In the first picture the people are working on something together, *whereas/despite* in the second picture the woman is presenting something.
5 The *main/serious* similarity between the pictures is that the people seem to be studying.
6 *Another/Other* similarity between the pictures is the age of the people.
7 They all look happy and healthy, *too/in addition*.

2 Complete a student's description of two photos with the correct words. Use one word in each space.

1) _Both/The_ pictures show different traditions.
2) _____ the first picture there's a street festival. There are a lot of people who are 3) _____ colourful costumes. They look as 4) _____ they're having a really good time. 5) _____ are people on the side of the street watching them too. It's nice and sunny and a good day for everyone. The second picture 6) _____ a girl opening presents. Perhaps it's a family celebration 7) _____ a birthday or an anniversary. Another 8) _____ between the pictures is that everyone 9) _____ happy! However, there are some differences 10) _____. The first picture is outside in the town 11) _____ the second is inside a family home. But the 12) _____ difference between the pictures is that the first picture is probably of a national tradition but the second is probably a family one. In both pictures the people have chosen to go to these events because they like celebrating something from the past. It's important to keep traditions alive.

WRITING

1 Match the comments about writing a good story (1–4) with the extracts (a–d).

1 Use time phrases to give a clear time sequence.
2 Try to use some humour.
3 Use some interesting language: adjectives, adverbs and verbs.
4 Try to build up the suspense.

a There was a strange noise coming from behind the door. I felt cold with fear.
b After eating the doughnuts the little dog's tummy was as big as a football!
c We waited outside the hotel and after a while the man came out. Then he started walking along the path and we followed him for half an hour.
d The building was massive and the nearby houses seemed tiny in comparison. There was a spectacular view from the top floor as we gazed out over the town.

2 Complete the story with these time phrases.

a few minutes later   after   at first   before
on my first day   ~~one summer~~   then   next day
suddenly   throughout the morning

1) _One summer_ I went to stay with my grandmother and 2) _____ I noticed a door upstairs that was always locked. 3) _____ at breakfast I saw a key in a bowl on her kitchen table. Perhaps it was for the locked door! 4) _____ I was excited because I wanted to try it, but I needed to wait for my grandmother to go out. 5) _____ lunch granny went to do some work in the garden and I raced upstairs with the key. 6) _____ it wouldn't turn and 7) _____ I heard a click and the door opened. 8) _____ I heard the back door close. Granny had come back! I shut the door and ran into my bedroom and 9) _____ I heard her climbing the stairs. 10) '_____ you come downstairs, Charlie,' she said, 'could you lock the old bathroom again – I don't want the cat to get in there, there's a hole in the floor!'

3 Match the adjectives, adverbs and verbs (1–6) with more interesting ones (a–f).

1 big
2 frightening
3 look
4 cry
5 quiet
6 drink

a terrifying
b silent
c sip
d scream
e stare
f massive

4 Complete the sentences with the words (a–f) from Exercise 3 in the correct form.

1 When Eva saw the blood she started to _scream_ .
2 For one _____ moment, she thought she was going to fall.
3 The house was _____ . There were probably more than forty rooms.
4 The man _____ at her for a long time before leaving the shop.
5 I _____ the orange juice slowly and read my book in the sunshine.
6 The thief climbed the stairs _____ and went into the spare room.

5 Write a story for a competition in 140–190 words. Your story must begin with this sentence:

The last day of the holidays was hot and sunny so we decided to go for a walk across the fields near the site of an old Roman camp.

Your story must include:
• a dog
• a gold coin

Revision Unit 6

1 Choose the correct answers.

1 We all breathed a sigh of *pale/nerves/relief* when we saw that she was safe.
2 I had a lump in my *throat/mouth/tongue* at the end of the film.
3 The horrible sound sent *shivers/fears/shakes* down my spine.
4 My heart was *hitting/thumping/slapping*, I was so scared.
5 His constant whistling really *gets/goes/gives* on my nerves!
6 What time are you setting *in/out/away* tomorrow?
7 Have you *worked/taken/went* out the answer yet?
8 They *got/went/came* across some ancient remains in Spain last year.
9 He came *out for/up with/over to* some good ideas.
10 I think we should *come on/get on/keep on* searching for bones.

2 Complete the text with these words.

> bones brain claws elbow muscles neck
> skeletons skin skull ~~tail~~

Tyrannosaurus rex was the largest of all dinosaurs, measuring over 12 metres from its nose to the tip of its 1) _tail_. Scientists have been lucky enough to find several complete 2) _____ of this amazing creature and so have been able to study it in some detail. We know that its head was massive because the largest 3) _____ that has been found measures 1.5 metres. T. rex had a thick, strong 4) _____ to support its huge head. Its front legs were quite short, with an 5) _____ in the middle which could bend. At the end of its front legs were extremely powerful 6) _____, which it used for catching and killing smaller dinosaurs.
Its back legs were large and had huge, powerful 7) _____, which helped it to run fast. Although T. rex looks very heavy, in fact the huge 8) _____ in its legs were hollow, which kept its weight down and allowed it to run faster.
We obviously don't know what colour 9) _____ T. rex had, but scientists believe it was probably brown or dark green, like that of a modern crocodile.
Although T. rex had a huge head, the 10) _____ inside its head was relatively small, so unfortunately it wasn't the smartest of animals!

3 Unscramble and write the words in the correct column.

> ~~sasmvie~~ readdluf nowredluf iagnt fulwa
> nafsattic guhe retrbile ramlevlsou

bad	nice	big
1) _____	4) _____	7) _massive_
2) _____	5) _____	8) _____
3) _____	6) _____	9) _____

4 Complete the sentences with one word in each space.

1 Do you play any m_usica_l instruments?
2 We visited some interesting h_____l sites.
3 We couldn't walk for long in the b_____g heat.
4 Do you think it's important to study a_____t civilisations?
5 It's sunny now, but there was t_____l rain earlier!

5 Complete the sentences with the correct form of the words in capitals.

1 She refused to eat the food because it was so _disgusting_ .   **DISGUST**
2 I was _____ to see how much the place had changed.   **AMAZE**
3 I applied to get onto the show, but I didn't have any _____ .   **SUCCEED**
4 This film is really good _____ for the whole family.   **ENTERTAIN**
5 No one can explain his _____ disappearance.   **MYSTERY**
6 I think we should put up a few _____ to make the room look nice.   **DECORATE**
   _____ by the   **FASCINATE**
   ns are too simple _____ .   **SOPHISTICATED**

Revision Unit 6

6 Choose the correct answers.

1. The film *started/had started* when I *got/had got* to the cinema, so I missed the first ten minutes.
2. When I *met/had met* George, he *told/had told* me all about his problems.
3. Finally, we *arrived/had arrived* home and *were/had been* able to relax.
4. When I *went/had been* to Africa last year, it was the first time I *saw/had seen* elephants in the wild.
5. We *weren't/hadn't been* hungry in the evening because we *ate/had eaten* such a big lunch.
6. Sara *showed/had shown* me some photos which she *took/had taken* on holiday in Austria.
7. Lots of people *came/had come* to my party and they all *gave/had given* me presents.
8. I was delighted when I *discovered/had discovered* that I *won/had won* the competition.

7 Cross out one unnecessary word in each sentence.

1. We had known each other for ~~since~~ ten years.
2. I tried calling Sam yesterday morning, but he just had already left for school.
3. It was really exciting going to Brazil because we hadn't been already to South America before.
4. Max had gone just home because he was tired.
5. We had been there for since ten o'clock.
6. The concert had already started when I had got to the theatre.
7. It was the best film I already had ever seen.
8. When Jonathan called, we already had just finished eating.

8 Rewrite the sentences using the word given. Use between two and five words, including the word given.

1. I hadn't spoken to Mark before yesterday. **FIRST**
   Yesterday was the _first time I had spoken_ to Mark.
2. Julia left before we arrived. **ALREADY**
   Julia _____ when we arrived.
3. The train left a short time before we got to the station. **JUST**
   The train _____ when we got to the station.
4. I was in Paris for the first time. **BEFORE**
   I hadn't _____.
5. I had first met Jack when I was fifteen. **SINCE**
   I _____ I was fifteen.

9 Complete the sentences with the correct form of the words in brackets. Add extra words if necessary.

1. I think the ancient Greek civilisation is _more interesting than_ (interesting) the ancient Egyptian one.
2. Who do you think is _____ (good) singer in the world?
3. You need to work _____ (hard) this if you want to pass your exams!
4. Dan isn't _____ (clever) as he thinks he is!
5. My mum is one of _____ (patient) people I know.
6. That's _____ (bad) film I've ever watched!
7. Cara can work _____ (quickly) than anyone else I know.
8. The weather today isn't _____ (good) as it was yesterday.

10 Rewrite the sentences using the word given. Use between two and five words, including the word given.

1. Paul isn't quite as intelligent as his brother. **SLIGHTLY**
   Paul is _slightly less intelligent than_ his brother.
2. Gold coins are slightly more valuable than bronze ones. **AS**
   Bronze coins _____ as gold ones.
3. Leather shoes cost a lot more than canvas ones. **MUCH**
   Leather shoes are _____ canvas ones.
4. The monument wasn't nearly as big as I expected. **FAR**
   The monument _____ I expected.
5. Sara isn't as competitive as her sister. **LESS**
   Sara _____ her sister.
6. The site is slightly more popular now. **BIT**
   The site _____ now.

07 The feel-good factor

READING

1 Read the blog posts quickly and match the photos (1–4) with the people (A–D).

1 C
2 ......
3 ......
4 ......

2 Read the posts again and choose the correct answer, A, B, C or D.

Who:
1 did something to benefit other people? C
2 felt happy because of people's reaction to her achievement? ......
3 didn't take her friends' advice? ......
4 was encouraged by a particular friendship? ......
5 surprised people by her choice of free-time activity? ......
6 was not convinced she could succeed at something? ......
7 had no doubts about her ability? ......
8 tried something for a second time? ......

3 Choose the correct answer, true or false.

1 'A' believes that you need to be confident to be a good actor.
   True   **False**
2 'A' would like to continue to act in plays.
   True   False
3 'B' writes to a penfriend who she met in France.
   True   False
4 'B' has always worked hard at learning foreign languages.
   True   False
5 'C' knows that her habit is bad for her health.
   True   False
6 'C' wasn't the only one of her friends to have a challenge.
   True   False
7 'D' took her driving test more than once.
   True   False
8 'D' was surprised by her success.
   True   False

07 The feel-good factor

View previous comments   Cancel   Share   Post

A jeniwren

B Mandy53

C laurielu

D sportyBeth

Write a comment   Support

65

VOCABULARY
People and relationships

1 Complete the sentences with one word in each space.

1 C*ompetitors* are people who are taking part in a sport or competition.
2 Your o_____ are the people you are against in a sport or competition.
3 A c_____ is someone who teaches people how to do a sport.
4 Your p_____ g_____ is all the people you know who are the same age as you.
5 Your m_____ are your friends.
6 A school c_____ is a group of teachers and students who help to make decisions about the school.

2 Choose the correct answers.

1 Do you want to *take/have/get* part in the race next week?
2 Oh, no. I think I've *done/made/got* a silly mistake!
3 My brother started studying medicine, but he didn't like it so he changed *way/path/direction* and now he's doing law.
4 We walked all day and then *put out/got at/set up* camp near a river in the evening.
5 We couldn't *find/get/see* our way in the dark.
6 I hope I'll be able to *stand/run/walk* on my own two feet when I'm eighteen.
7 It doesn't taste very nice at the moment, but a little more salt should do the *task/trick/difference*.

3 Complete the article with one word in each space.

Is life getting you 1) *down*? We all feel depressed sometimes but don't worry – we've got lots of ideas to help cheer you 2) _____ .
- Go on a short holiday. We all need to get 3) _____ from home from time to time and when you get 4) _____ , you'll probably feel much better.
- Take up a new hobby. You might not feel very keen at first, but if you can find something you're interested in, it will gradually draw you 5) _____ , and you'll forget that you were ever depressed.
Good luck!

4 Choose the correct answer, A, B or C.

1 I'm absolutely hopeless ____ tennis!
 A for   B of   **C at**
2 My brother is hooked ____ computer games!
 A on   B at   C in
3 A lot of people are afraid ____ spiders.
 A for   B off   C of
4 I don't think you should be embarrassed ____ your appearance.
 A for   B at   C about
5 Jen is very popular ____ everyone at school.
 A with   B among   C for
6 I love it when my parents say that they are proud ____ me!
 A at   B for   C of

5 Complete the blog post with one word in each space.

View previous comments   Cancel   Share   Post

I was having a tough time at school last year. Problems with friends were getting me 1) *down*, so I started spending more and more time online. It was my way of getting 2) _____ from my problems, I guess, but after a few months I realised that I was completely addicted 3) _____ social media. It ruled my life! I didn't take part 4) _____ any activities at the weekend because I was worried 5) _____ missing an important chat with my online friends. I decided I needed to become more confident and learn to stand on my 6) _____ two feet. So I joined a local choir. I never thought I was brilliant 7) _____ singing and I was a bit anxious 8) _____ singing in front of other people. But it turns out that I've got quite a good voice. Now I'm really passionate 9) _____ singing. Even if I'm feeling a bit down, singing always cheers me 10) _____ . Why don't you give it a go?

Write a comment   Support

GRAMMAR
Modal verbs (1)

1 Choose the correct answers.

1. You spend too much time on your computer. You *should/can't* spend more time outdoors.
2. My parents were very strict when I was younger, so I *can't/couldn't* stay out late.
3. The bus leaves at nine, so we *mustn't/don't need to* be late.
4. Tom is great at scoring goals, but he *can't/couldn't* run very fast.
5. *Must/Would* you pass me the salt, please?
6. Thanks for the invitation, but I *shouldn't/had better* ask my parents before I say yes.
7. Do you think you *were allowed/will be allowed* to come with us next Saturday?
8. We *have to/needn't* worry about food, because my mum says she'll buy us pizzas.
9. My sister *can/was able to* swim when she was only three years old.
10. *May/Should* I open the window, please? I feel a bit faint and I need some fresh air.

2 Complete the email with one word in each space.

To: Tara Subject: Ice skating?

Hi Tara,
Do you think you 1) *will* be allowed to come ice skating with me on Saturday? You don't need 2) _____ worry about paying because my mum is paying for everything. It's my birthday treat! You must wear gloves, but you 3) _____ have to take your own skates – you can hire them there. I hope I'll 4) _____ able to stay on my feet this time. The last time I went skating, all I 5) _____ do was move around the edge, holding on! Anyway, I 6) _____ better get on with my homework now. I've 7) _____ to finish my geography project. See you on Saturday – I hope!
Mia

3 Read the conversations and choose the correct answer, A, B or C.

Stephan 1) *May* I go home early today? I 2) ____ finish an essay tonight.
Coach Yes, that's OK, but you 3) ____ be more organised in future. You 4) ____ to play in the team if you keep missing training.

Cara 5) ____ I go to Jo's party on Saturday?
Mum I'm not sure. Grandma's coming to visit, so you 6) ____ to spend some time with her.
Cara I know, but it's not fair. All my friends 7) ____ to go. I'll be the only one who misses it!
Mum Well, I guess it will be OK. But you 8) ____ make sure that you do all your homework on Saturday, before you go.
Cara Great. Thanks, Mum. Oh, and 9) ____ you wash my jeans for me, please? I want to wear them on Saturday.

	A	B	C
1	Would	**May**	Must
2	have got	mustn't	need to
3	must	have got	ought
4	can't	shouldn't	won't be able
5	Can	Must	Should
6	should	better	ought
7	allowed	can	will be allowed
8	needn't	had better	ought
9	should	can't	would

4 Rewrite the sentences using the word given. Use between two and five words, including the word given.

1. The teachers say we can't use our phones in class. **ALLOWED**
   We *aren't allowed to use* our phones in class.
2. Maria shouldn't work so hard! **OUGHT**
   Maria _____ so hard!
3. It won't be possible for me to come with you. **ABLE**
   I _____ come with you.
4. It isn't necessary to buy a ticket in advance. **HAVE**
   You _____ a ticket in advance.
5. You shouldn't invite too many people to the party! **BETTER**
   You _____ too many people to the party!
6. I must finish this essay tonight! **GOT**
   I _____ this essay tonight!

VOCABULARY
Being positive

1 Find eight adjectives to describe people. The words go across, down or diagonally. The first letter of each word is highlighted.

i	p	r	c	o	n	f	i	d	e	n	t
n	m	c	a	i	a	r	m	i	d	o	r
c	r	a	r	e	m	n	i	e	r	t	i
r	i	u	g	h	b	i	x	p	r	o	w
e	a	t	i	i	u	s	l	i	p	s	l
a	n	i	l	n	n	t	a	w	o	n	o
t	r	o	p	r	o	a	r	e	a	u	u
i	l	u	a	m	b	i	t	i	o	u	s
v	o	s	n	o	l	p	m	i	c	s	p
e	a	t	s	p	a	c	t	i	v	e	r
s	p	r	o	t	e	c	t	i	v	e	o

2 Complete the sentences with these adjectives.

> active ~~adventurous~~ aggressive ambitious competitive creative decisive protective self-sufficient supportive

1 My brother loves doing new and exciting things. He's very _adventurous_ .
2 I find it very difficult to make decisions about what to do. I'm not very _____ .
3 I definitely want to do well in life, so I guess I'm _____ .
4 My friends were all very _____ and helped me a lot last year when I was having problems.
5 I hate sitting around doing nothing. I prefer to be _____ !
6 My sister doesn't seem to need other people at all. She's completely _____ .
7 Leah doesn't care if she wins or loses games. She's not _____ at all.
8 My parents worry about me too much and they never want to let me do anything. I think they're too _____ of me.
9 I really don't like people who lose their temper and shout at others. There's no need to be _____ like that!
10 Anna is always making beautiful things. She's very _____ .

3 Choose the correct answers.
1 Sailing is quite a *danger/dangers/dangerous* sport.
2 I was beginning to *suspect/suspicious/suspicion* that Marty was the thief.
3 The high winds during the storm were very *destroy/destruction/destructive*.
4 My parents would be *fury/furious/furiously* if I failed all my exams.
5 Do you think that most teenagers *depend/depends/dependent* on their phones too much?
6 I'm really not interested in *fame/famously/famous* or wealth.
7 I think Lisa is a very *attract/attractive/attraction* person.
8 It's good to have lots of *differ/differs/different* hobbies, I think.

4 Complete the advert with the correct form of the words in brackets.

Circus skills for teenagers

Would you like to try something 1) _adventurous_ (adventure) this summer? If you are young and 2) _____ (act) and enjoy learning new skills, why not try one of our circus skills courses? Our 3) _____ (support) coaches will train you in all the main circus skills like juggling and riding a unicycle. And don't worry – although some of the activities look a bit 4) _____ (danger), we'll make sure you wear 5) _____ (protect) clothing so that if you fall you won't hurt yourself. Doing one of our courses will increase your 6) _____ (confide) and make you less 7) _____ (caution) about trying new things. So, if you have a 8) _____ (suspect) that you could be our next big star, go to our website at www.circusadventure.co.uk and sign up now!

GOLD EXPERIENCE

GRAMMAR
make, let, help

1 Put the words in the correct order to make sentences.

1 learn / by heart / us / the poem / The teacher / made
   The teacher made us learn the poem by heart.

2 exams / Talking / nervous / about / me / makes

3 let / get / Mum / me / won't / a part-time job

4 TV / Watching / relax / me / to / helps

5 Our coach / us / train / for two hours / made

6 my bad behaviour / I / apologise / made / to / for / was

2 Choose the correct answer, A, B or C.

1 Do you think they will ____ come to the party?
   A let you to
   B let you
   C made you

2 Joining a sports club can ____ make friends.
   A help to you
   B let you
   C help you to

3 We ____ clear up all the mess ourselves.
   A allowed to
   B were let
   C were made to

4 You ____ go on the trip if I don't want to!
   A can't make me
   B won't be made
   C don't help

5 We ____ look on the Internet for ideas.
   A let us
   B were let
   C were allowed to

6 Taking up climbing really ____ more confident.
   A was made   B made me   C let me

7 In the past, children ____ work from the age of twelve.
   A made them
   B were let
   C were made to

8 My parents said I was too young, so they ____ to the music festival.
   A not allowed to go
   B didn't let me go
   C helped me

3 Complete the text with the correct form of *help*, *let*, *make* or *be allowed*.

Drama is a great way to meet new people and improve your self-confidence. Teenager Natalie Jones says, 'I grew up with quite anxious parents. They didn't 1) ___*let*___ me go out very much because they were always worried about me. This 2) _____ me very shy and lacking in self-confidence.' Natalie saw an advert for a local drama group and decided she would like to join. 'I didn't know if my parents 3) _____ me do it, but as it was quite close to our home, they said it was fine,' she says. Natalie now says that doing drama has really 4) _____ her to become more confident. 'When you join a drama group, you 5) _____ to do all kinds of crazy things,' she says. 'It's hard at first, but after a while it 6) _____ you much more confident.' Natalie says that her joining the drama group has also 7) _____ her parents to become less anxious about her. 'They can see that I'm OK, so they worry a lot less,' she says. 'They've even said I will 8) _____ to go on the drama trip to Paris next year. I can't wait!'

4 Rewrite the sentences using the word given. Use between two and five words, including the word given.

1 Dan has to tidy his bedroom every week.   **MAKE**
   Dan's parents ___*make him tidy*___ his bedroom every week.

2 I won't be allowed to stay out that late.   **LET**
   My parents _____ out that late.

3 Do your teachers let you use the Internet in class?   **ALLOWED**
   Are _____ the Internet in class?

4 The prisoners had to work for eight hours a day.   **MADE**
   The prisoners _____ for eight hours a day.

5 Casper gave me some help with sorting out my computer.   **HELPED**
   Casper _____ out my computer.

6 I get angry when I see people being cruel to animals.   **MAKES**
   Seeing people being cruel to animals _____ .

LISTENING

1 7.1 **Listen to a girl talking about a difficult physical challenge. Which three activities does she not mention in the interview?**
1 swimming underwater
2 jogging in the rain
3 playing football
4 climbing walls
5 diving from a height
6 running up hills
7 working out at the gym
8 training to follow orders like soldiers

2 7.2 **Listen again and choose the correct answer, A, B or C.**
1 Who is the Tough Mudder assault course for?
   A people who want some hard physical tests
   B experienced soldiers
   C people who want to join the army
2 Why do people take part in Tough Mudder?
   A to earn some money
   B to win a prize
   C to achieve something difficult
3 For her next attempt Ella needs to
   A buy better equipment to help her finish well.
   B find another team to do it with.
   C do more intensive training in advance.
4 For Ella the least enjoyable part of the course was
   A swimming in very cold water.
   B getting up and down the hills quickly.
   C getting over some high walls.
5 Ella's boyfriend thought
   A Ella wasn't well enough prepared for the course.
   B he could have done better than Ella.
   C Ella was going to come last.
6 What is Ella's advice?
   A Don't try a challenge unless you're prepared.
   B Nothing is impossible.
   C Never let down your team mates.

SPEAKING SKILLS

1 Look at the photo and complete the conversations with the words in the box.

agree idea right say so sure true that

1 **A:** The photo's of a celebration. I think it's a person's birthday.
   B: I _agree_. You're right.
2 **A:** Maybe he organised it himself.
   B: I don't think _____. I think he had some help.
3 **A:** You need to spend a long time organising a big celebration like this.
   B: That's _____.
4 **A:** I would love a party like this.
   B: I can't _____ I agree.
5 **A:** It costs a lot of money, too.
   B: I'm _____ it does.
6 **A:** I think that cake will be absolutely delicious.
   B: I'm not sure about _____. It looks very sweet!
7 **A:** Everyone loves birthday parties.
   B: You're _____ there.
8 **A:** Let's talk about the preparations now.
   B: That's a good _____.

07 The feel-good factor

2 Look at the photos. Read the task and prepare a one-minute talk.

The photos show people experiencing a feel-good moment at different events. Compare the photos and say how difficult it was to prepare for this event.

WRITING

1 Choose which sentence, A or B, is appropriate for an informal email.

1. A Dear Mrs Banks
   B Hi Debbie
2. A Good to hear from you
   B It was kind of you to write to me
3. A Let me know what you think
   B Please send me your opinions
4. A Yours faithfully
   B Speak soon
5. A Thank you very much
   B Thanks
6. A Bye for now
   B Best regards

2 Complete the sentences giving advice with one word.

1. Have you ___thought___ of telling your friend about the problem?
2. Perhaps you _____ explain why you feel this way to your parents.
3. How _____ asking your teacher for some help with your work?
4. It _____ be a good idea to organise a party for everyone.
5. Why _____ you make a list of things to do and start at the top?
6. _____ to think about the good things that can happen and not the bad.

3 Match the explanations (a–f) with the advice (1–6) in Exercise 2.

a Then you'd probably find it easy to catch up. ____
b It's often best to write things down. ____
c That's what friends are for. 1
d It's a good way for people to get to know each other. ____
e There are always some in every situation. ____
f They will probably be pleased to try and help. ____

4 Read part of an email you have received from Anna, an English-speaking friend. Choose five things you should include in your reply to her.

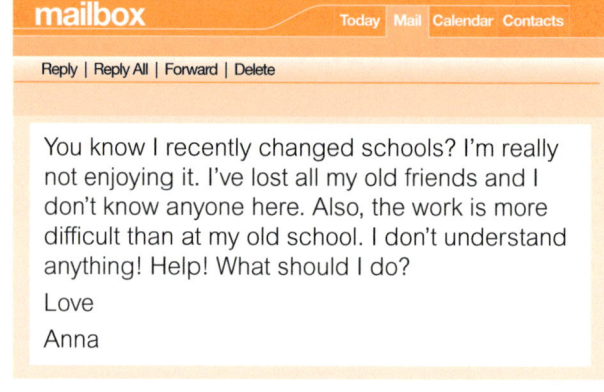

You know I recently changed schools? I'm really not enjoying it. I've lost all my old friends and I don't know anyone here. Also, the work is more difficult than at my old school. I don't understand anything! Help! What should I do?
Love
Anna

1 Wish her the best of luck.
2 Tell her how much you like your new school.
3 Suggest she meets her old friends from time to time.
4 Advise her to join a club at the school to make friends.
5 Tell her to revise all the work she did at her old school.
6 Suggest that she talks to her new teacher.
7 Sympathise but say that things will improve.
8 Describe your day at school today in detail.

5 Read Anna's email again and write your reply to her in 140–190 words.

Revision Unit 7

1 Complete the sentences with these words.

> camp coach ~~competitors~~ direction feet
> mates opponent part trick way

1 I chatted with the other _competitors_ at the start of the race.
2 I'd love to take _____ in a big sporting event.
3 If you don't like what you are doing, you can change _____ and try something else.
4 We found a good place to set up _____ for the night.
5 It's considered good manners to shake hands with your _____ at the end of the game.
6 My tennis _____ is always telling me that I should be more aggressive when I play.
7 It was hard to find our _____ without a map.
8 I'd like to get a job so that I can stand on my own two _____ .
9 I usually get together with my _____ at the weekend.
10 I don't know why my football team always loses. Maybe getting one or two new players would do the _____ and we might start to win!

2 Complete the definitions with one adjective in each space.

Someone who …
1 enjoys adventures is a_dventurous_ .
2 shows a lot of aggression is a_____ .
3 makes decisions easily is d_____ .
4 has a good imagination is i_____ .
5 enjoys competing and winning is c_____ .
6 tries to protect other people is p_____ .
7 suffers from anxiety is a_____ .
8 is good at supporting other people is s_____ .
9 has a lot of ambition is a_____ .
10 is good at making or creating things is c_____ .

3 Read the article and choose the correct answer, A, B, C or D.

I was always very bad 1) _at_ team sports like football and rugby. It really used to 2) ___ me down at school, and I was always 3) ___ of making a fool of myself in front of my peer group. But about six months ago I decided to take up running. I wasn't very 4) ___ on it at first because I found it quite tiring, but as I got fitter, it kind of drew me 5) ___ more and more. I started to find it easier and so I became more 6) ___ about it. Now I would say that I'm 7) ___ to running! I run four or five times a week and I'm very 8) ___ of myself because I've just entered my first marathon. Wish me luck!

1 **A** at   B in
  C about   D on
2 A let   B make
  C get   D take
3 A embarrassed   B worried
  C anxious   D afraid
4 A keen   B brilliant
  C popular   D passionate
5 A out   B in
  C at   D away
6 A good   B hooked
  C enthusiastic D popular
7 A hooked   B addicted
  C passionate   D happy
8 A proud   B happy
  C brilliant   D enthusiastic

Revision Unit 7

4 Complete the sentences with the correct form of the words in capitals.

1. I'd love to go to _different_ countries all over the world. **DIFFER**
2. If you have a _____ health problem, you should go to the doctor. **PERSIST**
3. The big slide is a very popular _____ at the water park. **ATTRACT**
4. I wouldn't really like to be _____. **FAME**
5. I hate being _____ on my parents for money! **DEPEND**
6. We must do what we can to prevent the _____ of the rainforest. **DESTROY**
7. My dad was _____ when I accidentally broke a window. **FURY**
8. It's important to eat healthily and be _____. **ACT**
9. I have a _____ that Clive knows more than he's telling us! **SUSPECT**
10. My sister is very _____ about trying new things. **CAUTION**

5 Choose the correct answer, A, B or C.

1. I wasn't hungry after such a big lunch, so I ___ eat anything in the evening.
   A can't **(B)** couldn't C shouldn't
2. My dad can't give us a lift to the station on Saturday, so we ___ get the bus.
   A will have to B had to C have to
3. Luckily, we ___ score a goal in the last minute, so we won the game.
   A ought to B can C were able to
4. I need to lose weight, so I ___ stop eating chocolate!
   A had to B must C better
5. ___ you open the door for me, please?
   A Would B Should C Must
6. We ___ work hard to prepare for our exams.
   A were let B were made to C allowed to
7. That kind of stupid behaviour really ___ angry!
   A helps me to be B lets me be C makes me
8. It was the last day of school, so we ___ go home early.
   A were allowed to B allowed us C let us

6 Rewrite the sentences using the word given. Use between two and five words, including the word given.

1. I could read when I was four years old. **ABLE**
   I _was able to read_ when I was four years old.
2. We have to train three times a week. **MAKES**
   Our coach _____ three times a week.
3. My parents don't let me stay at my friend's house. **ALLOWED**
   I _____ at my friend's house.
4. We should start training for the race. **BETTER**
   We _____ for the race.
5. It would be a good idea to check the details online. **OUGHT**
   We _____ the details online.
6. I wasn't allowed to go out last night. **LET**
   My parents _____ out last night.
7. It won't be necessary for you to be there. **NEED**
   You _____ there.
8. The teachers didn't let the children play outside. **MADE**
   The children _____ inside.

7 Rewrite the sentences correctly.

1. I was made see that my behaviour wasn't acceptable.
   I was made to see that my behaviour wasn't acceptable.
2. When I was younger, I wasn't let to have a TV in my room.
   _____
3. We've got plenty of time. We don't need hurry.
   _____
4. Do you think you will able to help us tomorrow?
   _____
5. I must to spend more time on maths this term!
   _____
6. We don't allowed to have games consoles at school now.
   _____
7. Our teachers always make us to turn off our phones in class.
   _____
8. The concert last night was free, so we don't have to pay.
   _____

73

08 Magic numbers

READING

1 Read the article. Choose the correct answer, true or false.

1 Calculators were allowed in the writer's primary class.
   True   False
2 The writer agrees with one of the speakers.
   True   False
3 The writer had big problems with both reading and maths.
   True   False
4 The writer's classmates helped him when he had problems.
   True   False
5 The writer heard a discussion about using calculators on the radio.
   True   False
6 The primary school maths teacher sometimes uses a calculator.
   True   False
7 The Kumon Method is a recent development in teaching maths.
   True   False
8 Children who follow this method attend after-school classes.
   True   False
9 The people in the interview disagree about using calculators in class.
   True   False
10 The teacher's class experiment involved making food.
   True   False

2 Read the article again and choose the correct answer, A, B, C or D.

1 How did calculators help the writer at school?
   A They helped him keep up with the rest of the class.
   B He became better at maths than his classmates.
   C He started to look forward to maths lessons.
   D He developed an interest in gadgets.
2 What does *see eye-to-eye* mean in paragraph 2?
   A to show your feeling to another person
   B to look directly at another person
   C to agree with another person's opinion
   D to discuss things with another person
3 The primary school teacher thinks calculators are important because
   A people use them in real life.
   B they help students pass tests.
   C we'll need them in our future jobs.
   D we won't need to do any mental sums at all.
4 In the Kumon Educational Method
   A students can work with other students all over the world.
   B students follow a special programme in class.
   C students become advanced very quickly.
   D students go at their own speed.
5 The maths experiment shows that
   A sometimes old-fashioned teaching methods are the best.
   B enjoying an activity helps students learn better.
   C the main aim of a maths lesson is to have fun.
   D primary school children need to get dirty from time to time.
6 What do you think is the best title for the article?
   A The magic of calculators
   B Maths isn't for everyone
   C Divided opinions about calculators
   D Good practical experiments for maths lessons

GOLD EXPERIENCE

Managing maths

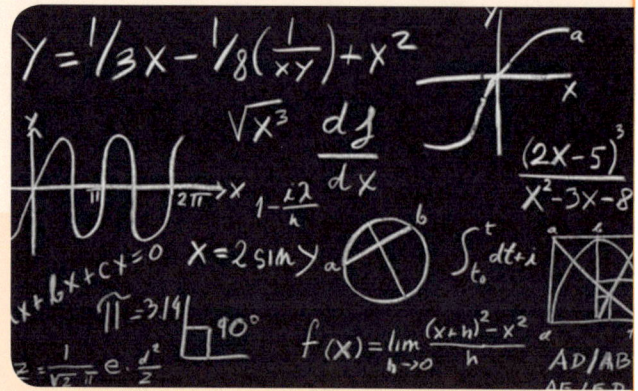

Maths is definitely not an easy subject for everyone. I have to say that it was a real nightmare for me at school. I had a lot of problems with the subject when I started school and I dreaded maths lessons. Reading was fine, but my brain didn't seem able to deal with numbers as well as my classmates, and I quickly fell behind. Not only that, but the others used to laugh at me when I just came up with answers out of the blue. I said anything because my mind was totally blank! However, my life was saved by the magic of the calculator. With this amazing little gadget I could solve the problems in class as quickly as anyone else. I just had to learn what calculations I needed to make. I'm convinced that without calculators, my education would have suffered. They gave me the confidence to move forward and not trail behind the class.

The other educationalist was a supporter of the Kumon Education Method. This is a method developed by a Japanese man, Toru Kumon, in 1978 to help his children who were having problems with maths at school. It is a special programme for after-school maths learning which allows children to progress through various levels, individually – not as part of a group. It aims to develop basic to advanced maths skills to give children confidence – without the need to rely on calculators! Today its popularity has spread across the world and more than 4,340,000 students follow the programme in over 7,500 centres

VOCABULARY
Maths

1 Complete the sentences with one word in each space.

1 Twenty _divided_ by two is ten.
2 Six _____ by two is twelve.
3 Seven _____ four is three.
4 Eight _____ two is ten.
5 If you _____ seven to ten, the answer is seventeen.
6 If you _____ five from twenty, the answer is fifteen.

2 Complete the puzzle with words related to maths.

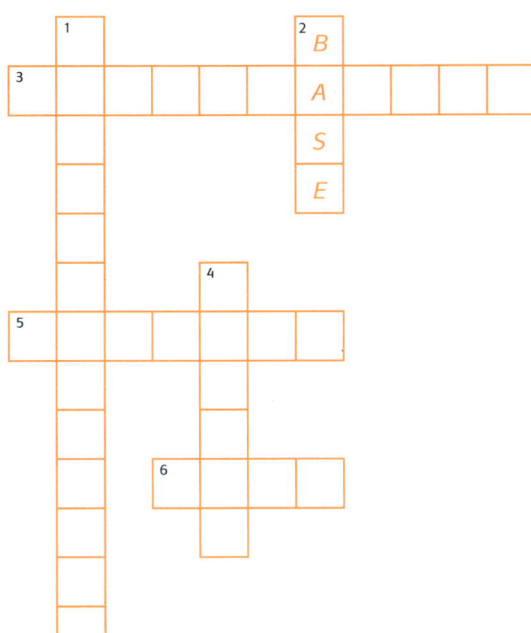

Across
3 sums that you do with numbers, to work out an answer
5 a way in which a particular feature repeats itself in a regular way
6 the number 0

Down
1 someone who studies maths
2 the number that is used to build a number system, for example ten in the decimal system
4 a set of numbers which increases or decreases in a particular way

3 Look at the pictures and write the words.

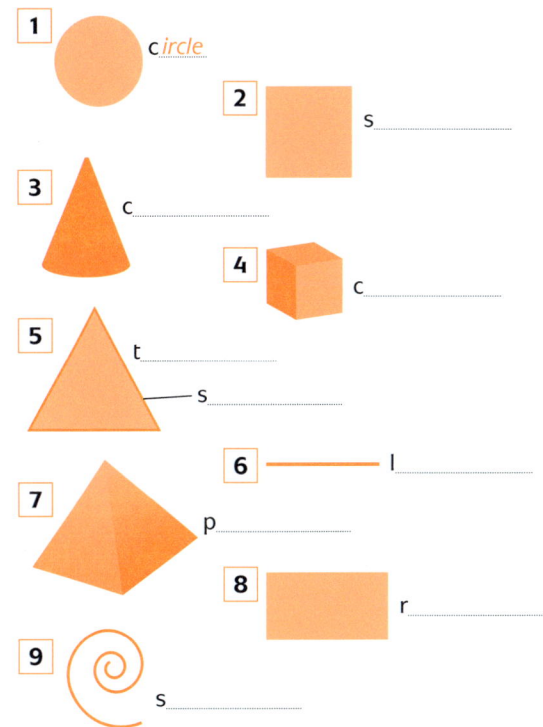

1 c_ircle_
2 s_____
3 c_____
4 c_____
5 t_____
  s_____
6 l_____
7 p_____
8 r_____
9 s_____

4 Complete the sentences with these words.

> deep   depth   height   high   length   ~~long~~
> wide   width

1 How _long_ is your garden, from the house right to the bottom of the garden?
2 Giant sequoia trees are the tallest trees in the world. They can reach a _____ of eighty-five metres.
3 Be careful – the water is very _____ here.
4 We measured the _____ of the room, from one side to the other.
5 What's the _____ of the race track, from the start to the finish?
6 At over 800 metres _____, the Burj Khalifa building in Dubai is the tallest building in the world.
7 It's a long way to the other side, so the river is too _____ for me to swim across.
8 You should never dive into a swimming pool until you have checked the _____ of the water.

76 GOLD EXPERIENCE

08 Magic numbers

GRAMMAR
The passive

1 Put the words in the correct order to make sentences.

1 Most / maths / are / children / at / school / taught
   Most children are taught maths at school.

2 The Internet / used / for / been / twenty-five / has / years
   _____

3 Calculators / cannot / the exam / used / be / in
   _____

4 All / copied / Tom's answers / were / from / his classmate
   _____

5 chosen / teacher / This textbook / our / was / by
   _____

6 The results / uploaded / the website / to / be / will
   _____

2 Read the article and choose the correct answer, A, B or C.

Amazing maths facts

1 Einstein once *said* that pure mathematics is the poetry of logical ideas.
2 An ancient animal bone _____ with marks on it which suggest that people were using mathematics in 35,000 BC.
3 We _____ very much about how maths was used in ancient Egypt.
4 A decimal system of mathematics _____ in China as early as the first century AD.
5 Because of the importance of computers, more mathematicians _____ in the future.
6 Some languages _____ a word for zero.
7 Most early counting systems _____ on the number ten because people have ten fingers which they used for counting.
8 Most of the mathematical notation that _____ today was invented in the sixteenth century.

	A	B	C
1	(A) said	B was said	C has been said
2	A found	B has found	C has been found
3	A don't know	B aren't know	C aren't know
4	A is used	B was used	C was using
5	A will needed	B will need	C will be needed
6	A don't have	B didn't had	C aren't had
7	A based	B were based	C being based
8	A used	B is used	C use

3 Rewrite the sentences in the passive.

1 Will they build a new school here?
   Will *a new school be built here* ?

2 I've arranged a visit to a museum for next week.
   A visit _____.

3 Someone wrote a new book on this subject.
   A new book _____.

4 Galileo didn't discover this theory.
   This theory _____.

5 You can find more maths books in the library.
   More maths books _____.

6 Someone had already solved this problem.
   This problem _____.

7 They might discover new planets in the future.
   New planets _____.

8 A celebrity opened the new exhibition.
   The new exhibition _____.

4 Complete the text with the correct form of these verbs.

> become ~~can/find~~ can/use have move
> replace teach tell use

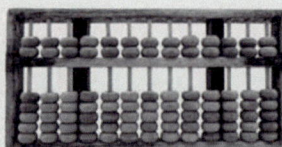

The suanpan, or abacus, is a traditional Chinese counting machine. The first description of a suanpan 1) *can be found* in a text dating back to the second century and the devices 2) _____ in China and other countries since that time.
To use a suanpan, the beads 3) _____ to different positions to indicate different numbers. The beads on the lower part of the machine 4) _____ a value of one and the value for the beads on the upper part is five.
As well as simple adding and subtracting, the suanpan 5) _____ for more complicated tasks such as multiplying and dividing. Children in China 6) _____ how to use these machines until the 1990s. When electronic calculators first 7) _____ available, they were not very reliable and stories 8) _____ of suanpan operators beating electronic calculators in competitions. Nowadays, however, electronic calculators are much better and faster, so people no longer use suanpans. They 9) _____ by these more modern devices.

77

VOCABULARY
Thinking skills

1 Complete the sentences with these words.

> advice   equipment   experience
> imagination   ~~information~~   intelligence
> knowledge   logic   news   research

1. The book has a lot of _information_ about how the human body works.
2. Scientists are doing a lot of _____ into this disease in the hope that they can find a cure.
3. I always watch the _____ on TV because I like to know what's happening in the world.
4. I've worked in a shop before, but I don't have any _____ of working in a restaurant.
5. Reading books helps to improve your _____ of a particular subject.
6. Can you give me some _____ about which computer I should buy?
7. His argument wasn't clear and there seemed very little _____ to it.
8. Carl draws some amazing pictures – he's got a great _____ .
9. Humans often assume that they have more _____ than other animals, but this isn't true – a lot of animals are very clever, too!
10. You don't need much _____ to do this experiment – just a bowl and a small gas burner.

2 Write C (Countable) or U (Uncountable).

1. We need more **light** in the room!   _U_
2. Please could you make a bit less **noise**?   ____
3. I've been to the USA several **times**.   ____
4. There were over thirty people in the **room**.   ____
5. I wanted to take some notes, but I didn't have any **paper**.   ____
6. I'm sorry, there's no **work** for you here.   ____

3 Choose the correct answers.

1. There are many *work/works* of art in the museum.
2. I didn't have enough *time/times* to finish my essay.
3. There were some strange *noise/noises* coming from outside.
4. Please turn the *light/lights* off when you go out.
5. There wasn't much *room/rooms* for people to sit down.
6. The teacher collected in all the exam *paper/papers*.

4 Read the article and choose the correct answer, A, B, C or D.

TAKE ANOTHER LOOK AT MATHS

Our modern world relies on mathematics, but very few mathematicians are well-known and maths very rarely makes it into the 1) _news_ . Most people think of maths as a scientific subject that uses only 2) ____ and no creativity. However, great mathematical discoveries are a result of 3) ____ as well as science. The Greek Pythagoras was one of the earliest mathematicians. He wanted to gain more 4) ____ of shapes and, using only very simple 5) ____ , he developed some important theorems to calculate the length and area of triangles. These principles are still used in engineering projects all over the world.

Carl Friedrich Gauss was a German mathematician of the eighteenth century whose great 6) ____ was recognised at a young age. He did a lot of 7) ____ into prime numbers. This might not seem very important to us, but in fact the science of prime numbers is used to keep the Internet safe from hackers.

Alan Turing was a British mathematician of the twentieth century. During the Second World War he helped to understand German secret codes. This gave the British access to secret 8) ____ about German plans and helped them win the war. After the war, Turing used his 9) ____ of numbers and codes to develop a computing machine – one of the earliest computers. So, maybe we should celebrate great mathematicians more and if you're looking for a career that could make a difference to the world, take my 10) ____ and consider studying maths!

1. A research   B information
   (C) news   D work
2. A logic   B think
   C brain   D advice
3. A creative   B imagination
   C artistic   D equipment
4. A knowledge   B fact
   C detail   D inform
5. A tool   B machine
   C device   D equipment
6. A intelligent   B intelligence
   C clever   D think
7. A knowledge   B research
   C experiment   D thought
8. A fact   B idea
   C information   D know
9. A experience   B advice
   C knowing   D secret
10. A advise   B support
    C suggest   D advice

GRAMMAR
Quantifiers and pronouns

1 Complete the sentences with *few*, *a few*, *little* or *a little*.

1 I need _a little_ more time to finish this job.
2 We decided to invite _____ friends round.
3 This theory was popular ten years ago, but there is _____ evidence that it is true.
4 Very _____ people do calculations in their heads nowadays.
5 The disaster happened ten days ago and there is now _____ hope of finding anyone alive.
6 The town is quite small, but there are _____ interesting places to visit there.
7 There's some cheese and _____ bread, so we can make a sandwich.
8 George doesn't go out much and he has very _____ friends.

2 Choose the correct answer, A, B or C.

1 ___ the computers in the library are broken.
   A Either   B Neither   **C Both of**
2 ___ student is given a password to gain access to the school website.
   A All   B Every   C All of
3 There were two questions to choose from in the exam, but I couldn't answer ___.
   A neither one   B every one   C either one
4 I tried all the machines, but ___ worked.
   A none of them
   B all them
   C either of them
5 ___ students love the new teacher.
   A All of   B All the   C Every
6 I tried calling Sam and Will, but ___ them answered their phone.
   A neither of   B neither   C either of
7 The examiner asked ___ a question in turn.
   A each of us   B each us   C every of us
8 Neither Paul ___ Simon is interested in maths.
   A neither   B or   C nor
9 This torch doesn't work, but it's OK because I've got ___.
   A other one   B another one   C other
10 Put those books beside ___ on the bookcase.
   A the other ones
   B other ones
   C the another ones

3 Complete the sentences with indefinite pronouns.

1 I haven't had _anything_ to eat all morning, so I'm really hungry!
2 I knocked on the door, but _____ answered.
3 I looked _____ for my calculator, but I couldn't find it.
4 Is there _____ interesting on TV tonight?
5 I looked through the pile of letters, but there was _____ for me.
6 It was a wonderful holiday – _____ was perfect – the beach, the hotel, the weather!
7 We couldn't agree on where to go, so in the end we didn't go _____.
8 There's _____ under the sofa. What do you think it could be?

4 Complete the text with one word in each space.

When it comes to thinking skills, one of the best known brains in the world is the fictional detective Sherlock Holmes. I've read a 1) _few_ of the books and I've seen 2) _____ the films, which I loved. In fact, there's 3) _____ film coming out soon and I'll definitely go and see that, too. Holmes takes on all kinds of criminal cases and 4) _____ of them is different. Sometimes there are plenty of clues to help him, but in other cases there are very 5) _____ clues, so he has to use his intelligence to find the criminal, with a 6) _____ help from his companion, Dr Watson. 7) _____ Holmes nor Watson are police officers, but they always seem to get better results than the police. In fact, there is 8) _____ in the police force who seems as good at solving crimes as Holmes. I'd definitely recommend the Sherlock films. 9) _____ seems to enjoy watching them and I've never met 10) _____ who doesn't like them.

LISTENING

1 8.1 Listen to people talking in six different situations. Match the recordings (1–6) with the topics they talk about (a–f).

1 c
2 ___
3 ___
4 ___
5 ___
6 ___

a a pastime
b a family relationship
c technology
d history
e fiction
f health

2 8.2 Listen again and choose the correct answer, A, B or C.

1 You hear two people talking about a computer problem. What does the girl say about the problem?
   A She's going to buy a new computer.
   B She fixed the problem once before.
   C She might ask a friend to help.

2 You hear someone reviewing a new book. Why does she recommend it?
   A It's better than the writer's first books.
   B It's about a city in Scotland.
   C It's hard to guess the killer.

3 You hear a guide talking about an old house. What is she doing in her talk?
   A talking about an event that may have happened here
   B giving facts about the house
   C describing the room they are visiting

4 You hear two friends talking about a puzzle. How does the boy help?
   A He tells the girl the answer.
   B He gives the girl a clue about the answer.
   C He offers to do the girl's homework.

5 You hear two friends talking about being twins. What annoys their teachers?
   A The sisters know what the teachers are thinking.
   B The sisters use a secret language in class.
   C The sisters answer each other's questions.

6 What does the doctor think caused the girl's illness?
   A some food she had on holiday
   B something she caught while travelling
   C some medicine she took on holiday

SPEAKING SKILLS

1 Look at the photos of people competing at different things. Complete what a student says about the photos with these words.

> ~~called~~ it kind know people place remember special thing

1 They're running together. What's it 1) _called_ ? It's a 2) _____ of race.
2 I think they're playing ... Oh, what is 3) _____ ? It's a 4) _____ type of game.
3 All the ... I can't 5) _____ the word. It's the 6) _____ who watch something.
4 They're putting things on the ... You 7) _____ . It's the 8) _____ we use when we're playing a game.
5 All the runners are on the ... It's the 9) _____ where people run a race.

2 Put the sentences (a–h) in the correct order (1–8).

a So do I. You have to run for a long time every day or a few times every week. ___
b Yes, what about a marathon? How can people prepare for that? ___
c Neither would I. I'm too lazy to practise. ___
d OK. We have to talk about preparing for these different events. _1_
e That's a good idea. People sometimes hurt their feet if they don't. ___
f You're right there. At least twice a week. And you should get the right shoes too. ___
g Well, I think that it's important to get lots of practice. ___
h I agree. It can be expensive, but it's important. But I wouldn't like to run a marathon. ___

08 Magic numbers

WRITING

1 Complete the sentences with these words.

> aim   ask   personally   recommend   score   ~~view~~

1 In my _view_ it's the best game on sale at the moment.
2 _____, I don't think you can get a more interesting game.
3 I'd definitely _____ this series to anyone who likes a challenge.
4 If you _____ me it's the best game the company has ever produced.
5 The _____ of the game is to _____ as many points as you can.

2 Complete the sentences with *when/if* or *so*.

1 _When_ you start, everyone has the same money.
2 Some questions are difficult _____ you might lose points.
3 _____ you're lucky and get to the top level, you get extra bonus points.
4 I landed on my friend's square _____ I had to pay her a lot of money.
5 _____ we finished, my friend was easily the winner.
6 My brother is a bad loser _____ he doesn't usually like playing games.

3 Read the writing task and think about what you should do. Choose the correct answer, true or false.

1 Start by explaining how you play the game.
   True   False
2 Use formal language.
   True   False
3 Say why the game is interesting.
   True   False
4 Give your opinion and recommendation.
   True   False
5 Divide your review into two long paragraphs.
   True   False
6 Give a detailed description of an occasion when you played the game.
   True   False
7 Include a short introduction and conclusion.
   True   False

4 You see this advert on an international student website. Write your review in 140–190 words.

Board Games

Are you fed up playing computer games? Want some interactive fun with friends or family?

We want to know what board games you play. Write a review of a game saying what you do in the game, whether you enjoy it and if you would recommend it and we'll put the most interesting ones on the website.

81

Revision Unit 8

1 Complete the words related to geometry then match them with the pictures (a–i).

1 c _i_ r _c_ l _e_   _c_
2 c _____ b _____
3 c _____ n _____
4 s _____ r _____
5 r _____ t _____ g l _____
6 s p _____ r _____ l
7 t r _____ g l _____
8 l _____ n _____
9 p _____ r _____ d

a _____
b
c
d
e
f
g
h
i

2 Complete the sentences with one word in each space.

1 That tall building is over 200 metres h _igh_ .
2 If you a _____ twenty to fifty, you get seventy.
3 Are you good at doing mathematical c _____ in your head?
4 The word for the number 0 is z _____ .
5 Are all three s _____ of the triangle the same length?
6 The water in the swimming pool is two metres d _____ .
7 Someone who studies mathematics is a m _____ .
8 If you s _____ fifteen from forty, you get twenty-five.
9 The w _____ of the river is so great here that you can't even see the other side.
10 These snakes can grow to a l _____ of nearly three metres.

3 Complete the sentences with these words.

> light lights noise noises paper ~~papers~~
> time times

1 The teacher collected in the _papers_ at the end of the test.
2 There isn't enough _____ for me to see clearly.
3 I can't concentrate in here – there's too much _____ .
4 Where have you been? I called you five _____ this morning, but you didn't answer your phone.
5 I don't want to sleep in that house again – I heard strange _____ in the night!
6 There was a power cut and all the _____ went out.
7 I've got a pen, but I haven't got any _____ .
8 Hurry up! We don't have much _____ .

4 Choose the correct answer, A, B, C or D.

1 Mathematicians often try to find _____ in numbers.
  A zero   **(B) patterns**
  C bases   D calculations
2 We need a lot of expensive _____ to do this job.
  A logic   B research
  C equipment   D imagination
3 I found out some useful _____ about the company.
  A information   B knowledge
  C imagination   D advice
4 What's the _____ of the tallest tree in the world?
  A wide   B high   C height   D long
5 My uncle doesn't have a job at the moment, so he's looking for _____ .
  A work   B works   C task   D job
6 Tom has got a lot of _____ of working with animals.
  A equipment   B experience
  C information   D imagination
7 We need to do some _____ to find out more about the problem.
  A knowledge   B experience
  C advice   D research
8 We use _____ ten in our mathematical system.
  A series   B plus   C pattern   D base

GOLD EXPERIENCE

Revision Unit 8

5 Complete the sentences with the correct form of the verbs in brackets.

1. The James Bond books ___were written___ (write) by Ian Fleming.
2. I couldn't believe it when I _____ (tell) that my uncle was a spy!
3. Last year they _____ (spend) many months trying to find out the secret information.
4. Some very clever gadgets _____ (can / use) to listen to people's conversations.
5. I bought this book last week, but I _____ (not / read) it yet.
6. They have been in the meeting for three hours, but a decision _____ (not / reach) yet.
7. We all hope that a cure for this disease _____ (will / find) soon.
8. By the time I arrived home, all the cake _____ (eat)!
9. You _____ (can / earn) quite a lot of money working as a secret agent.
10. Spies _____ (employ) by governments all over the world nowadays.

6 Rewrite the sentences using the word given. Use between two and five words, including the word given.

1. People eat fish all over the world. **EATEN**
   Fish ___is eaten___ all over the world.
2. Someone has published a new book on this subject. **BEEN**
   A _____ on this subject.
3. Rembrandt painted this portrait. **BY**
   This _____ Rembrandt.
4. We will announce the results later today. **BE**
   The _____ later today.
5. They clean the windows once a month. **ARE**
   The _____ once a month.
6. You can buy tickets online. **BOUGHT**
   Tickets _____ online.
7. They were upset because a fire had destroyed their home. **BEEN**
   They were upset because their _____ a fire.
8. They arrested the two spies last week. **WERE**
   The _____ last week.

7 Complete the sentences with these words. There are three words which you don't need.

> ~~a few~~ a little another anything anywhere
> both either little neither none nor
> nothing other

1. My sister's English is very good, but she still makes ___a few___ mistakes.
2. I haven't got _____ to wear to the party on Saturday!
3. _____ James nor Dan went to the match last weekend.
4. I'm really hungry, but there's _____ to eat in the fridge!
5. Sara and Emma _____ love the James Bond movies.
6. I can't find my keys _____!
7. One of my shoes is here, but I don't know where the _____ one is!
8. I've read two books by Ian Fleming, but I didn't like _____ of them.
9. Would you like _____ milk in your coffee?
10. I tried all the batteries, but _____ of them worked!

8 Complete the text with one word in each space.

The World Sudoku Championship 1) ___is___ organised each year 2) _____ the World Puzzle Federation. The first competition 3) _____ held in 2006 and there has been one 4) _____ year since then. The event started with only a 5) _____ countries represented, but now teams from all over the world take part. The next championship will 6) _____ held in the UK and it is expected to be the biggest yet.
The competition consists of around fifty puzzles which 7) _____ solved 8) _____ the competitors, working to finish as quickly as possible. 9) _____ of the puzzles are easy, of course, but some are more difficult than others.
The most successful players are Thomas Snyder of the USA and Jan Mrozowski from Poland. The championship has 10) _____ won by 11) _____ of these players three times.

09 All change

READING

1 Read the article. Choose the correct answer, true or false.

1 Becky and Steve have two children.
   True   False
2 The children are two years old.
   True   False
3 Becky's old kitchen was unsafe for children.
   True   False
4 Becky and Steve hired a local company to rebuild their house.
   True   False
5 The team built an extra room.
   True   False
6 Becky and Steve's children are boys.
   True   False
7 The rebuilding cost the family a lot of money.
   True   False
8 The garden is still too small for children to play in.
   True   False

2 Read the article again. Complete the spaces (1–8) with the correct sentences (a–h).

a She said it felt like a prison.
b The main problem was giving the family more space.
c So the family were no longer confined to the living room.
d She was left to look after the three toddlers on her own.
e imagine how they felt when they learned that Becky was going to have not one, not two but three babies!
f Since 1999 they have helped all sorts of people, from the disabled to the unemployed, from young parents to elderly pensioners.
g Becky was in tears because her life was going to be a lot, lot better than it had been.
h In addition to this they built on an extra room at the back for the washing machine and dishwasher and then they got to work on the top floor.

3 Match the words in the article (1–7) with their meanings (a–g).

1 cramped
2 update
3 basic
4 roomy
5 loft
6 terraced
7 stylish

a joined to other houses
b simple, with no luxuries
c smart and attractive
d with not enough space
e make more modern
f part of a house under the roof
g with plenty of space

SAVE OUR HOUSE

Having a baby is a dream come true for most families, and Becky and Steve were no exception. However, they knew things were going to be difficult because they lived in a very small, cramped terraced house with only two bedrooms. 1) __e__ Steve made a promise to redecorate and update the house, but when the babies arrived he simply didn't have enough time. Two years later, with the house still in the same condition, life was becoming a nightmare for Becky. Steve was away a lot of the time earning money to support his big family. 2) _____ With all three babies in the same bedroom, it was almost impossible to get them to sleep at the same time – because they woke each other up. Downstairs, the kitchen was very basic and so dangerous that Becky spent all her time in the small living room with the children. 3) _____

Then, earlier this year Becky's mother-in-law wrote to the TV series DIY SOS. This is a programme where a team of designers and builders help people who have big problems with their homes.

4) _____ . In a short time, the team arrived, sent Becky and the triplets to stay with her mum and started to renovate the old building. However, it wasn't a straightforward job at all.

Creating the perfect house for Becky and the family was an enormous challenge. 5) _____ They had to take out the old chimney and fireplaces to make the rooms bigger and they needed to replace nearly all the walls and the stairs because they were in very bad condition. 6) _____ The team created another bedroom in the loft, but to do this, they had to take off the roof as well! By the end of the week the team had changed nearly everything in the house. The result was amazing – the whole building felt much more roomy. The extra room allowed the little boy, Archie, to sleep away from his sisters and give everyone some peace and quiet. The new kitchen was stylish and safe – with the cooker lifted higher up. 7) _____

When Becky, Steve and the children saw the finished house the team felt that it was definitely worth all the hard work. 8) _____ Even the garden was now child-friendly, with raised flower beds and a sand play area. All the local builders, electricians and roofers who helped renovate the house gave their time unpaid to make this dream come true.

This is a really excellent series which makes an enormous difference to people's lives. The programme about Becky and Steve's house can be seen this Wednesday. You must watch it. It's about human nature at its very best.

VOCABULARY
Homes and furniture

1 Complete the words for different kinds of homes with the missing vowels.

1. v _i_ ll _a_
2. l _ _ g h t h _ _ _ _ s _
3. b _ ng _ l _ w
4. l _ g c _ b _ n
5. bl _ ck _ f fl _ ts
6. c _ r _ v _ n
7. _ gl _
8. t _ nt
9. t _ rr _ c _ d h _ _ s _
10. c _ tt _ g _
11. s _ m _ -d _ t _ ch _ d h _ _ s _
12. h _ _ s _ b _ _ t
13. d _ t _ ch _ d h _ _ s _
14. m _ n s _ _ n

2 Complete the definitions with one word in each space.

1. A _cottage_ is a small house in the countryside.
2. A _____ of _____ is a large building where a lot of people live.
3. A _____ is a small house made of wood.
4. A _____ is a very large house.
5. An _____ is a house made of snow and ice.
6. A _____ is a house on one level, with no upstairs.
7. A _____ is a home made of cloth, that you can carry around with you.
8. A _____ house is a house that is joined to other houses on both sides.
9. A _____ is a home on wheels which you can move from place to place.
10. A _____ house is a house that is not joined to any other houses.
11. A _____ is a home on a boat.
12. A _____ is a building on the coast, with a light to warn ships about dangerous rocks.
13. A _____ is a house where you can stay on holiday.
14. A _____-_____ house is a house that is joined to one other house.

3 Complete the sentences with these words.

curtains   cushions   dishwasher   lampshade
light switch   mattress   ~~washbasin~~
washing machine

1. Where's the _washbasin_ ? I need to wash my hands.
2. Can you turn the light on, please? The _____ is just by the door.
3. Those colourful _____ look delightful on the sofa!
4. I'll put the dirty clothes in the _____ .
5. That old lamp looks nice with its new _____ .
6. We're having some new _____ made for the window in our bedroom.
7. Can you load the plates and bowls into the _____ , please?
8. This bed is really uncomfortable – I think it needs a new _____ .

4 Choose the correct answers.

1. There's loads of space in this room – it's *tiny/enormous*!
2. Their flat is very small and *spacious/cramped*.
3. Your room is so *messy/tidy*! Why don't you ever put your clothes away?
4. The bathroom is *tiny/roomy* – you can hardly move in it!
5. I like to keep my room nice and *untidy/neat*, so I never leave my clothes on the floor.
6. Although it's only small, their flat feels quite *tiny/roomy*.

86 GOLD EXPERIENCE

GRAMMAR
Zero, first and second conditionals

1 Match (1–8) with (a–h) to make sentences.

1 If we lived in a bigger flat, — d
2 If you need money,
3 If you could live anywhere in the world,
4 We would pay less for electricity
5 I get bored
6 If I were you,
7 We won't move to a bigger house
8 We'll go for a walk

a when all my friends are away.
b I'd buy a rug to brighten the room up.
c where would you choose?
d we would invite people to stay more often.
e if the weather's fine.
f if we had solar panels on the roof.
g you can get a job.
h unless we win the lottery.

2 Choose the correct answers.

1 If you want the room to look more modern, you *have to/had to/will have to* change the furniture.
2 If my dad earned more money, we *lived/will live/would live* in a bigger house.
3 This room feels very small when it *will get/got/gets* messy.
4 If I were you, I *put/'ll put/'d put* some shelves on the wall.
5 We wouldn't live in Madrid if my dad *doesn't/didn't/wouldn't* have a job there.
6 My mum won't let me go out unless I *tidy/will tidy/tidied* my room.
7 I'd have a big TV in my room if I *was/am/will be* allowed.
8 If my dad *gets/will get/got* a job in London, we'll have to move house.
9 If you *can/could/would* speak Chinese, would you like to live in China?
10 If you *won't like/don't like/wouldn't like* these curtains, we'll change them.

3 Complete the sentences with the correct form of these verbs.

> apologise   be   get   not let   need
> not spend   see

1 If my brother _gets_ a job in New York, he'll move there.
2 We'll buy a cupboard if you _____ somewhere to keep all your things.
3 If you _____ a piece of furniture you really liked, would you buy it?
4 If I don't finish my homework, my mum _____ me go out later.
5 If I were you, I _____ too much money on clothes.
6 I won't invite Jack to my party unless he _____ to me for what he said.
7 Our flat is lovely and light when the weather _____ sunny.

4 Complete the conversation with the correct form of the verbs in brackets.

Freya Oh, this is lovely. If I 1) _had_ loads of money, I 2) _____ (spend) all my time on holiday!
Gina You 3) _____ (get) bored if you 4) _____ (do) nothing all day, every day! You wouldn't enjoy it.
Freya That's not true. If I 5) _____ (can) choose, I 6) _____ (live) in a little cottage by the sea and spend all my time just relaxing.
Gina Wouldn't you miss your friends if you 7) _____ (do) that?
Freya Maybe. But I wouldn't miss school. I hate it when we 8) _____ (have) loads of homework!
Gina Yes, but you 9) _____ (never / get) what you want from life unless you 10) _____ (put) the time and effort in now. If I were you, I 11) _____ (work) hard at school and try to get a good job. If you 12) _____ (manage) to do that, you 13) _____ (be able to) have plenty of holidays!
Freya I guess you're right. But I can still dream!

VOCABULARY
Going places

1 Complete the texts with one word in each space.

We arrived at the airport early, which was a good thing because we went to the wrong 1) t<u>erminal</u> first! Luckily, it wasn't too far to get to the right place. Then our plane was delayed, so we spent over three hours waiting in the 2) d_____ lounge! We were so relieved when they finally announced that our 3) f_____ was leaving. We had bad weather while we were in the air, but luckily we had a very experienced 4) p_____ flying the plane, so it was fine.

I was waiting for my train on the 5) p_____ and when it came into the station I couldn't believe how crowded it was! I managed to find a 6) c_____ with a few seats, but when the 7) g_____ came round to check our tickets, I realised that mine had dropped out of my pocket! Then the train was delayed because a tree had fallen onto the 8) t_____ . The only good thing was that they offered a free meal to all the 9) p_____ in the 10) d_____ c_____ !

I loved every minute of going on a cruise ship, from the minute we sailed out of the 11) p_____ to when we sailed back in three weeks later! The 12) c_____ we slept in was quite spacious and during the day it was lovely sitting up on the 13) d_____ enjoying the sunshine and looking out over the sea. The 14) c_____ were all really nice and friendly, too.

2 Choose the correct answers.

1 I came *to/into/for* contact with loads of people when I was travelling.
2 We had to keep *costs/prices/spend* to a minimum while we were away.
3 You should definitely *take/have/get* advantage of the opportunity to travel.
4 Paris is well-known *to/in/for* its restaurants.
5 We were *going/heading/travelling* for London when the car broke down.
6 It didn't take us long to *go through/get away/go in* customs.
7 We could really relax once we were *on the board/in board/on board* the ship.
8 We should arrive *to/at/for* our destination in about half an hour.
9 We saw some really lovely countryside *on way/at the way/on the way* to Scotland.
10 The city is *named for/called for/named after* an ancient king.

3 Read the blog and choose the correct answer, A, B, C or D.

💬 View previous comments   Cancel   Share   Post

Day 18 – India
We've arrived in India! It's been a tiring day. Our 1) <u>*flight*</u> was delayed, unfortunately, and it took us ages to go through 2) ____ when we landed. Then we got on a train and there were no seats in any of the 3) ____, so we had to stand! Still, the great thing about travelling in this way is that you come into 4) ____ with all kinds of people. Everyone was very friendly, including the 5) ____ who checked our tickets. He didn't charge us more even though we had the wrong tickets! We also saw some amazing sights on the 6) ____ , including wild elephants!
Anyway, we've finally arrived 7) ____ our destination, Jaipur, and we'll soon be 8) ____ for our hostel. We chose quite a cheap one, to keep costs to a 9) ____ , so let's hope it's OK. We'll let you know!

Write a comment   Support

1   A   fly   B   air
    C   travel   (D) flight
2   A   departure   B   port
    C   customs   D   passport
3   A   compartments   B   cabins
    C   decks   D   platforms
4   A   meeting   B   contact
    C   opportunity   D   discussion
5   A   pilot   B   crew
    C   guard   D   passenger
6   A   way   B   path
    C   travel   D   board
7   A   in   B   on
    C   for   D   at
8   A   going   B   getting
    C   heading   D   coming
9   A   minimum   B   maximum
    C   small   D   reduced

 All change

GRAMMAR
Third conditional

1 Match (1–7) with (a–g) to make sentences.

1 We wouldn't have missed the train — d
2 If we'd bought our tickets in advance, ...
3 We would have sat up on deck ......
4 If the dining car hadn't been closed, ...
5 We would have caught our flight ......
6 The trip wouldn't have been so expensive ......
7 If we'd had more time in New York, ...

a if the weather had been sunny.
b we might have had a meal on the train.
c if we hadn't stayed in five-star hotels.
d if we'd got up earlier.
e we'd have been able to do some shopping.
f if we'd gone to the right terminal.
g they might have been cheaper.

2 Choose the correct answer, A, B or C.

1 We would have travelled by plane if it ...... so expensive.
  A isn't   **B hadn't been**   C hasn't been
2 If it hadn't rained all the time, we ...... our holiday more.
  A would enjoy   B had enjoyed
  C might have enjoyed
3 If we ...... so many souvenirs, we could have gone through customs more quickly.
  A don't buy   B hadn't bought   C didn't buy
4 The guard wouldn't have reported us if ...... the right tickets.
  A we'd bought   B we would have bought
  C we would bought
5 If we'd set out earlier, ... have something to eat at the airport.
  A we'd have been able to
  B we were able to
  C we would been able to
6 If the train ...... less crowded, we would have found a seat.
  A was   B would be   C had been
7 We could have gone on a longer trip if ...... up more money.
  A we'd saved up   B we would have saved up
  C we would save up
8 I ...... so ill on the boat if the sea had been calmer.
  A would have felt   B wouldn't have felt
  C didn't feel

3 Complete the text with the correct form of the verbs in brackets.

Subject: **Missed flight!**

Hi Jenna,
We're still at the airport and it's all my fault. If I 1) *had got up* (get up) earlier, we 2) .... (leave) home at six this morning, as we had planned. If we 3) .... (leave) at the right time, we 4) .... (not arrive) with so little time to spare before our flight. And, of course, if I 5) .... (not be) in such a hurry to pack this morning, I 6) .... (remember) that you're not allowed to take liquids in your hand luggage. Of course, when we went through the security checks I had to unpack my bag to take all my shampoo and stuff out! If that 7) .... (not happen), my parents 8) .... (might not be) so stressed. And, of course, if we 9) .... (all / be) more relaxed, we probably 10) .... (not make) the mistake of going to the wrong gate. So, we've got to wait for six hours for the next flight – not a good day!

4 Rewrite the sentences using the word given. Use between two and five words, including the word given.

1 I stayed in because I was tired.   **IF**
  If I hadn't been tired, I wouldn't have stayed in.
2 We didn't have any money so we couldn't get a taxi.   **COULD**
  If we'd had some money, ... a taxi.
3 I'm glad we set out early, so the roads weren't busy.   **WOULD**
  The roads .... if we'd set out later.
4 I forgot my camera, so I didn't take any photos.   **FORGOTTEN**
  If .... my camera, I would have taken some photos.

89

LISTENING

1 9.1 Listen to a student talking about spending time in another country. Put the events in the correct order (1–8).

a   I bought a lot of clothes. ___
b   We lived in London. _1_
c   Dad spent weekends in England. ___
d   We went to an International school. ___
e   We moved to Manchester. ___
f   We moved to England. ___
g   My brothers got into trouble at school. ___
h   We moved to Paris. ___

2 9.2 Listen again and complete the sentences with one or two words in each space.

1   The name of Suzanne's teacher is Miss _Turner_ .
2   Her dad's job is with a ___ company.
3   He was moved to Paris ___ years ago.
4   At that time Suzanne and her family were living in ___ .
5   Suzanne's dad travelled between England and France for ___ .
6   In Paris, their house was very close to a ___ .
7   At their school in Paris, the main language was ___ .
8   The thing Suzanne missed most about England was her ___ .
9   Suzanne didn't go to many ___ while she was in Paris.
10 The family spent a lot of their free time at ___ because of the good weather.

SPEAKING SKILLS

1 Match the questions (1–6) with the answers (a–f).

1   Would you like to live in another country? _b_
2   Has your town changed a lot in the last five years? How? ___
3   Do you have any pets? What sort of animals? ___
4   What gadget have you bought recently? ___
5   What do you think is most difficult for children when they start school? ___
6   What would you like scientists to invent in the future? ___

a   I think it's the change of routine.
b   Not really because I'm happy where I am.
c   I think they should find a way to get rid of all our rubbish.
d   Quite a lot, yes. There are several new hotels and shopping malls.
e   I got a new phone because I dropped my old one in the river.
f   I used to have some fish when I was young, but now we've got two dogs.

2 Match your answers (a–f) in Exercise 1 with these follow-up statements (1–6).

1   This one was a lot more expensive but it's very fast and can do lots of things. _e_
2   We've got more things to throw away because of new technology, so technology should deal with the rubbish. ___
3   They're wonderful and I take them for walks every day. ___
4   I don't like change very much. ___
5   Everything is at a different time and you can't choose what to do. ___
6   Unfortunately we've lost a big park we used to have, too. ___

3 Prepare your own answers to the same six questions.

1 Would you like to live in another country? Why/Why not?
2 Has your town changed a lot in the last five years? How?
3 Do you have any pets? What sort of animals?
4 What gadget have you bought recently? What's it like?
5 What do you think is most difficult for children when they start school? Why?
6 What would you like scientists to invent in the future? Why?

4 Read the task and prepare your comments for each point. Choose two of the topics and speak aloud. Can you speak for one minute?

> Here are some changes we sometimes experience in our lives.
> Why might these changes be difficult for us?
> 1 moving to another country
> 2 going to a new school
> 3 moving house
> 4 going to university
> 5 starting a job

WRITING

1 Match sentences (1–6) from a semi-formal email with the follow-up sentences (a–f).

1 Thanks for your letter.   *c*
2 It was great to hear your news. ___
3 Sorry I haven't written recently. ___
4 How are you? ___
5 Please write soon. ___
6 What's the new house like? ___

a I hope you've recovered from that bad cold.
b I can't wait to see it.
c I got it just before school this morning
d I've been revising for an exam.
e I'd love to know how you're getting on.
f It sounds like your new house is really lovely.

2 Choose the words that best describe what the writer is doing in each sentence.

complaining (x2)   describing (x2)   inviting (x2)
giving advice (x2)   giving opinion (x2)

1 It's a really old building with big rooms and high ceilings.   *describing*
2 If I were you I'd ask your parents to redecorate your room. ___
3 Would you like to come and stay for a few days? ___
4 I think it's the best place I've ever lived in. ___
5 We're having a house warming party at the weekend. You'd be very welcome. ___
6 I'd love to live here forever. ___
7 I've got nowhere to put all my clothes. ___
8 There's a small river at the bottom of our garden and beyond that there are lovely green fields. ___
9 It's really hard to get a phone signal in this area. ___
10 Perhaps you should get a dog now that you live in the country. ___

3 Read the essay task and write your letter in 140–190 words.

This is part of a letter you have received from your English-speaking friend, Belle. Read it carefully and write a reply.

> I suppose you've been in your new house now for about a month. Do write and tell me what it's like. Is it in a nice area and have you got a big bedroom? Do you miss your old house? I can't wait to hear from you!
>
> Write soon
>
> Belle.

Revision Unit 9

1 Complete the crossword with words related to travel or furniture.

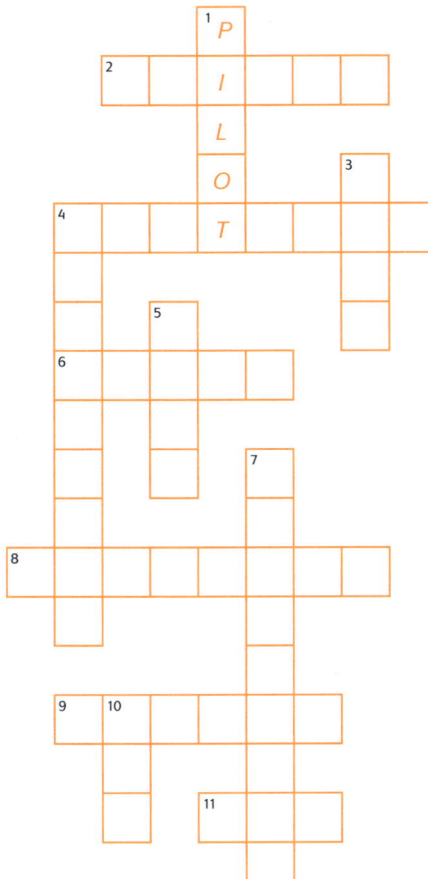

Across
2 a journey in a plane
4 the place where you wait for a train at the station
6 a narrow board attached to a wall that you can put things on
8 a building where people wait to get on a plane
9 a piece of electrical equipment that you can keep food in to keep it cool
11 a piece of equipment for controlling water flow

Down
1 someone who operates the controls of an aircraft
3 all the people who work on a ship or plane
4 someone travelling on a train, boat or plane
5 the top level of a ship that you can walk or sit on
7 a room on a train where you can eat a meal
10 a small carpet that you put on the floor

2 Complete the sentences with these words. There are two words which you don't need.

> carpet   curtains   cushions   dishwasher
> drawer   duvet   light switch   stool   tap
> ~~washbasin~~

1 You can wash your hands in the _washbasin_ .
2 It's dark in here. Where's the _____?
3 I was cold in bed last night. My _____ isn't very thick.
4 Open the _____ so we can see out of the window.
5 The cutlery is in a _____ in the kitchen.
6 I can sit on this little _____ .
7 Remember to load the _____ at the end of the meal.
8 He left muddy footprints on the _____ !

3 Look at the pictures and write the words.

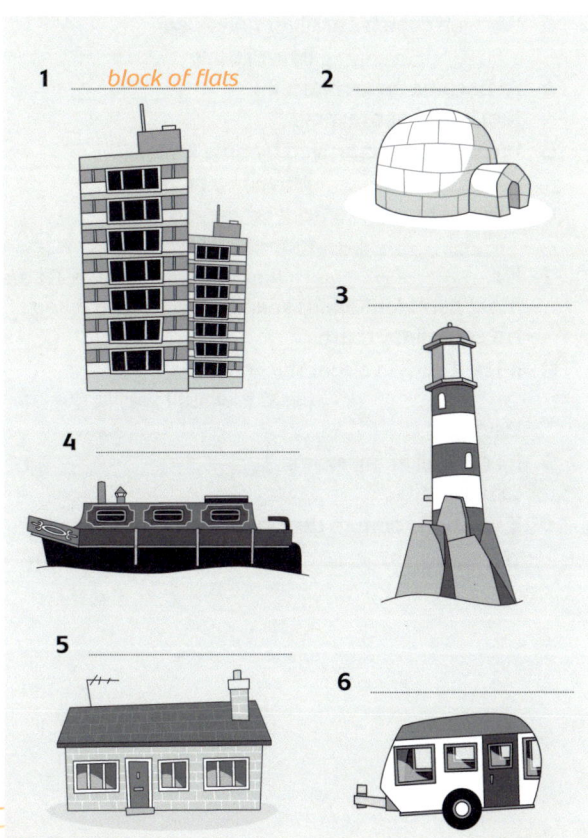

1 _block of flats_
2 _____
3 _____
4 _____
5 _____
6 _____

Revision Unit 9

4 Choose the correct answers.
1 Their kitchen is lovely and *spacious*/*untidy*, so there's plenty of room for cooking.
2 They sailed to the USA on a really big ship – it really was *tiny*/*enormous*!
3 My sister's flat is quite small and *roomy*/*cramped*.
4 I like my room to be nice and *tidy*/*tiny*. I can't stand it when it's messy.
5 We should arrive at our *opportunity*/*destination* at ten thirty.
6 Once everyone is *on*/*at* board, the ship can leave.
7 The train was delayed due to a problem with the *port*/*track*.
8 I love coming *into*/*to* contact with lots of different people.
9 We really need to *have*/*keep* our costs to a minimum.
10 This is a wonderful opportunity and you should take advantage *of*/*for* it.

5 Complete the sentences with the correct form of the verbs in brackets.
1 My sister always ____*gets*____ (get) bad-tempered when she's tired.
2 If I were you, I _____ (save up) and get a new phone.
3 We won't catch our flight unless we _____ (leave) now.
4 I'd become an architect if I _____ (be) better at drawing.
5 We would have arrived by now if we _____ (travel) by plane.
6 Life can be very difficult when you _____ (not have) any money.
7 If I _____ (know) more French, I'd be more confident about speaking to people when I'm on holiday there.
8 If I had known about this museum, I _____ (visit) it when I was in the city last year.
9 If I do well in my exams, I _____ (go) to university.
10 If you had come to the cinema with us yesterday, you _____ (might / enjoy) the film.

6 Rewrite the sentences using the word given. Use between two and five words, including the word given.
1 I'm not very good at singing, so I can't be in a band. **BETTER**
If ___*I was better*___ at singing, I could be in a band.
2 My advice is to share a flat with friends. **YOU**
If I _____ share a flat with friends.
3 I'm poor, so I don't buy many clothes. **RICH**
If I _____ more clothes.
4 We didn't win the money, so we didn't go on holiday. **MIGHT**
We _____ if we'd won the money.
5 We won't get to the station on time if we don't leave now. **UNLESS**
We won't get to the station on time _____ now.
6 You didn't pack last night, so we left late this morning! **COULD**
We _____ this morning if you'd packed last night.
7 It might rain tomorrow, so we'll stay at home. **IT**
We'll stay at home _____ tomorrow.
8 I won't call you unless the flight is delayed. **ONLY**
I _____ if the flight is delayed.

7 Rewrite the sentences correctly.
1 If I would have bought a ticket, I might have won a prize.
If I had bought a ticket, I might have won a prize.
2 The party won't be fun unless my friends will come.
3 If we don't leave soon, we don't get there on time.
4 I might been able to help you if you'd asked me earlier.
5 If I were you, I start saving up for your holiday now.
6 If the train been less crowded, we would have enjoyed the journey more.
7 I'll text you if the train would be delayed.
8 If I would have a car, I would be able to drive you to the station.

93

10 Inspiration

READING

1 Read the article. Choose the correct answer, true or false.

1 The International Space Station started more than twenty years ago.
   True   False
2 There hasn't been a British astronaut at the Space Station before.
   True   False
3 Astronauts' ability to taste is affected by gravity.
   True   False
4 The competition is for chefs.
   True   False
5 Astronauts sometimes eat English breakfasts in the Space Station.
   True   False
6 Children in the US can see immediately how spiders are behaving in space.
   True   False
7 Spiders are active at different times on earth and in space.
   True   False
8 Spiders become more aggressive in space.
   True   False

2 Read the article again. Choose which sentence (a–g) fits each space (1–7) in the text.

a Too often, science appears impractical and irrelevant to today's young people, but this project is really inspirational. ____
b Teachers also find it challenging to make their lessons interesting and fun. ____
c This means that their food tastes even worse! ____
d These are just two of the things that the students discovered. ____
e The experiment involved comparing their behaviour on earth and their behaviour on the ISS. ____
f They don't take up a lot of room and they are light to carry. ____
g It is perhaps the most important science laboratory in the world. _1_

3 Find words in the article with the following meanings.

1 related to science   *scientific*
2 something that creates interest and new ideas
3 something difficult but interesting
4 moved to a different place
5 encourage
6 finding out about
7 round in shape
8 built

GOLD EXPERIENCE
94

LIVING IN SPACE

INSPIRATION FROM SPACE

Since 1998 the International Space Station has been the temporary home for dozens of astronauts. 1) *It is perhaps the most important science laboratory in the world*. Experiments of all kinds have been conducted here to help our knowledge of science to progress on earth. However, as well as helping the scientific world, the ISS has also been used as an inspiration for many students who are studying science subjects at school. Science is an important subject and often very difficult for students. 2) ………. Here are two ways that the ISS is inspiring a new generation of young scientists in the classroom.

A SPACE DINNER

Not long ago, Major Tim Peake was the first British astronaut to be sent to work on the ISS for six months, and before going he set British students a challenge. Eating meals on the ISS is usually really boring. Food is dehydrated and put into small air tight packages so that they can easily be transported. 3) ………. When they eat, the astronauts have to mix the food with water and then suck it – often through a straw – like we drink coca cola! The food isn't interesting to look at or to taste. The astronauts have a problem with their sense of taste and smell because in zero gravity, the blood goes to their heads and their noses get blocked. 4) ………. So, Tim Peake wanted school children to design some meals that are fun, healthy and suitable for using in space. The competition was for seven to fourteen year olds and the five winners got the chance to work with a very famous chef – Heston Blumenthal – to create exciting menus for astronauts. The space dinners also had to have a British theme to them. However, a traditional English breakfast with bacon and sausages is unlikely ever to appear on the ISS! Tim Peake believes that if young people are involved in a project like this, it will motivate them to engage more with science. 5) ……….

SPIDERS IN SPACE

In another fascinating experiment recently conducted in the USA, students were involved in researching golden orb spiders. Studying spiders is nothing new, but this project was a bit different! 6) ………. Film of the spiders on the ISS was downloaded for the students to watch in class and so that they could look out for any differences that being in zero gravity in space might have on the spiders. Their results showed that the spiders' webs in space are a different shape to those in their classrooms – they are more circular. They also constructed their webs at different times. Spiders in space made their webs following a certain timetable, whereas spiders on earth made webs all the time. 7) ………. Most importantly for them, they found that spiders in space did not change into mini monsters or anything else that they might see in a Spiderman movie! Educationalists have praised the experiments and say that projects like this are extremely motivating for students in science classes.

VOCABULARY
Science

1 Complete the crossword with words related to science.

```
1 S P E C I E S
```

Across
1. a type of animal or plant
5. someone who does scientific work in order to discover new facts
7. the top or outside layer of something
8. a place where scientists work and do experiments

Down
2. a disease on a part of your body that is caused by a bacteria or virus
3. a scientific instrument that makes small things look bigger
4. to do with medicine
6. a very small structure that all living things are made of

2 Complete the sentences with one word in each space.

1. Can you speak a bit louder? My _hearing_ isn't very good.
2. I could hear the s_____ of bees in the garden.
3. I love the t_____ of chocolate!
4. You should wear glasses if your s_____ isn't very good.
5. Lambs wool is very soft to t_____.
6. You have to have perfect v_____ in order to become an aircraft pilot.
7. There was a horrible s_____ of rotten fish!

3 Complete the definitions with these words.

> delicate   durable   flexible   invisible
> man-made   transparent   waterproof

1. Something that is _man-made_ is not natural, but has been produced by people.
2. Something that is _____ can bend easily.
3. If something is _____, you cannot see it.
4. Something that is _____ is not strong and will break easily.
5. If something is _____, it will last for a long time.
6. Something that is _____ does not allow water to pass through it.
7. If something is _____, you can see through it.

4 Read the article and choose the correct answer, A, B, C or D.

We are all accustomed to the 1) _sight_ of honeybees buzzing around flowers in the summer time. In fact, these amazing creatures have always been an 2) ____ to people for their seemingly endless ability to work. Bees have a very good sense of 3) ____, so they can find sources of nectar from scented flowers even if they are several kilometres away. Their wings look 4) ____, but in fact they are very strong – strong enough to carry the weight of the bee and an equal amount of nectar and pollen. Bees can't speak, of course, but they have the 5) ____ to communicate with each other by doing 'dances' to show other members of the hive where flowers can be found. The honey that bees produce has wonderful 6) ____. It is sweeter than any 7) ____ food and also full of goodness. In the past, it was used for 8) ____ purposes.

1. **A** sight   B vision   C see   D view
2. A infection   B inspiration   C instruction   D intention
3. A smell   B hearing   C taste   D vision
4. A durable   B invisible   C medical   D delicate
5. A property   B power   C material   D taste
6. A structures   B surfaces   C properties   D researchers
7. A man-made   B durable   C invisible   D flexible
8. A medicine   B treat   C ill   D medical

GRAMMAR
-ing forms and infinitives

1 Choose the correct answers.

1. I enjoy *to visit/visiting* the zoo.
2. Some insects seem *to move/moving* very quickly.
3. Do you expect some species of animal *to become/becoming* less common in the future?
4. I think we had better *go/to go* home now.
5. I really don't know what *do/to do* now.
6. Professor Higgins agreed *to help/helping* us.
7. Tim prefers *work/working* alone.
8. I can't imagine *to live/living* in a world without animals.
9. My sister suggested *applying/to apply* to a college abroad to improve my French.
10. I'm not sure who *ask/to ask* about joining the science club.

2 Complete the sentences with the correct form of the verbs in brackets.

1. These creatures appear _to have_ (have) some amazing powers.
2. My uncle wants me _____ (help) him with some experiments.
3. Carl suggested _____ (take) a camera with us so we could take some photos.
4. We've decided _____ (go) to South America next year.
5. How do you know about this? It's supposed _____ (be) a secret!
6. Jack has invited me to his party, but I'd prefer _____ (watch) a DVD with a few friends.
7. I'm not sure how _____ (get) to the city centre by bus.
8. We could watch TV, but I'd rather _____ (play) on the computer.
9. Does the experiment involve _____ (kill) animals?
10. _____ (use) animals in medical experiments is wrong in my opinion.

3 Complete the sentences with the correct form of these words. Add any other words that are necessary.

> better / take   ~~decide / do~~   forget / water
> hate / be   involve / work   love / watch
> rather / study   supposed / go

1. Scientists wanted to find out more about these creatures, so they _decided to do_ some experiments.
2. I'd love to do a job that _____ with animals.
3. I'm really interested in nature and I _____ documentaries about animals.
4. Come on – hurry up! I _____ late!
5. I think we _____ some food with us because we might get hungry later.
6. Why is your little brother still up? He _____ to bed at seven o'clock!
7. All my plants died because I _____ them.
8. My parents want me to do medicine at university, but I _____ biology.

4 Complete the text with one word in each space.

Subject: New job!

Hi Jack,
Guess what? I've got a job working at the zoo in the summer holidays! I decided 1) _to_ apply because my brother worked there last year and he said it's really interesting. The only problem is that they want 2) _____ to work in the snake house! I'm not very happy about that. I don't really like snakes and I wouldn't know 3) _____ to do if one escaped! I 4) _____ rather work with the elephants! They 5) _____ supposed to be really intelligent animals, aren't they? Anyway, I guess I 6) _____ better accept any job they're willing to give me. I just hope I don't 7) _____ to touch the snakes!

VOCABULARY
Experiments

1 Choose the correct answers.

1. Animal behaviour is a very interesting *topic*/*topical*.
2. It isn't *logic*/*logical* to start at number five!
3. We need to find a *practice*/*practical* solution to this problem.
4. I'd love to study *biology*/*biological* at university.
5. I think she is an *inspiration*/*inspirational* singer.
6. Most people nowadays don't believe in *magic*/*magical*.
7. This badge is *magnet*/*magnetic*, so it will stick to the fridge.

2 Complete the sentences with these words.

> basic   dramatic   electric   microscopic
> panic   ~~plastic~~   scientific

1. Things that are made of _plastic_ don't break down in the soil.
2. The water looks clear to us, but in fact there are millions of _____ creatures in it.
3. The _____ problem is that we don't have enough money.
4. Don't _____ if there's a fire, just leave the building as quickly as possible.
5. The film has a very _____ ending.
6. Some _____ experiments have been done to test this theory.
7. The house was without _____ power for a while during the storm.

3 Complete the sentences with the correct form of the words in capitals.

1. Sometimes _biological_ weapons are used in wars. **BIOLOGY**
2. His new car is a bright _____ blue colour. **METAL**
3. Some scientists have experimented with using _____ energy to power machines. **MAGNET**
4. Many TV documentaries are very _____ for young children. **EDUCATION**
5. I think that one day we will all drive _____ cars. **ELECTRICITY**
6. I've never been very _____ – I can't even draw a simple picture! **ART**

4 Look at the underlined stress on the words in the table. Write these words in the correct column according to their stress pattern.

> magnetic   magical   dramatic   electric
> practical   scientific   biological   microscopic

ar-<u>tis</u>-tic	<u>lo</u>-gic-al

5 Complete the article with the correct form of the words in brackets.

Bird song is one of the 1) _natural_ (nature) sounds we associate with summer. It has always been enjoyed and admired for its beauty and has been 2) _____ (inspiration) to poets over the centuries. Different birds produce a great variety of songs – from the sweet and 3) _____ (music) song of the blackbird to the loud and 4) _____ (drama) hoot of the owl. However, there are simple 5) _____ (biology) reasons for why birds sing. 6) _____ (science) studies have shown that birds sing either to attract a mate, to make a claim on their territory or to warn other birds of danger. So there is nothing 7) _____ (magic) about bird song – it is just a form of communication like any other.

GRAMMAR
have/get something done

1 Choose the correct answer, A, B or C.

1 I went to the dentist yesterday and ____ .
  A had cleaned my teeth
  B got my teeth clean
  C had my teeth cleaned

2 If you can't see that, you should ____ .
  A get your eyes tested
  B have your eyes test
  C have your eyes testing

3 My computer's broken, so I'm ____ .
  A getting repaired   B having repair it
  C getting it repaired

4 My sister is really upset. She ____ last Saturday.
  A stole her bag   B had her bag stolen
  C got her bag stolen

5 Have you ____ yet?
  A had decorated your bedroom
  B got your bedroom decorate
  C had your bedroom decorated

6 Your hair is too long. You should ____ .
  A get cut   B have cut it
  C get it cut

2 Complete the sentences with the correct form of *have/get something done*.

1 We *get the windows cleaned* (get / the windows / clean) every week.
2 My glasses are broken, so I need to _____ (have / them / mend).
3 My dad _____ (have / his car / take) from outside his office last week.
4 You can order a new computer online and _____ (get / it / deliver) to your home.
5 When we do an experiment, we always _____ (have / the results / check).
6 That's a lovely photo. Why don't you _____ (get / it / frame)?
7 I had to _____ (have / a tooth / take out) at the dentist yesterday.
8 After the burglary last month, we _____ (have / new locks / fit) on all the doors.

3 Complete the text with the correct form of *have* and these verbs and phrases.

> a mini science lab/install   a TV/fix
> the walls/paint   your dream/make
> ~~your perfect room/design~~

Fancy a new bedroom? Just sit back and relax. You can 1) *have your perfect room designed* by our expert designers. Just tell them what you want. For example, you can 2) _____ to the wall opposite your bed, so you can sit in bed and watch your favourite programmes. If you're into science, why not 3) _____ in one corner of the room? You can 4) _____ any colour of your choice. Once you've decided on your dream room, just relax and 5) _____ a reality by our expert fitters.

4 Rewrite the sentences using the word given. Use between two and five words, including the word given.

1 The hairdresser cut my hair yesterday.   **HAD**
  I *had my hair cut* yesterday.
2 Someone stole my microscope from the laboratory.   **STOLEN**
  I _____ from the laboratory.
3 You should ask someone to check your computer for viruses.   **GET**
  You should _____ for viruses.
4 I'd prefer to study languages.   **RATHER**
  I _____ languages.
5 You should turn the music down a bit.   **BETTER**
  You _____ the music down a bit.
6 We don't know what we can do about this problem.   **TO**
  We don't know _____ about this problem.

LISTENING

1 **10.1 Listen to a student presentation. Choose the correct answer, true or false.**

1 The talk is about wild animals.
   True   False
2 The first invention the girl mentions is modern gadgets.
   True   False
3 The biggest difficulty for the scientists was making this invention safe.
   True   False
4 The inventor was inspired to develop his invention when he touched his hair one day.
   True   False
5 The second invention has helped people on the road.
   True   False
6 The inventor of Velcro was going through a forest when he had the idea for it.
   True   False
7 Velcro is an invention that people use every day.
   True   False
8 The inventor of Velcro was from the USA.
   True   False

2 **10.2 Listen again and complete the sentences (1–10) using one word or number from the presentation in each space.**

1 The students have spent several _lessons_ studying animal inspired inventions.
2 This invention has even helped people in hospital with _____ problems.
3 The subject of electricity was extremely interesting for _____ scientists.
4 The _____ whose method became most popular in the end was Tesla.
5 He got his first idea from his _____ .
6 The second invention is useful for people when it's very _____ .
7 Percy Shaw invented cat's eyes in _____ .
8 The cat he saw was on a _____ by the side of the road.
9 _____ are a popular modern item of clothing that uses Velcro.
10 After hunting, Mestral's dog was covered in flower _____ .

SPEAKING SKILLS

1 Match the statements (1–6) with the follow-up sentences (a–f).

1 I don't think zoos are a good thing. _d_
2 Animals can definitely make our lives better. ___
3 People say that some dogs are dangerous but I don't agree. ___
4 Using animals in laboratories is cruel in my opinion. ___
5 A lot of people don't eat meat these days because they don't want to kill animals. ___
6 Some people have pets and they treat them like children. ___

a They put clothes and jewellery on them and I think they look silly.
b Some, like dogs, help people who are disabled.
c I would never buy cosmetics that have been tested on animals.
d Animals should live in the wild and be free.
e It's the owners who make them like this.
f They think they can get all the right things from vegetables and fish.

2 Choose the best answer for an exam, A, B or C.

1 What recent invention do you think has been very important in our lives?
   A I don't know. Can you ask me another question please?
   B I have two smart phones and I like them very much.
   (C) I would say the tablet computer because it's small and you can take it everywhere with you.
2 How can teachers make science a more interesting subject for their students?
   A I think it's a very boring subject and I don't pay attention.
   B Science is very important for students and they need to start learning it when they are young.
   C Teachers should do lots of funny experiments to show that science is amazing.
3 Do you think that new technology is difficult for older people to use? Why/Why not?
   A Yes. It's very difficult for them because they're old.
   B It's difficult because maybe they don't use it as often as young people do. However, you can learn about it at any age.
   C I would like to teach old people how to use computers. I know a lot about them and it would be interesting for me.

10 Inspiration

4 What invention would you like to see in the next few years?
  A I think it would be wonderful to get somewhere very quickly. For example, to step into a room and immediately you're somewhere different.
  B Perhaps we will all live on another planet because ours is very polluted.
  C I don't think that's a very interesting question. Nobody knows what's going to happen in the future.

WRITING

1 Match the situations (1–4) with the personal reactions (a–d).

1 He didn't hesitate and took out a twenty pound note. _b_
2 The rejection letter came two days later. ____
3 Most of the action took place in a small Devonshire village. ____
4 The weather forecaster explained the whole situation with admirable clarity. ____

a That's the kind of job I'd love to do.
b I'll never forget his generosity.
c The film reminded me a lot about my own childhood.
d I felt a complete failure.

2 Match the situations (1–4) with the exclamations (a–d).

1 The singer called out my name from the stage and everyone sang Happy Birthday to me. _b_
2 The film is about a man who met his wife while he was cycling across the USA. ____
3 An old lady in the town has rescued fifteen dogs and cats in the last ten years and found new homes for them all. ____
4 First we ran out of petrol, and then as we were walking to the garage it started to rain. ____

a What a horrible evening it was!
b What an amazing experience!
c What a kind person she is!
d What an interesting story!

3 Write exclamations for the situations (1–4) using the words given and these adjectives.

> beautiful   difficult   expensive   ~~horrible~~

1 It was raining heavily and it was really windy too. (weather)
   What horrible weather! .
2 We could see right across the fields to the beach. (view)
   _____ .
3 I had to choose whether to go climbing or kayaking. (decision)
   _____ .
4 Everything in the shop was over £100. (shop)
   _____ .

4 Read the writing task and decide in which paragraph (A–D) the sentences (1–4) would go.

You have seen this advertisement on an international students' website.

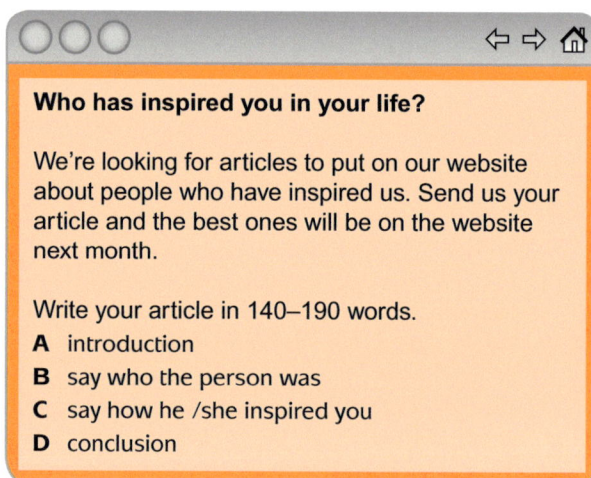

Who has inspired you in your life?

We're looking for articles to put on our website about people who have inspired us. Send us your article and the best ones will be on the website next month.

Write your article in 140–190 words.
A introduction
B say who the person was
C say how he /she inspired you
D conclusion

1 I later went on to study French at university. I now work as a translator at the United Nations. _D_
2 I don't know where she is today but thank you Miss Winters. I shall always be grateful. ____
3 She replaced my old French teacher when I was thirteen. I loved her lessons. ____
4 People have inspired me at different times in my life. ____

5 Read the writing task again. Make notes and then write your article.

Revision Unit 10

1 Unscramble and write the words related to science.

1 Cotton is not a very strong _material_ (atremial).
2 Your body is made up of millions of _____ (lelcs).
3 We looked at the skin under a _____ (mcriocspoe).
4 It's better to buy things that are _____ (draubel) because they will last for a long time.
5 We studied the _____ (rsutctrue) of the eye in our biology lesson.
6 The curtains were so thin that they were almost _____ (anstrpaertn).
7 Oil will float on the _____ (ursfcea) of water.
8 You should go to the doctor if you have a _____ (deicmla) problem.
9 Metal is strong, but not very _____ (lefelibx).
10 In stories, people can sometimes make themselves _____ (isvniielb).

2 Complete the sentences with these words. There are two words which you don't need.

> hear   hearing   see   ~~sight~~   smell   sound
> taste   touch   vision

1 Seeing thousands of these butterflies in the air is an amazing _sight_ .
2 My grandad always has the TV very loud because he's got such bad _____ .
3 Silk is so lovely and soft to _____ !
4 I could hear the _____ of an aeroplane in the distance.
5 Do you have a _____ of what life will be like in thirty years?
6 The sauce had a delicious creamy _____ .
7 There was a horrible _____ when he took his boots off!

3 Complete the text with the correct form of the words in brackets.

mailbox   Today | Mail | Calendar | Contacts
Reply | Reply All | Forward | Delete
To: **Andy**   Subject: **Guess what!**

Hi Andy,
I saw an amazing 1) _sight_ (see) down by the river this morning! A kingfisher! Have you ever seen one? Their wings are a really bright 2) _____ (metal) blue colour. This one was sitting above the river, then it suddenly did a 3) _____ (drama) dive into the water and caught a fish! It was really 4) _____ (magic) to watch! I've just found some information about them online and it seems they have a 5) _____ (nature) ability to catch fish, even when they're very young. I think they are 6) _____ (inspiration) creatures!
Love,
Carly

4 Choose the correct answer, A, B, C or D.

1 There were some dirty marks on the _____ of the glass.
  A structure   **B surface**
  C property   D power
2 There are thousands of different _____ of insects.
  A creatures   B animals
  C cells   D species
3 The doctor gave me some cream to treat the _____ on my skin.
  A infection   B illness
  C sickness   D medical
4 Scientific experiments are usually carried out in a _____ .
  A microscope   B laboratory
  C material   D surface
5 One useful _____ of rubber is that it is very flexible.
  A property   B character
  C skill   D ability
6 I'd love to work as a _____ and try to discover new drugs.
  A species   B laboratory
  C researcher   D medical

GOLD EXPERIENCE

Revision Unit 10

5 Choose the correct answer, A, B or C.
1. Do you enjoy ___ new places?
   A discover   B to discover   **C discovering**
2. ___ too much chocolate isn't good for you.
   A Eat   B Eating   C To eat
3. I've decided ___ a doctor.
   A to become   B become   C becoming
4. I don't know how ___ this machine!
   A use   B to use   C using
5. My parents expect me ___ with jobs at home.
   A to help   B helping   C help
6. I haven't got any money, but I would rather ___ a weekend job.
   A not get   B don't get   C can't get
7. It's late. I think we had better ___ playing music now.
   A to stop   B stop   C stopping
8. Owls are able ___ their prey in the dark.
   A see   B seeing   C to see

6 Complete the messages with one word in each space.

Messages — **Jane**

Help! There's a huge spider in the shower! I don't know what 1) _to_ do!

Oh, no! I guess you had 2) _____ try and move it!

No way! I don't want 3) _____ touch it! I'd 4) _____ just not have a shower!

Is your sister there? She might know 5) _____ to get it out.

No, she's gone to the police station. She 6) _____ her bag stolen this morning, so she's gone to report it. Guess it's just a bad day all round! :(

7 Cross out one incorrect word in each sentence.
1. I enjoy ~~to~~ spending time with my grandparents.
2. The guide showed us where we to go.
3. My friend always wants to chat online, but I would to prefer to meet face-to-face.
4. I lent Mike £5 last week, so he had don't better not ask me for any more money!
5. Jack wants me to go out to the cinema with him, but I would rather to stay at home.
6. My parents want me to I become a scientist.
7. The exam is tomorrow, so you had better and revise this evening!
8. We're cutting up a mouse in our biology lesson tomorrow, but I would don't rather not watch!

8 Rewrite the sentences using the word given. Use between two and five words, including the word given.
1. The dentist checked my teeth yesterday.   **GOT**
   I _got my teeth checked_ yesterday.
2. I think you ought to phone Sally.   **BETTER**
   I think _____ Sally.
3. The doorman told us where we should put our coats.   **TO**
   The doorman told us _____ our coats.
4. I don't want to have a big meal.   **RATHER**
   I _____ a big meal.
5. Someone broke Sara's glasses last week.   **BROKEN**
   Sara _____ last week.
6. You should ask someone to check the car as soon as possible.   **GET**
   You should _____ as soon as possible.
7. We mustn't be late!   **HAD**
   We _____ late!
8. Everyone says it's a great film!   **SUPPOSED**
   It _____ a great film!

103

11 The art of make-believe

READING

1 Read the article. Choose the correct answer, true or false.

1. The article gives advice about how to succeed in the theatre.
   True   **False**
2. As a child the writer wanted to be like Princess Kate.
   True   False
3. The writer's interest in the arts was influenced by a member of her family.
   True   False
4. The writer showed great ability when she was still very young.
   True   False
5. She gave up dancing when she was a teenager.
   True   False
6. She had a very confident personality.
   True   False
7. The attitude of the writer's husband stopped her from being an actor.
   True   False
8. Her child has different ambitions to her mother's.
   True   False

A life in the theatre

A Ask any little girl what she wants to be when she grows up and I bet she'll say something like a princess or a ballerina. At least that's what kids used to say when I was young. I suppose today it could be a pop star or a film actress, but because Wills and Kate are so popular – that's Prince William and the Duchess of Cambridge – I guess that being a princess is still up there as an ambition for little girls! However, mine was the second alternative. It was my mother who got me interested in dancing. She took me along to ballet classes almost as soon as I could walk and before long I was enjoying pretending to be a flower in the school's annual ballet show.

B I progressed rapidly from being one of many flowers to dancing solo, so I must have shown some talent at an early age. I thoroughly enjoyed the long hours of training and the challenge of doing ever more difficult things like jumping, pirouetting and soon going 'en pointe'. I wanted to be a ballerina and nothing was going to stop me. But something did. In those days there was a height limit for ballerinas and after measuring my parents and myself, I was told by the top ballet school in the country that I was going to grow too tall. I was just eleven years old and my dream was shattered.

C However, as I had already been a performer, I couldn't stop wanting to be on a stage. Later, as a teenager, I started acting and found that I loved it almost as much as dancing. But people couldn't understand it. I was actually a very shy person and they couldn't see how I could stand up on a stage in front of huge audiences. Personally, I think it was my ballet experiences that helped me. I seemed to come alive on the stage and didn't think about the people watching me at all. Also, when you act or dance, you're not yourself but someone else with their emotions – and for an actor, their words as well! What I enjoyed most about performing was the ability to touch people in the audience – to make them laugh … or cry. There's nothing better than seeing an audience in tears!

D Sadly, the dream of becoming a professional actor also died when I got married to Jack, a lovely guy from my hometown. I didn't have the freedom to travel and audition for parts in different areas of the country. Most actors are based in London and we couldn't move there because of Jack's job. So, I turned my frustration to writing plays instead. Now, it's my words that touch audiences, not my performances. I love doing this and many, many actors have spoken my words on television as well as on stage and in films. I have a little girl of my own now, whose dream is not to be a ballerina – but a racing driver. Oh well!

11 The art of make-believe

2 Read the article again and match the questions (1–10) with the paragraphs (A–D).

Which paragraph mentions:
1 the benefits of pretending to be different characters? C
2 taking pleasure in hard work? ___
3 the changing attitude of children to the future? ___
4 the influence of a relationship on a career path? ___
5 surprising others with a choice of hobby? ___
6 the advantages of living in a central location? ___
7 the ability to ignore spectators? ___
8 the effect of a prediction on an ambition? ___
9 reaching a wide range of different audiences? ___
10 an early interest in the arts? ___

VOCABULARY
Creative arts

1 Choose the correct answers.
1 My mum told me to stop messing *up/around* and get on with my homework.
2 Is that story true or did you make it *up/out*?
3 The magazine *comes/gets* out every Thursday.
4 Those drawings are really good, so don't throw them *up/away*.
5 If you want a career in the arts, you just have to go *on/for* it!
6 I'd love to *do/have* a go at animation.
7 How do you *make/rate* our chances of winning?
8 You can *take/make* my place if you want.
9 I had plans for a new computer game, but they didn't *go/come* to much.
10 Do you think your dreams will ever *come/get* true?

2 Complete the sentences with one word from each box.

artistic   cartoon   fantasy   ~~learning~~   vivid

characters   ~~experience~~   imagination   skill   world

1 At the film studio, they taught us a lot about film-making. It was a great *learning experience*.
2 The film creates a complete _____ _____ of castles and monsters.
3 James is really good at writing stories. He's got a very _____ _____.
4 It's an animated film with _____ _____, not actors.
5 You must need a lot of _____ _____ to do those very detailed drawings.

3 Choose the correct answer, A, B, C or D.

Animation workshops

Do you love watching 1) *cartoons* on TV? Or maybe you have your favourite 2) ___ that you read every week? If you would like to learn how to turn your hobby into a career, come to one of our animation workshops!

People often make the mistake of thinking that to work in animation you have to be good at 3) ___. It isn't true. Of course, having a lot of artistic 4) ___ is useful, but it isn't absolutely necessary. There are plenty of other ways to create great animated 5) ___ – think of Wallace and Gromit or Toy Story! One thing you do need, though, is lots of ideas and a vivid 6) ___ so that you can 7) ___ some great story lines!

If you've got a passion for animation, sign up for a workshop now! You'll be 8) ___ away! It's a great learning 9) ___ and at the end of the three days you'll have some fantastic 10) ___ to take home with you!

1 A sketches   B drawings
   C cartoons   D comics
2 A drawing   B comic
   C character   D paint
3 A drawing   B skill
   C experience   D sketch
4 A skill   B fantasy
   C artwork   D drawing
5 A paints   B characters
   C crayons   D imagination
6 A imagination   B experience
   C skill   D artwork
7 A go over   B make up
   C do up   D get on
8 A taken   B pushed
   C blown   D pulled
9 A skill   B imagination
   C experience   D world
10 A crayons   B imagination
   C paints   D artwork

GRAMMAR
Reported speech

1 Choose the correct answers.

1 'I love that comedy show.'
  Sara said that she *loved*/loves that comedy show.
2 'There won't be any tickets left.'
  Jack told us that there won't/wouldn't be any tickets left.
3 'I've never been to a concert at that venue.'
  Paula said she has never been/had never been to a concert at that venue.
4 'The tickets aren't selling very quickly.'
  Mark said that the tickets aren't selling/weren't selling very quickly.
5 'You must go and watch him perform.'
  Ana said that we must/had to go and watch him perform.
6 'You should listen to their music.'
  Pete said that we should/will listen to their music.
7 'I watched a play on TV the previous night.'
  Carla said that she has watched/had watched a play on TV the previous night.
8 'You ought to go to more live performances.'
  Leo told me that I ought to/had ought to go to more live performances.

2 Rewrite the sentences in reported speech.

1 'You're a great singer.'
  Paul told ___*me that I was*___ a great singer.
2 'The show has already started.'
  They said that the show _____.
3 'It will be difficult to get tickets.'
  Sam said that _____ to get tickets.
4 'We must leave at five.'
  My dad said that _____ at five.
5 'All the actors gave amazing performances.'
  Jess said that all the actors _____ amazing performances.
6 'Let's go for a pizza before the show.'
  Liam suggested that we _____ for a pizza before the show.
7 'You ought to practise your guitar more.'
  My mum told me that _____ my guitar more.
8 'I'm not going to the concert.'
  My brother told me that _____ to the concert.

3 Read the conversation and complete the text with the correct verb forms. Add any other necessary words.

Carl Hi, Ana. How are you?
Ana Fed up! I really wanted to get into the school orchestra this year, but they didn't accept me.
Carl Oh, that's a shame, because you can play the violin really well.
Ana Thanks. But it doesn't matter. I'll probably get in next year. I know I ought to practise a bit more.
Carl Hey, I know something that will cheer you up. There's a concert on at the O2 Arena on Saturday.
Ana Great! Let's go and have a coffee and talk about it!

Ana said that she 1) ___*was*___ fed up because 2) _____ to get into the school orchestra, but they 3) _____. Carl said that it 4) _____ because Ana 5) _____ the violin really well. Anna thanked him and said that it 6) _____. She said she 7) _____ the following year. She said that she knew that 8) _____ practise more. Carl said he 9) _____ something that 10) _____ Ana up. He told her that 11) _____ a concert on at the O2 Arena that Saturday. Ana suggested that 12) _____ and had a coffee and talked about it.

4 Complete the blog post with one word in each space.

View previous comments   Cancel   Share   Post

Well, I guess it's my lucky day! I went for an audition for the X-Factor today and guess what? I got in! The judges listened to me singing, then told 1) ___*me*___ that I had a lot of talent and that I 2) _____ performed really well! One of the judges said that I 3) _____ the best singer they'd heard that day! How about that? I talked to the judges afterwards and told 4) _____ about my dreams of becoming a famous singer. They 5) _____ I've definitely got what it takes, but they told me I 6) _____ to take my singing more seriously if I really wanted to make it big! They suggested that I 7) _____ get a personal singing teacher. They also said 8) _____ I ought to think about my image more. Any ideas, anyone?

Write a comment   Support

VOCABULARY
Live entertainment

1 Unscramble and write the words related to entertainment.
1 Do you like _classical_ (lascalsic) music?
2 I'd love to go to a film _____ (ripermeè) and see all the stars!
3 Some very famous _____ (tsac) have performed in this theatre.
4 Wembley Stadium is a very good _____ (neveu) for concerts.
5 My grandma appeared in a _____ (whos) on Broadway when she was young!

2 Complete the email with these words.

> audience   box office   interval   ~~open-air~~
> row   seat   sold out   stage

mailbox Today | Mail | Calendar | Contacts
Reply | Reply All | Forward | Delete
To: Jo   Subject: Rock-n-roll!

I saw a great rock concert last night! It was at an 1) _open-air_ amphitheatre and luckily for us it didn't rain! I had a great 2) _____ right near the front. I wasn't in the front 3) _____, but I was still quite close to the band. It was so exciting when the lights went out and the band came onto the 4) _____! It was an amazing concert and the 5) _____ went wild when the band played some of their big hits. I was talking to some other fans during the 6) _____ and it seems there's another concert coming soon. Do you fancy going? We should be able to get some tickets at the 7) _____ because I don't think it's 8) _____ yet.

3 Choose the correct answers.
1 This arena is a great *setting/fame* for rock concerts.
2 I love that band – I'm a member of their *music-lovers/fan club*.
3 I'd like to know a little bit more about the *comedy/background* to this show.
4 The band sounded awful because the *audience/acoustics* were so bad.
5 A lot of young people dream of achieving *fame/stage*.
6 A lot of famous *musicians/music-lovers* have performed in this venue.
7 My cousin goes to loads of concerts – he's a real *music-lover/fan club*!

4 Read the notice and choose the correct answer, A, B or C.

Drama Club

This notice is for everyone involved in the school 1) _play_. Don't forget that there's a 2) ___ tomorrow evening after school. And it's for everyone – people playing the main 3) ___ and those who have just got small parts. Please make sure you're there on time! You should all know your 4) ___ by now, but someone will be there to help you if you forget one or two words. It's really important to know all your words before you get up on the 5) ___ in front of a live 6) ___. And don't forget that we're performing a 7) ___, so come in a good mood and ready to have a laugh!
We're still looking for people to help out with other aspects of the show. We need people to help put out 8) ___ in the hall and we'd also like some volunteers to help serve tea and coffee during the 9) ___. We're also looking for one or two more 10) ___ for the band, so if you can play the guitar or violin, please come along!

1	A role	**B play**	C stage
2	A rehearsal	B première	C setting
3	A lines	B acts	C roles
4	A acts	B lines	C settings
5	A stage	B play	C show
6	A fan club	B audience	C venue
7	A classical	B role	C comedy
8	A seats	B shows	C lines
9	A audience	B interval	C background
10	A musicians	B music-lovers	C fan clubs

GRAMMAR
Reporting orders and requests

1 Choose the correct answers.

1 'Don't forget to post the letter!'
My mum *reminded*/*begged* me to post the letter.
2 'Please, please come with us!'
My friends *ordered*/*begged* me to go with them.
3 'Stand back!'
The police officers *ordered*/*allowed* us to stand back.
4 'You should work harder.'
My teacher *permitted*/*advised* me to work harder.
5 'Please can you help me?'
My friend *asked*/*warned* me to help her.
6 'Yes, of course you can go to the concert.'
My parents *persuaded*/*allowed* me to go to the concert.

2 Choose the correct answer, A, B or C.

1 The police ordered the crowd ____ .
 A that they leave
 (B) to leave
 C leave
2 Martin ____ for him.
 A said me to wait
 B asked to wait
 C told me to wait
3 My friend ____ anyone her secret.
 A told me don't tell
 B asked not to tell
 C warned me not to tell
4 My parents ____ to the festival.
 A didn't allow me to go
 B didn't permit me go
 C didn't allow I go
5 My teacher ____ all my revision until the last minute.
 A encouraged me don't leave
 B advised me not to leave
 C warned me that I don't leave

3 Rewrite the sentences in reported speech.

1 'You really should study music.'
My teachers persuaded *me to study music* .
2 'Don't be late home.'
My dad warned me ____ .
3 'Can you lend me some money?'
My sister asked me ____ .
4 'Hand your homework in on Monday.'
The teacher told us ____ .
5 'You shouldn't stay up so late.'
Sam advised me ____ .
6 'Stop making so much noise!'
My dad ordered us ____ .
7 'Remember to bring your sports clothes to school.'
The teacher reminded us ____ .
8 'Don't give up playing the guitar.'
My parents persuaded me ____ .

4 Rewrite the sentences using the word given. Use between two and five words, including the word given.

1 Jack told me I should take up acting. **ENCOURAGED**
Jack *encouraged me to take up* acting.
2 'Please don't eat all the cake,' Martha said to her friends. **ASKED**
Martha ____ all the cake.
3 'Remember to do the shopping,' Paul's aunt said to him. **REMINDED**
Paul's aunt ____ the shopping.
4 'I don't think you should accept the role', Tara's agent said to her. **ADVISED**
Tara's agent ____ the role.
5 'Do Exercise 5 for homework,' the teacher said to the students. **TOLD**
The teacher ____ Exercise 5 for homework.
6 'Don't spend all your money,' my mum said to me. **WARNED**
My mum ____ all my money.

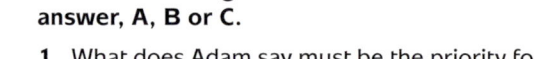

LISTENING

1 Complete the sentences with these words. You do not need one of the words.

> calm   challenge   passion   priority
> ~~stunt~~   talent

1 A difficult or exciting activity in a film is called a ___*stunt*___.
2 People describe the most important thing they have to do as a _____.
3 I love doing sport – it's my _____ in life.
4 Something that is difficult to do is often described as a _____.
4 If a person is doing something dangerous, they should stay _____ under pressure.

2 🔊 **11.1** Listen to an interview with Adam Elliot, who is a stunt performer in films. Which picture (A–F) is **not** mentioned in the interview?

A

B
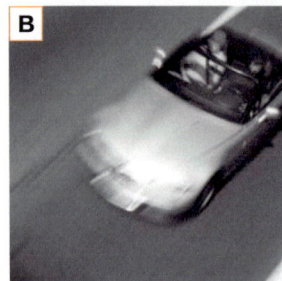

C

D

E

F

3 🔊 **11.2** Listen again and choose the correct answer, A, B or C.

1 What does Adam say must be the priority for a stunt performer on a film?
  A making it look real
  (B) making sure a stunt is safe
  C having the ability to use a range of skills
2 Adam became a stunt performer because
  A it had a high salary.
  B it had always been his dream.
  C it was recommended by his teacher.
3 According to Adam, what's the most difficult part of the job?
  A the long hours
  B the right clothes
  C the uncomfortable conditions
4 What does Adam say about having to keep fit?
  A He enjoys all forms of exercise and sport.
  B He finds it impossible to control his diet.
  C He understands why it is important for his job.
5 How did Adam feel about working on his first stunt in *The Escape*?
  A He was pleased with the final result.
  B He was grateful for how much it taught him.
  C He was glad he didn't actually have to perform it.
6 Adam gives the example of a stunt in *The Big Robbery*
  A to show some strange problems stunt performers can have.
  B to describe how angry directors can get with stunt performers.
  C to explain how complicated a stunt can be.
7 What does Adam think is most important for a stunt performer?
  A being well-trained
  B being a good organiser
  C being able to work anywhere

109

SPEAKING SKILLS

1 Put the words in the correct order.

1 I / well, / start / shall
   Well, shall I start?

2 you / one / think / this / what / about / do
   ?

3 would/ it / interesting, / wouldn't / be / this
   ?

4 like / would / start / to / you
   ?

5 do / better / think / be / which / you / would
   ?

6 make / now / perhaps / decision / should / a / we
   .

2 Complete the conversations with the correct phrases from Exercise 1.

1 **A:** *This would be interesting, wouldn't it?*
   B: Yes, I agree. It would be fascinating to try.

2 **A:**
   B: Well, if you ask me, I think it's a terrible idea.

3 **A:**
   B: OK. Go ahead.

4 **A:**
   B: You're right. So which do you want to go for?

5 **A:**
   B: In my opinion this course would be more popular with teenagers.

6 **A:**
   B: Sure. Let's think about this one first. For me, it would be really interesting and appeal to lots of people.

3 Read the speaking task and match the jobs (1–5) with the photos (A–E).

A  B  C  D  E

1 news reader   *D*
2 camera man ___
3 reality TV show presenter ___

What do you think are the good and bad points of doing these jobs?

4 director ___
5 soap opera actor ___

4 Read the speaking task again and match students' comments (a–e) with the jobs (1–5) in Exercise 3.

a Oh, one of the best things about this job is that you can go to lots of different locations and film different types of things. You need to have a lot of technical knowledge too. ___

b I think this is a great job because you can order everyone around and tell them what to do! Everyone respects you. ___

c You keep up to date with everything, learn a lot and all you have to do is look at a camera and read a script! No worries about forgetting anything. *1*

d Well, it's a steady job isn't it? And you become a celebrity very quickly. I think it's well paid too. And if you forget something you can start again. ___

e It's a cool job because they're very popular shows and millions of people watch them, plus you get to meet and talk to lots of different people and celebrities too. ___

11 The art of make-believe

WRITING

1 Choose the correct words to complete the sentences.

1 Generally *speaking/talking*, I thought the show was very good.
2 There were some problems but they did well in the *finish/end* and the audience clapped for a long time.
3 They played a lot of different instruments and the music *sounded/seemed* very good.
4 I'd definitely recommend to *go/going* to see the film.
5 It's a *pity/sorry* that the music was so loud.
6 There were a few boring moments, but *despite/on the whole* it was worth watching.
7 *Although/However* the cast were all young, they did very well.
8 The show finished *by/with* a brilliant song, written by the students' teacher.

2 Complete the sentences with these adjectives.

~~disappointing~~ exciting flat impressed
influential nervous professional proud

1 I found the concert _disappointing_ because my favourite band didn't take part.
2 The lead actor looked a little _____ in front of such a large audience, but he did well.
3 The storyline was very _____ and I couldn't stop watching for a moment.
4 I think the audience were enjoying the show, but the atmosphere in the theatre was a bit _____ .
5 I was extremely _____ by the performance and I would love to see it again.
6 Although the film was made by a group of students, it was a very _____ production.
7 When I realised that the film was made in my local town, I felt very _____ .
8 There were some _____ people from the music industry in the audience, so we all wanted to play well.

3 Read the task and complete the example sentences with the correct words.

You see this announcement on your school website.

> **Write a review! What do you watch on TV?**
>
> We would like to post some reviews of TV programmes on the website. So, choose a programme that's been on TV recently and write a review, saying what the programme is about, what you think about it and why you would or wouldn't recommend it to other viewers. Then send it to us!
>
> Write your review in 140–190 words.

I was   It's a   It's about   ~~It's on~~
It's set in   It stars

1 _It's on_ Channel 4/every Friday/once a month/Monday evenings.
2 _____ Marc Warren/a new actor/two famous actors/an ex-sports champion.
3 _____ documentary/detective series/soap opera/reality show.
4 _____ impressed/disappointed/excited/amazed.
5 _____ London/a European country/the countryside/a hotel.
6 _____ wild animals/a celebrity's life/people who live in hot countries/a policeman who solves murders.

4 Read the task again and write your review.

Revision Unit 11

1 Complete the sentences with one word in each space.

1 I'd never performed on a s_tage_ in front of so many people before.
2 We had a great view because we were sitting in the front r_____.
3 We went to an e_____ of landscape paintings at the art gallery.
4 There's a fifteen minute i_____ in the middle of the performance.
5 The show was a great success and the a_____ all cheered at the end.
6 To be a writer, you need a very vivid i_____.

2 Complete the definitions with these words. There are two words which you don't need.

> acoustics   box office   fan club   musician
> music-lover   ~~première~~   role   seat

1 A _première_ is the first performance of a play or film.
2 A _____ is someone who plays music.
3 A _____ is a place where you can buy tickets for a performance.
4 A _____ is a chair you sit on to watch a performance.
5 A _____ is an organisation for people who like a particular singer, actor, etc.
6 A _____ is someone who enjoys listening to music.

3 Choose the correct answers.

1 I did a rough *sketch/paint* of the house.
2 Some children like to live in a fantasy *place/world*.
3 What day does the magazine usually *come/go* out?
4 Do you dream of achieving *stage/fame*?
5 I want that old comic – don't throw it *away/off*!
6 Going on the course was a great *learn/learning* experience.
7 One day your dreams may *get real/come true*!
8 If you want to become a famous pop singer, just *go at/go for* it!

4 Read the advert and choose the correct answer, A, B, C or D.

Brigstock Festival

There's something for everyone at the Brigstock Festival of the Arts. You can hear all kinds of music, from 1) _classical_ to rock. There's a great variety of 2) ____ in different 3) ____ all around the town, including the magnificent Royal Hall, which has wonderful 4) ____. There are also 5) ____ performances in Queen's Park, which is a wonderful 6) ____ for concerts.
There's plenty for kids to do, too. There are play areas where they can 7) ____ around with paints or crayons. There are also more formal workshops where they can 8) ____ a go at drawing cartoon 9) ____ and 10) ____ up stories about them. You should book early for these, as they tend to get sold 11) ____ quite quickly.
For more information or to find out more about the 12) ____ to the festival, visit our website at www.brigstockarts.co.uk.

1 A acoustics   (B) classical
   C audience   D animation
2 A shows   B lines
   C roles   D rows
3 A plays   B rehearsals
   C venues   D stages
4 A background   B setting
   C acoustics   D fame
5 A air   B open-air
   C interval   D rehearsal
6 A setting   B role
   C play   D show
7 A touch   B mess
   C go   D use
8 A use   B take
   C make   D have
9 A lines   B roles
   C characters   D plays
10 A getting   B going
   C having   D making
11 A out   B up
   C off   D away
12 A setting   B background
   C play   D seat

112 GOLD EXPERIENCE

Revision Unit 11

5 Rewrite the sentences in reported speech.

1 'I love going to the theatre!'
Mary said that _she loved_ going to the theatre.
2 'I've already seen that film.'
Stacey said that she _____ that film.
3 'We aren't going to the concert.'
They told me they _____ to the concert.
4 'There may be some tickets left.'
They told us at the box office that there _____ some tickets left.
5 'You must see them perform live!'
Clare told me that I _____ them perform live.
6 'I'll book the tickets online.'
Sam said that he _____ the tickets online.
7 'Let's watch a DVD.'
Paul suggested that we _____ a DVD.
8 'You ought to read this book.'
Sara told me that I _____ this book.

6 Choose the correct answer, A, B or C.

1 'Tidy your room immediately!'
My mum ___ my room immediately.
A told me to tidy
B said me to tidy
C asked me tidy
2 'Please, please help us!'
They ___ them.
A persuaded me help
B begged me to help
C ordered me to help
3 'Don't let the microphone get wet.'
Dan ___ the microphone get wet.
A permitted me to let
B advised me don't let
C warned me not to let
4 'Yes, you can go to the festival.'
My parents ___ to the festival.
A allowed me to go
B permitted me go
C reminded me to go
5 'Can you pay for the tickets?'
Rob ___ for the tickets.
A advised me to pay
B persuaded me that I pay
C asked me to pay
6 'Remember, you mustn't be late.'
My dad ___ late
A persuaded me to be
B reminded me not to be
C encouraged me to be

7 Complete the text with one word in each space.

HOW DO YOU BECOME A SUCCESSFUL COMEDIAN?

We spoke to young comedian Andy Roberts. He told us that he 1) _had_ started performing at a young age. He said a friend had advised him 2) _____ become a comedian because he 3) _____ always making jokes at school. It seems his parents weren't so keen. They advised him 4) _____ to try and make a living from performing, but Andy's heart was set on a career in comedy and he knew it was something he 5) _____ to do. At the age of sixteen, an agent suggested that he 6) _____ start by trying to do some shows in small venues close to home. The agent said 7) _____ Andy would know fairly soon whether he was popular with audiences. Audiences loved him and a lot of people who saw his early shows wrote to him and encouraged 8) _____ to continue performing. He now performs all over the country and has just been offered his own TV show!

8 Rewrite the sentences using the word given. Use between two and five words, including the word given.

1 'I've never heard of that band.' **HAD**
Emily said that she _had never heard_ of that band.
2 'You should become a professional musician,' my mum said to me. **ADVISED**
My mum _____ a professional musician.
3 'Let's meet outside the theatre,' Mike said. **SUGGESTED**
Mike _____ outside the theatre.
4 'You should go to drama college,' Stella's dad told her. **ENCOURAGED**
Stella's dad _____ to drama college.
5 Jack thought the show started at seven. **THINK**
'I _____ at seven', Jack said.
6 'Please don't mess around during rehearsals,' the teacher said to us. **TO**
The teacher asked _____ during rehearsals.

12 Find your voice

READING

1 Read the article about the BBC School Report project and choose the correct answer A, B or C.

The article is about:
- A The history of the School Report project.
- B The benefits of the School Report Project.
- C The future of the School Report project.

2 Read the article again and find two items on the list that are <u>not</u> mentioned.
1. when it began
2. the date of this year's School Report
3. how often it happens
4. the teachers' views
5. some students' views
6. the number of schools that take part
7. the best School Report
8. the skills required

3 Choose which sentence (a–g) fits each space (1–6) in the text. You do not need one of the sentences.

- a Another was to give students a voice and the chance to research and comment on issues that are important to them.
- b They give advice on researching, writing stories and developing editing skills in order to produce the best materials that they can.
- c This is good news for teachers and students alike.
- d They also say that even their shyer students gain in confidence when they take part.
- e In spite of this, students manage to work together well and have produced some excellent stories.
- f Well, these days secondary school students all over the UK have a chance to find out.
- g It was extremely successful and since then more than 200,000 students, aged between eleven and sixteen, have taken part.

4 Find words or phrases in the article that match these definitions.
1. talking about something to a camera _presenting_
2. problems
3. take part in
4. make people aware of something
5. when something started
6. unchanging /permanent

12 Find your voice

School Report

Have you ever watched a news report on TV and wondered just how much work went into creating and developing what we see on the screen? 1) __f__ Every year students can take part in a project organised by the BBC, called School Report, where they produce their own news reports to put on their school website on a particular day. However, the audience is much wider than just the visitors to that school website. On that day the BBC links up to all the schools that are participating and viewers all over the UK can go online and watch the reports. That could be millions of people!

Before the School Report Day, teachers work with students to help them prepare. 2) ____ The students also need to learn about filming and interview techniques, and presenting to a camera. However, after this the teachers are just guides. The students are in control of the issues they choose to write about and do everything themselves.

2016 will see the tenth anniversary of this amazing project. It was started in 2006 with 120 schools participating to see how it might work. 3) ____ . Last year more than 1,000 schools were involved.

So, why was it started and how useful is it to students? One reason behind the launch of the project was to encourage students to learn more about the media and the world of journalism. 4) ____ In addition to this, getting involved in the School Report raises students' awareness of the news, politics and how events are reported. On last year's School Report Day a wide range of issues were discussed. As well as interviews with top politicians, there were also reports about teenagers' addiction to social media and why dancing was not only an interest for girls!

Both teachers and students value the project highly. Teachers say that working on something like this gives their students a sense of responsibility and independence. 5) ____ And from the students' point of view, it is an incredible experience which allows them to develop a whole range of skills; from journalism and using cameras to interviewing and being a news presenter on the big screen, with all the nervousness that goes with it. One student pointed out that he hadn't realised how much work went into research in order to gets the facts right, and other students mentioned the value of learning to work in a team and their pride in the finished reports.

It seems that the School Report is now a fixed annual event and more and more schools will be participating in the future. 6) ____ Any project which encourages young people to learn more about politics and social issues and also to express themselves and their views should be admired and respected. The experience will help students develop important skills for the workplace such as team work and leadership. It may also produce some of our future journalists and the faces that we will see presenting the news on our TV screens in a few years' time!

VOCABULARY
Values

1 Choose the correct answers.

1 Tom will never *argue/admit* when he's wrong about something.
2 What's your *view/speech* on asking for help with your homework? Do you think it's always wrong?
3 Her essay *concluded/discussed* that cheating in exams is never acceptable.
4 I think we should *discuss/argue* this topic further.
5 What's the best way to *conclude/prepare* for exams?
6 Nathan is always *arguing/discussing* with his dad about politics – they never agree!
7 Paul is quite an interesting *discussion/individual*.

2 Complete the sentences with the correct form of the words in capitals.

1 James put forward some very convincing _arguments_ in his speech. **ARGUE**
2 Elena always speaks with great _____. **CLEAR**
3 Good _____ is really important when you're speaking in public. **PREPARE**
4 You should try to bring all your ideas together in your _____. **CONCLUDE**
5 We had some very interesting _____ about human rights. **DISCUSS**
6 I'd be terrified if I had to give a _____ in public. **SPEAK**

3 Complete the puzzle and find the mystery word.

1 E Q U A L I T Y
2
3
4
5

1 a situation in which all people have the same rights
2 the quality of being strong
3 a duty you have to do something or be in charge of something
4 a feeling of admiration for someone because of their qualities or skills
5 the quality of being honest

Mystery word: _____

4 Complete the sentences with these words.

advice   difference   ~~freedom~~   rights
skills   truth

1 The people protested in the streets and demanded _freedom_.
2 In some countries, human _____ aren't respected.
3 Do you believe that an individual can really make a _____ in the world?
4 I often ask my parents what I should do, but I don't often follow their _____!
5 I try to be honest, but sometimes it's kinder not to tell the _____.
6 I really enjoy learning new _____.

5 Complete the text with one word in each space.

Eastleigh Youth Club

At Eastleigh Youth Club we believe 1) _in_ helping young people to grow into confident adults. Our members can take 2) _____ in lots of fun activities or just chill out and chat. We run football teams for boys and girls. We believe that team sports help you learn to stick 3) _____ and stand up 4) _____ each other. We don't focus 5) _____ winning, though. We think it's important to take pride 6) _____ doing well, but also accept losing with a smile! At Eastleigh we stand 7) _____ fairness. We encourage our members to show respect 8) _____ each other and to speak 9) _____ if they see others behaving badly. We try to help all our young people to have confidence 10) _____ themselves and to feel confident about the future.

116 GOLD EXPERIENCE

GRAMMAR
Modal verbs (2)

1 Choose the correct meaning, A, B or C for each sentence.

1 Paul may be at football practice.
   - A I'm sure that Paul is at football practice.
   - **B** It's possible that Paul is at football practice.
   - C It's impossible that Paul is at football practice.
2 It can't be Sam's coat.
   - A It's possible that it's Sam's coat.
   - B I'm sure it's Sam's coat.
   - C It's impossible that it's Sam's coat.
3 It should be fun!
   - A I expect it will be fun.
   - B I expect it was fun.
   - C I don't think it will be fun.
4 We might not get tickets for the concert.
   - A I'm sure we won't get tickets.
   - B We'll probably get tickets.
   - C It's possible that we won't get tickets.
5 She must be very nervous.
   - A She definitely isn't very nervous.
   - B I'm sure she's very nervous.
   - C It's possible that she's very nervous.
6 They could win the competition.
   - A It's possible that they will win.
   - B They were able to win.
   - C It's impossible for them to win.

2 Choose the correct answers.

1 I *may/must* go to the party, but I'm not sure yet.
2 No, that *can't/mustn't* be Jed's bike – it's too old!
3 I'd love to go and see that film, but I *might not/couldn't* have time – I've got exams this week.
4 I'm sure she *can/must* feel scared when she has to give a speech.
5 There will be some good speakers, so it *must/should* be interesting.
6 I can't find my purse. *Could/May* it be in your bag?
7 I don't know how much the tickets cost, but they *may not/mustn't* be too expensive.
8 I'm not sure whose bag it is. I suppose it *could/can* be Ana's.

3 Read the conversation and choose the correct answer, A, B or C.

Max Are you going to join the debating society?
Lucy I'm not sure. I 1) *might* go along. I think it 2) ___ be interesting.
Max Hmm. I find the idea pretty terrifying, though. I mean, 3) ___ you've got the confidence to speak in front of an audience?
Lucy Yes, I think so. I mean, if you've done your preparation properly, you just get up and speak, don't you? It 4) ___ be that scary!
Max Yes, but it 5) ___ be difficult when people disagree with you.
Lucy I think you worry too much. It 6) ___ be as bad as you think. Why don't we both go along and give it a go?
Max Yes, you 7) ___ be right. OK, I'll come with you!

1 A can   B must   **C** might
2 A should   B must   C can
3 A Could   B Do you think C Can
4 A can't   B mustn't   C couldn't
5 A might not B couldn't   C must
6 A may not   B mustn't   C couldn't
7 A can   B could   C should

4 Rewrite the sentences using the word given. Use between two and five words, including the word given.

1 I'm sure my bus pass is here somewhere! **MUST**
   My bus pass ___*must be here*___ somewhere!
2 It's possible that you won't like the film. **MIGHT**
   You _____ the film.
3 Is it possible that Jem is ill? **COULD**
   _____ ill?
4 I'm sure the tickets don't cost that much! **CAN'T**
   The _____ that much!
5 I expect you will have a wonderful time. **SHOULD**
   You _____ a wonderful time.
6 Is she a good speaker, in your opinion? **THINK**
   Do _____ a good speaker?

VOCABULARY
Issues: fair or unfair?

1 Choose the correct answers.

1. It's a very *formal/informal* event, so you can wear jeans if you want.
2. You must make sure your writing is *legible/illegible* in the exam.
3. These creatures are so small that they are *visible/invisible* without a microscope.
4. My brother annoys me because he's so *mature/immature* – he laughs at really stupid things!
5. It isn't *responsible/irresponsible* to throw paper in the bin – you should recycle it!
6. You might win a prize if you're *lucky/unlucky*!
7. I can't understand this decision – it seems *rational/irrational* to me!
8. Going for a pizza together was *planned/unplanned* – we just decided on our way home that we would do it!

2 Complete the sentences with the negative form of the adjectives in brackets.

1. I find learning _irregular_ verbs very difficult! (regular)
2. I think it's very _____ to leave without saying goodbye to everyone! (polite)
3. My mum is always complaining that my bedroom is _____ . (tidy)
4. Our old car was very _____ – it was always breaking down! (reliable)
5. You don't get any marks for an _____ answer. (correct)
6. I think it's _____ not to tell a shop assistant when they've made a mistake with your change. (honest)
7. Why are you going to go all the way home when you have to be back here in an hour? It's _____ . (logical)
8. My dad complained to the restaurant because he was _____ with his meal. (satisfied)

3 Complete the sentences with the correct form of these words.

correct   formal   legal   necessary
possible   ~~reliable~~   responsible   visible

1. No one will give Tyler a job because he's so _unreliable_ . He never arrives on time!
2. It wasn't really an interview – more of an _____ chat about the job.
3. It's _____ to drive a car without a driving licence.
4. I think it's _____ to have pets if you don't have time to look after them.
5. We've already put up ten posters and I think that's enough. It's _____ to put up any more.
6. There's too much vocabulary here – it's _____ to learn it all!
7. I thought Marco was from Portugal, but that was _____ – he's from Spain.
8. The mountain was _____ because of the thick fog.

4 Complete the blog post with the correct form of the words in brackets.

> View previous comments   Cancel   Share   Post
>
> **Film downloads – my view**
>
> What are your views on downloading music and films without paying? We all know it's 1) _illegal_ , but some people argue that it's OK. They think it isn't 2) _____ (honest) because it isn't really like stealing. They also believe they can get away with it. Very few people are 3) _____ (luck) enough to be caught, as it's virtually 4) _____ (possible) for the police to keep an eye on what everyone's doing online. I don't agree with this point of view, though. I think it's 5) _____ (fair) to the actors who've worked hard to make films when we just download and watch them without paying. It's also 6) _____ (necessary), as it really isn't very expensive to download films legally. Also, I think that if you're 7) _____ (satisfy) with the amount you have to pay for a movie, you should speak up and complain rather than breaking the law. So, for me, taking anything without paying for it is always 8) _____ (accept). Let me know what you think!
>
> Write a comment   Support

12 Find your voice

GRAMMAR
Reply questions and question tags

1 Choose the correct answers.

1. **A** I'm going to take part in my first debate next week.
   B *Do you?/Are you?* Good luck!
2. **A** It wasn't a very interesting talk.
   B *Was it?/Wasn't it?*
3. **A** I'll be late to football practice tomorrow.
   B *Will you?/Are you?* Why's that?
4. **A** I haven't spoken in public before.
   B *Didn't you?/Haven't you?*
5. **A** She won't win the trophy!
   B *Will she?/Won't she?* Why not?
6. **A** I'm not very good at giving speeches.
   B *Are you?/Aren't you?* That surprises me.

2 Write reply questions.

1. **A** All the speeches were really boring!
   B *Were they?* What a pity!
2. **A** She didn't seem very confident.
   B _____ That's a shame.
3. **A** It won't matter if we're a bit late.
   B _____ Oh, that's good.
4. **A** The debate could go on for two hours!
   B _____ That seems like a long time!
5. **A** My parents helped me prepare my speech.
   B _____ You're lucky!
6. **A** I'm not interested in that issue.
   B _____ Why not?
7. **A** Most people weren't listening!
   B _____ How rude!

3 Complete the questions with these question tags. There are two question tags which you don't need.

> did they   didn't they   do you   don't you
> hasn't he   have you   ~~isn't she~~   shall we
> wasn't he   will we

1. Anna's a great speaker, *isn't she* ?
2. You enjoy giving speeches, _____ ?
3. They didn't ask many questions, _____ ?
4. Let's discuss this later, _____ ?
5. Dad was working late last night, _____ ?
6. We won't have time to prepare, _____ ?
7. Your brother's got a lot of friends, _____ ?
8. You've never met Paul, _____ ?

4 Complete the conversation with the correct question tags and reply questions.

Mia I think we should start a debating club at school.
John 1) *Do you* ? Why's that?
Mia Well, most people of our age are interested in serious issues, 2) _____ ? So, a debating club would encourage them to discuss their ideas, 3) _____ ? Most schools have got debating clubs already.
John 4) _____ ? And are they popular?
Mia Yes, very popular.
John I find that surprising. I mean, most people feel quite shy about speaking in public, 5) _____ ?
Mia That's true. But public speaking can help you to overcome your shyness. Mr Evans talked to us about it last term.
John 6) _____ ? I don't remember that.
Mia Yes. He's quite keen to start a debating club.
John 7) _____ ? OK. Let's go and talk to him then, 8) _____ ?

LISTENING

1 12.1 Listen to five people talking about different class discussions and presentations. Choose the correct speaker (1–5) for each topic.

1 What do the different political parties believe?
Speaker: 1 2 3 (4) 5
2 What influence does television have on children?
Speaker: 1 2 3 4 5
3 Will our weather continue to get worse in the future?
Speaker: 1 2 3 4 5
4 Will we still read paper books in the future?
Speaker: 1 2 3 4 5
5 Should lessons begin later in the morning?
Speaker: 1 2 3 4 5

2 12.2 Listen again and match the speakers (1–5) with the statements (a–h). You do not need three of the statements.

Speaker 1   _c_   Speaker 4 _____
Speaker 2 _____   Speaker 5 _____
Speaker 3 _____

a This person doesn't have strong feelings about a particular topic
b This person finds it difficult to make a decision.
c This person changed their mind after a discussion.
d This person has strong views that they believe won't change.
e This person trusts another person's views as a basis for their opinion.
f This person has defended his point of view in a recent debate.
g This person would like more information before reaching a decision.
h This person thinks some people change their opinions too quickly.

SPEAKING SKILLS

1 Read the sentences for speculating about photos. Complete them with these words.

can't   ~~looks~~   maybe   might   must   need

 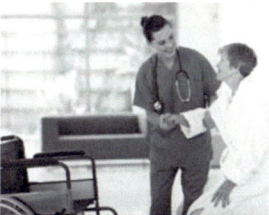

1 It _looks_ as if the people are tourists.
2 I think she _____ be in hospital for an operation.
3 Or _____ they're in a city and they're lost.
4 She _____ be very ill because she's smiling.
5 Perhaps the people _____ some help.
6 It's clear that they _____ be asking the policeman for help.

2 Complete the sentences with the correct questions tags.

1 That would be very interesting, _wouldn't it_ ?
2 We've talked about that already, _____ ?
3 That's a good idea, _____ ?
4 We don't need to talk about all of them, _____ ?
5 That's not really very important, _____ ?
6 Let's go on to the next one now, _____ ?

3 Complete the useful phrases for giving a talk with suitable words.

1 I'm _here_ today to talk to you about selfishness.
2 I don't think that it's _____ to say that.
3 I know a lot of people _____ that …
4 Another _____ I'd like to make is …
5 And finally we mustn't _____ that …
6 That's all. Thank you for _____ .

4 Read the question and prepare a one-minute talk about it. Use some of the phrases in your talk.

Some people say that we are too selfish these days and only think about ourselves. What do you think?

12 Find your voice

WRITING

1 Complete the sentences with the correct words or phrases.

> although   conclusion   ~~on the one hand~~
> on the other hand   overall   whereas

1 I don't know where I want to get a job.
1) _On the one hand_ I'd like to live near my parents but 2) _____ I'd like to travel to different countries and use my languages. So, I don't know.

2 3) _____ I started learning English six years ago, I still don't speak it well.

3 My mum says it's a good idea to do volunteer work when you're a teenager,
4) _____ my dad says I should concentrate on working for school exams.

4 In my opinion, there are good and bad points about leaving school early, but
5) _____ I would say that it's better to stay until you've passed all your exams.

5 In 6) _____ I would say that it's a difficult decision to make and needs very careful thought.

2 Read the essay question below and some notes for it (1–10). Put the notes into the best paragraphs (A–E).

> Is it better for very old people to live in a special home or with their families?

A	introduction	
B	special care	
C	happiness	
D	cost	
E	conclusion	1

1 living with family always best answer
2 big problem today
3 need to sell home
4 live longer today
5 very ill
6 close to relatives
7 love grandchildren, like to help
8 attention all the time
9 relaxed, familiar place
10 family out at jobs

3 Read the essay question in Exercise 4 below and decide if the sentences 1–4 would be appropriate (A) or not appropriate (NA) to include in the essay.

1 I don't like politicians because I think they make bad decisions and they don't consider the effect of those decisions.   _NA_

2 People need to be able to trust politicians.   _____

3 I'm not sure that I would tell my best friend if I saw her boyfriend with another girl. It's difficult.   _____

4 Friends should always be loyal no matter what happens; they have to support each other.   _____

4 Make notes and then write your essay in 140–190 words.

> You have recently had a discussion in your English class about whether it's important for people to always tell the truth. Your teacher has asked you to write an essay, answering the following question: People should always tell the truth. Do you agree?
>
> Write about:
> • politicians
> • friends
> • your own ideas

Revision Unit 12

1 Complete the crossword.

Across
4 a person
7 writing or words which you can't read
8 a talk that you give in public about a topic

Down
1 the state of being united
2 which you can't see
3 the quality of being clear
5 another word for rude
6 the state of being free

2 Complete the sentences with the correct form of the words in capitals.

1 The secret to exam success is doing enough _preparation_. **PREPARE**
2 I thought it was an interesting essay, but I didn't agree with the _____. **CONCLUDE**
3 Jenna and Paula are always having _____ about animal rights. **ARGUE**
4 We had a very interesting _____ about climate change. **DISCUSS**
5 Sometimes Tina behaves in quite a strange, _____ way. **RATIONAL**
6 Cycling without a helmet isn't _____, but it's very foolish! **LEGAL**
7 Most people would say it's _____ to copy homework from other people. **HONEST**

3 Complete the sentences with these words.

admit   equality   honesty   human rights
respect   responsibility   ~~unity~~

1 Everyone in the club disagrees about this issue – there's no _unity_ at all!
2 I think it's important to be honest and _____ you've made a mistake.
3 It's your _____ to feed the cat every day, so don't forget!
4 We encourage our students to have _____ for each other and to treat each other fairly.
5 There is a principle of _____ before the law, which means that the law treats all citizens in the same way.
6 If you take money that you find to a police station, you may be rewarded for your _____.
7 Some governments don't respect the _____ of their citizens enough.

4 Complete the text with one word in each space.

Speaker's Corner

Speaker's Corner in London is known as a place where people can speak 1) _out_ about anything that is on their mind. Londoners take pride 2) _____ the fact that many famous people have spoken on this spot, including Karl Marx. Anyone has the right to stand up and talk about anything that they believe 3) _____. For example, some people might feel it is important to 4) _____ the truth about a political scandal. Others might want to focus 5) _____ an environmental issue such as global warming. Whatever your beliefs, Speaker's Corner gives everyone the opportunity to stand 6) _____ for their values and feel that they are 7) _____ a difference. All you need is to 8) _____ plenty of confidence in yourself – and a good loud voice!

Revision Unit 12

5 Choose the correct answer, A, B or C.

1 I'm not sure where Jess is right now. She _may be_ playing tennis.
   A can be   **B** may be   C must be
2 I'm worried that my team ___ their game.
   A mustn't win   B couldn't win   C may not win
3 I don't know whose bike that is. ___ Tim's?
   A Could it be   B Can it be   C Must it be
4 I'm not sure who the celebrity guest is going to be. It ___ a famous singer.
   A can be   B mustn't   C might be
5 Liam ___ very confident about the exam if he's decided not to do any revision!
   A can be   B must be   C couldn't be
6 That building ___ a school, surely? It's much too small!
   A can't be   B mustn't be   C might not be
7 Why don't you come ice skating with us? It ___ fun!
   A must be   B can be   C should be
8 ___ it's difficult to speak in public?
   A Can you think
   B Do you think
   C Must you think

6 Rewrite the sentences using the word given. Use between two and five words, including the word given.

1 It's possible that I'll be late this evening. **COULD**
   I _could be late_ this evening.
2 I'm sure it's very scary standing up in front of so many people. **MUST**
   It _____ standing up in front of so many people.
3 It's possible I won't come to the party on Saturday. **MIGHT**
   I _____ to the party on Saturday.
4 It's possible that Stella has a bike that you can borrow. **MAY**
   Stella _____ that you can borrow.
5 It isn't possible that it's Maria's phone! **BE**
   It _____ Maria's phone!
6 If we leave at nine, I expect we'll get there by eleven. **SHOULD**
   If we leave at nine, _____ by eleven.

7 Write reply questions.

1 'I haven't finished yet.'
   '_Haven't you?_'
2 'The film starts at seven thirty.'
   '_____'
3 'I'll make some pizzas for everyone.'
   '_____ How kind!'
4 'John wasn't very enthusiastic about the idea.'
   '_____'
5 'I can lend you my phone.'
   '_____ That would be great!'
6 'Cara and Jo didn't win their game last night.'
   '_____ That's a shame.'

8 Complete the sentences with the correct question tags.

1 *Mission Impossible* is an American film, _isn't it_?
2 Some governments don't respect human rights, _____?
3 Your brother has decided to become a politician, _____?
4 Her speech won't be too long, _____?
5 You gave your speech yesterday, _____?
6 Let's meet at six thirty, _____?

9 Complete the conversation with the correct question tags and reply questions.

Leah I'm really nervous about giving my speech.
Josh 1) _Are you_? I don't think you should worry. You've given speeches before, 2) _____?
Leah Well, only to my class. I've never given one to the whole school before.
Josh You're going to talk about money and sport, 3) _____?
Leah Yes. And I haven't practised it yet!
Josh 4) _____? Well, if you want to practise it now, I'll listen to it.
Leah 5) _____? That would be great!
Josh No problem. You'll feel much more confident once you've practised, 6) _____?

NOTES

NOTES

NOTES

NOTES

Pearson Education Limited
Edinburgh Gate
Harlow
Essex CM20 2JE
England
and Associated Companies throughout the world.

www.english.com/goldxp

© Pearson Education Limited 2016

The right of Sheila Dignen and Lynda Edwards to be identified as authors of this Work has been asserted by them in accordance with the Copyright, Designs and Patents Act 1988.

All rights reserved; no part of this publication may be reproduced, stored in a retrieval system, or transmitted in any form or by any means, electronic, mechanical, photocopying, recording, or otherwise without the prior written permission of the Publishers

First published 2016

ISBN: 9781292159485

Set in ITC Mixage
Printed by Neografia, Slovakia

Acknowledgements
The publishers would like to thank Jacky Newbrook for her contribution to this new edition. The publishers and author would like to thank the following people for their feedback and comments during the development of the material:

Elif Berk, Turkey; Alan Del Castillo Castellanos, Mexico; Dilek Kokler, Turkey; Trevor Lewis, The Netherlands; Nancy Ramirez, Mexico; Jacqueline Van Mil-Walker, The Netherlands

The publishers would like to thank the following for their kind permission to reproduce their photographs:

(Key: b-bottom; c-centre; l-left; r-right; t-top)

123RF.com: 7106108800 31tr, 34, 45br, 110l, Dmitriy Shironosov 60tr; **Alamy Images:** Simon Balson 80tl, blickwinkel 6, Cultura Creative 28, Ulrich Doering 69, dpa picture alliance 85, Ersoy Emin 122, Eddie Gerald 88, David Grossman 107, H. Mark Weidman Photography 112, Ingram Publishing 119, Kuttig - Travel 97, Mint Images / Tim Robbins 5tc, Keith Morris 64bc, OnTheRoad 120tc, Photofusion Picture Library 116b, Pictorial Press Ltd 110cl, Niels Quist 120tl, Relaximages 68, Richard Splash 41cl, Kumar Sriskandan 67, Colin Underhill 27, Westend61 GmbH 24; **Bahamas Tourist Office:** 109br; **Corbis:** 60tl, Ocean / 237 / Paul Bradbury 71b, Tetra Images / Rob Lewine 70; **FLPA:** David Tipling 98; **Fotolia.com:** Ermolaev Alexandr 38, arenaphotouk 11cl, Amy Nichole Harris 58, Mike Lane 102, Monkey Business 26, Tyler Olson 60br, Enrico Della Pietra 59, Pink Badger 77, Tomispin 19, WavebreakMediaMicro 64tc; **Getty Images:** Carmen MartA-nez BanAs 113, Peter Bischoff 109t, Blend Images 25, Phil Boorman 53, ESA 95t, Fuse 71t, gbh007 72, Hemera / 360 / Anthony Harris 5bc, Kisgorcs 8cr, David Paul Morris 17; **Glow Images:** Robert Harding 66; **Imagestate Media:** John Foxx Collection 29br, 109cl; **Pearson Education Ltd:** Jon Barlow 13, Sophie Bluy 21cr, Gareth Boden 14r, 15br, 47, 48cl, 91cl, Miguel Domínguez Muñoz 11br, 114tr, 114c, 114b, 115, Jules Selmes 14l, 14cl, 15tl, 15cr, 29cl, 39, 84, 91b, Sozaijiten 44tr, Studio 8 14cr, 15cl; **PhotoDisc:** Martial Colomb 54bl; **Rex Shutterstock:** Blend Images 106, John Powell 9, Adrian Sherratt 49, Simon Tang 23; **Shutterstock.com:** 110c, Iveta Angelova 41r, Anneka 74, Noam Armonn 7, Artiomp 121c, Paul Banton 44br, Bikeriderlondon 109bc, Joggie Botma 109cr, Brisbane 114tl, Marcel Clemens 44bl, 94bl, Creativa 29cr, Robert Crum 5b, David Davis 111, DM7 62, Dotshock 5t, 48br, Dragon Images 21b, Eldeiv 118, Elena Elisseeva 64t, Mike Flippo 18, FotograFFF 90cr, David Fowler 60bl, Frenzel 35, Filip Fuxa 81b, Goodluz 60tc, GVictoria 29c, iurii 94br, Jule_Berlin 61, Dmitry Kalinovsky 104, katatonia82 30t, kingfisher 103, Lasse Kristensen 83, Lite Choices 90tr, michaeljung 120tr, Dudarev Mikhail 33, Monkey Business Images 21cl, R. Nagy 90b, Neelsky 95b, Ollyy 64b, Pavel L Photo and Video 110r, Pixsooz 86, Poznyakov 29bl, Pressmaster 30b, Daniel Prudek 96, Luis Santos 45cr, Elzbieta Sekowska 44tl, Rui Vale Sousa 45cl, Stocklite 121b, Patrizia Tilly 81t, Camelia Varsescu 109bl, Vectomart 54br, wavebreakmedia 80tr, withGod 110cr, Olena Zaskochenko 45tl, Terrie L. Zeller 31tl; **The Kobal Collection:** Aardman Animations 105, Silver Pictures 79; **Walter & Linda Zimmerman:** 20

Illustrated by: Caron Painter (Sylvie Poggio) 8; Andrew Painter 56, 89, 99; Ned Woodman 57, 92

Cover images: *Front:* **Alamy Images:** TongRo Images

All other images © Pearson Education

Every effort has been made to trace the copyright holders and we apologise in advance for any unintentional omissions. We would be pleased to insert the appropriate acknowledgement in any subsequent edition of this publication.

Title Page to be designed

Answer Key

01 Inside or outside?

Reading

Exercise 1
2 C   3 A   4 A   5 B   6 B   7 B   8 A

Exercise 2
2 D   3 A   4 D   5 B   6 A   7 C   8 C

Exercise 3
1 (a) passion   2 rewarding   3 specialise   4 freedom
5 tough   6 satisfying   7 forester   8 rare

Vocabulary 1

Exercise 1
2 relaxing   3 well-paid   4 seasonal   5 full-time
6 rewarding   7 satisfying   8 stressful

Exercise 2
2 full-time   3 seasonal   4 well-paid   5 satisfying
6 part-time   7 relaxing   8 rewarding

Exercise 3
2 keeps   3 getting   4 outdoors   5 with   6 prove

Exercise 4
2 incredible   3 comfortable   4 terrible   5 sensible
6 understandable   7 reliable

Exercise 5
2 punctual   3 organised   4 practical   5 flexible
6 reliable   7 suitable

Grammar 1

Exercise 1
2 isn't wearing   3 is getting   4 don't often see
5 don't understand   6 is always telling   7 is raining
8 always enjoy

Exercise 2
2 My brother is always borrowing my things.
3 I usually do my homework after dinner.
4 Do they live in London?
5 My friends are waiting for me right now.
6 Where are you going?
7 It is often sunny in July.
8 The hero jumps out of the aeroplane.
9 Do you have an evening job?
10 Who is she talking to?

Exercise 3
2 am watching
3 is always
4 Do you live
5 is always using
6 aren't studying
7 Are you looking after
8 are making

Exercise 4
2 Do   3 not   4 at   5 as   6 aren't   7 at   8 don't
9 always

Vocabulary 2

Exercise 1
2 earrings   3 flip-flops   4 gloves   5 necklace   6 scarf
7 apron   8 goggles

Exercise 2

w	c	a	j	k	i	p	l	u	r	o
e	a	o	e	p	i	a	f	r	n	u
a	s	t	w	l	y	t	l	a	r	t
t	u	g	e	f	l	e	a	b	s	f
t	a	r	l	r	v	o	t	a	c	i
y	l	o	l	a	p	i	s	t	o	t
h	y	h	e	m	i	r	h	e	a	l
j	s	t	r	i	p	y	o	r	t	p
w	o	r	y	y	i	b	e	o	r	t
b	a	g	g	y	m	l	s	a	f	e

Exercise 3
2 e   3 b   4 f   5 c   6 g   7 a

Exercise 4
2 hairstyle   3 image   4 logo   5 wristband   6 scarf
7 tracksuit bottoms   8 designer label

Exercise 5
2 C   3 D   4 B   5 A   6 C   7 D   8 A

Grammar 2

Exercise 1
2 Money   3 TV   4 the cinema   5 Life
6 Mount Everest   7 the Pacific Ocean   8 work

Exercise 2
2 a   3 a   4 the   5 a   6 the   7 a   8 the   9 a   10 a

Exercise 3
2 A   3 B   4 C   5 A   6 B   7 A   8 B

Exercise 4
2 the   3 the   4 the   5 a   6 a   7 the   8 theatre

Exercise 5
2 the   3 The   4 a   5 a   6 the   7 a   8 –   9 the

Listening

Exercise 1
2 b   3 f   4 c   5 a   6 d

Exercise 2
2 C   3 A   4 B   5 C   6 A

Speaking Skills

Exercise 1
2 in, especially
3 fact
4 on, at
5 shopping, can't
6 To, Actually

Exercise 2
2 a   3 d   4 f   5 b   6 c

Exercise 3
Model answer:
My name's Pippa and I'm from England. I go to college and I'm studying languages. I love speaking Spanish and French and I'd like to be a teacher. Our college day starts at 8.30 but I can't stand getting up early. I belong to lots of clubs so I go to bed quite late most nights. I'm a big sports fan and I'm pretty good at swimming. I swim nearly every night for two or three hours. I'm not really into music a lot. I like listening to some pop music while I'm doing my homework, but in fact I can live without it. I've got quite a big family and we're all keen on sports, so we spend a lot of time at the weekend outside watching football matches or other competitions. My best friend is Carolina – she's from Spain and we chat online all the time. It's very good for my Spanish.

Writing

Exercise 1
2 a   3 e   4 d   5 c

Exercise 2
2 However   3 in addition   4 On balance   5 in spite of

Exercise 3
2 B   3 B   4 D   5 D   6 C   7 D   8 B   9 D   10 C

Exercise 4
Model answer:
People often say that life in the country is much better than life in the city and one reason is because children can go to small village schools and get a better education. I've been to both a village school and a city one and I don't think that I completely agree.

It's true that at a village school there are usually small classes and the teachers know all the children. It's easier for the children to tell the teachers when they don't understand things. In addition, the teachers know when there are problems like bullying or family problems.

At a big city school however, I think there are more opportunities. There are more teachers, more equipment like computers and science laboratories and you can learn lots of different subjects. I agree that big classes aren't always a good thing, but personally, I really liked being in a big class. I had lots of friends and I met different types of people.

So, on balance, I think there are both benefits and downsides to village and city schools. However, in my view I believe that in spite of the noise and the numbers, a city school is better for a good education.

Revision Unit 1

Exercise 1
2 suitable 3 satisfying 4 sensible 5 stressful

Exercise 2
2 A 3 C 4 C 5 A 6 B 7 C 8 A

Exercise 3
2 apron 3 hoodie 4 gloves 5 goggles 6 hairstyle
7 short-sleeved 8 scarf

Exercise 4
2 baggy 3 outfit 4 kit 5 plain 6 necklace
7 flip-flops 8 designer label

Exercise 5
2 rewarding 3 stripy 4 spotty 5 understandable
6 organised 7 paid 8 flexible 9 yourself 10 reliable

Exercise 6
2 don't often see
3 is working
4 goes
5 is becoming
6 always wears
7 am trying
8 is always telling
9 don't agree
10 am enjoying

Exercise 7
2 We usually buy our lunch in the canteen.
3 What are you doing at the moment?
4 I play tennis most weekends.
5 I'm watching TV at the moment.
6 I don't often cycle to school.
7 My sister is always borrowing my things!
8 I'm sorry, I don't understand you.
9 They don't often visit their grandparents.
10 Karl is applying for a job in a local supermarket because he needs some money.

Exercise 8
2 – 3 a 4 – 5 the 6 a 7 the 8 the 9 – 10 –

Exercise 9
2 a 3 a 4 Are 5 don't 6 at 7 The 8 doesn't
9 don't

02 Making it happen

Reading

Exercise 1
2 False 3 True 4 False 5 False 6 False
7 True 8 False

Exercise 2
2 C 3 D 4 D 5 A 6 B 7 C 8 C 9 A 10 D

Vocabulary 1

Exercise 1

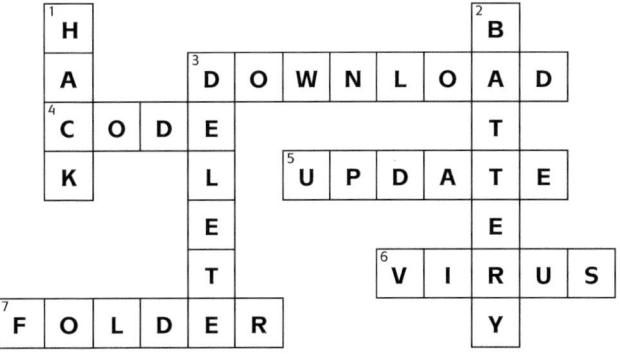

Exercise 2
2 software 3 touch screen 4 signal 5 online
6 virtual 7 connection 8 website

Exercise 3
2 charge 3 scroll 4 access 5 click 6 downloaded
7 update 8 hacked

Exercise 4
2 f 3 a 4 b 5 d 6 e

Grammar 1

Exercise 1
2 I didn't enjoy the exhibition.
3 We were watching a movie when you phoned.
4 Did you read that article about computers?
5 I'm sorry, were you sleeping?
6 Where were you going when I saw you?
7 I didn't pay for the software.
8 She was working on her laptop at the time.

Exercise 2
2 was studying 3 was living 4 left 5 spent
6 returned 7 got 8 was working 9 decided
10 formed

Exercise 3
2 would watch
3 used to love
4 didn't use to
5 used to text
6 used to live
7 Did you use to
8 didn't use to have
9 they used to
10 taught herself

Exercise 4
2 B, C 3 A 4 B 5 B 6 A 7 B 8 A, B
9 B 10 B

Vocabulary 2

Exercise 1
2 transmitter 3 scanner 4 collector 5 competitor
6 inventor 7 player 8 employer

Exercise 2
2 amplifier 3 generator 4 photocopier 5 adviser
6 refrigerator 7 programmer 8 narrator

Exercise 3
2 player 3 amplifier 4 instructor 5 calculator
6 generator 7 inventor 8 photocopier

Exercise 4
2 redo 3 disagree 4 replay 5 re-read 6 disapproves
7 re-record 8 disobey 9 dislike

Exercise 5
2 player 3 inventor 4 receiver 5 transmitter
6 re-recorded 7 disliked

Grammar 2

Exercise 1
2 himself 3 ourselves 4 yourself 5 herself
6 yourselves 7 themselves 8 itself 9 themselves

Exercise 2
2 each other 3 each other 4 himself 5 herself
6 each other 7 themselves 8 each other 9 myself
10 themselves

Exercise 3
2 yours 3 his 4 hers 5 theirs 6 ours 7 mine

Exercise 4
2 myself 3 yourself 4 each 5 themselves
6 ourselves 7 yours

Listening

Exercise 1
a, d, f

Exercise 2
2 pictures
3 assistant
4 twelve/12
5 software
6 words
7 printer
8 NASA

Speaking Skills

Exercise 1
2 h 3 a 4 f 5 b 6 g 7 c 8 d

Exercise 2
2 A 3 C 4 B 5 C 6 A 7 B

Writing

Exercise 1
2 benefit
3 Personally
4 downside
5 opinion
6 balance
7 fact
8 spite

Exercise 2
2 a 3 g 4 h 5 b 6 e 7 d 8 f

Exercise 3
Model answer:
It's definitely true that computers are everywhere in our lives today. Most people think that this is a good thing but others say that we rely on them too much. I have to say that I think they are probably right.

Our lives would be very difficult without computers. We use them at work and at school, for communicating with people and for all sorts of buying and selling. And one of the main reasons we use computers is to find out information. Computers help us do things quickly and soon everyone will need to be able to use them.

However, because we are using computers more and more, we are losing some skills that we used to have. For example, we don't often write letters any more or look up information in books.

Personally, I think computers are important, but we must remember that they are just machines. They cannot replace people. In addition, they can go wrong. Then we have to depend on our other skills. So, on balance, I think we should take advantage of the ways computers can help us, but we must not rely on them too much.

ANSWER KEY: GOLD EXPERIENCE WORKBOOK B1+

Revision Unit 2

Exercise 1
2 tweet 3 delete 4 access 5 program 6 charge
7 download 8 hack

Exercise 2
2 B 3 D 4 C 5 C 6 A 7 D 8 C

Exercise 3
2 on 3 in 4 up 5 down

Exercise 4
2 amplifier 3 calculator 4 transmitter
5 generator 6 narrator 7 instructor 8 inventor

Exercise 5
2 distrust 3 competitors 4 disconnect 5 replay
6 employer 7 scanner 8 disapprove

Exercise 6
2 was raining
3 was watching
4 didn't try on
5 designed
6 was doing
7 bought

Exercise 7
2 used to get
3 won
4 would go
5 used to have
6 Did you use to see
7 didn't use to

Exercise 8
2 B 3 B 4 C 5 B 6 C 7 B 8 C

Exercise 9
2 taught herself to
3 enjoyed themselves
4 write to each other
5 friend of mine
6 use to be so / use to be as
7 while I was eating
8 used to live

Exercise 10
2 used 3 yourself 4 each 5 would 6 didn't
7 use 8 yours

03 True story?

Reading

Exercise 1
2 False 3 False 4 False 5 True 6 True 7 False

Exercise 2
a 5 b 8 c 1 d 3 e – f 2 g 7 h 6 i 4

Vocabulary 1

Exercise 1
2 achievement 3 feeling 4 hope 5 vote
6 recognition 7 offer 8 grin

Exercise 2
2 A 3 B 4 A 5 C 6 B 7 C 8 B 9 B 10 A

Exercise 3
2 weakness 3 strength 4 relief 5 nerves 6 feats
7 tense 8 sweaty 9 positive 10 negative

Grammar 1

Exercise 1
2 She has been on TV a few times.
3 I have been practising all morning.
4 She hasn't been feeling well recently.
5 Have you ever met a celebrity?
6 What have you been doing?
7 It's the worst book I have ever read.
8 It's the first time she has performed on stage.
9 I have never won a competition.

Exercise 2
2 still 3 yet 4 since 5 ever 6 already 7 for
8 never 9 just 10 ever

Exercise 3
2 has been trying
3 has sent
4 have rejected
5 has ever happened
6 have been writing
7 has told
8 has already started
9 has been thinking

Exercise 4
2 have been writing poems for
3 has just left
4 haven't seen Sam since
5 has been raining for
6 haven't eaten meat for
7 best book I have ever

© 2016 PEARSON PHOTOCOPIABLE

Vocabulary 2

Exercise 1
2 crept 3 vanished 4 spotted 5 yelled 6 remained
7 waved

Exercise 2
2 happily 3 quietly 4 frequently 5 never 6 often
7 eventually 8 immediately 9 yesterday 10 here
11 outside 12 there

Exercise 3
2 The man shouted at us angrily.
3 We never watch talent shows on TV.
4 You must call me immediately if anything happens.
5 Sally is always cheerful.
6 They were waiting for us by the bus stop.

Exercise 4
2 truthful 3 nervously 4 noise 5 hopeful
6 suspiciously 7 happy 8 professionally

Exercise 5
2 suddenly 3 immediately 4 strength 5 calmly
6 nervous 7 feeling 8 eventually 9 seriously
10 hopefully

Grammar 2

Exercise 1
2 B 3 C 4 B 5 B 6 C 7 B 8 C 9 C 10 B

Exercise 2
2 Don't tell anyone this secret.
3 She read the letter to us.
4 They brought us some warm clothes.
5 My uncle has found a part-time job for me.
6 He showed all his friends the photos.
7 I've bought a present for you.
8 I can send you the concert details.

Exercise 3
2 to 3 for 4 her 5 them 6 for 7 us 8 to

Exercise 4
2 lent me this
3 sent that text to
4 sold me this
5 showed me his new
6 offered his old phone to
7 gave me this

Listening

Exercise 1
2 D 3 C 4 A 5 B

Exercise 2
1 False 2 True 3 False 4 False 5 True

Exercise 3
a 5 b – c 3 e 2 f 4

Speaking Skills

Exercise 1
2 has just started/'s just started
3 have been
4 has not seen/hasn't seen
5 has played/'s played
6 has had/'s had

Exercise 2
2 though 3 looks 4 Both 5 main 6 whereas
7 Another

Exercise 3
a 5 b 4 c 2 e 7 f 6 g 3

Exercise 4
1 show/depict 2 In 3 are 4 main 5 as 6 However
7 whereas/while 8 Another 9 feeling/very 10 or

Writing

Exercise 1
2 c 3 a 4 f 5 b 6 e

Exercise 2
2 f 3 e 4 d 5 a 6 b

Exercise 3
2 e 3 a 4 d 5 f 6 c

Exercise 4
c, f

Exercise 5
Model answer:
It started as just another ordinary day. It was another Monday morning and another journey to school by train. I sighed deeply as I set off for the station. Where was the adventure in my life? I felt as though I were a mouse running around in a cage. My life was like a prison and I wasn't going to escape – ever!

I put my ticket into the machine and walked slowly onto the platform. It was crowded and I hardly noticed the man standing beside me. He was tall, I remember, and he was standing quietly.

Suddenly there was noise at the other end of the platform. Then three men started pushing through the crowd. Everyone moved back to let them through. The first man pointed at me and yelled, 'That's him! Stop him!'

I was so shocked I jumped backwards and knocked the tall man down. 'I'm so sorry…' I began to say but then the man put his foot on the tall man's back. 'Well done boy,' he smiled. 'You've just caught a thief!'

I wanted some adventure in my life and that day I certainly got it!

Revision Unit 3

Exercise 1
2 vote 3 feats 4 sweaty 5 recognition 6 nerves
7 negative 8 grin 9 achievement 10 weakness

Exercise 2
2 A 3 A 4 C 5 B 6 C 7 B

Exercise 3
2 spot 3 remain 4 vanish 5 wave 6 yell
7 creep

Exercise 4
2 reference 3 feeling 4 achievements
5 relief 6 noisily 7 hopefully 8 mysteriously
9 dangerously 10 truthfully

Exercise 5
2 have read
3 have been looking
4 haven't tried
5 have been training
6 have sold
7 have been calling
8 has been raining

Exercise 6
2 A 3 C 4 C 5 A 6 B 7 B

Exercise 7
2 already 3 yet 4 have 5 us 6 for 7 ever
8 have 9 for

Exercise 8
2 first time I have been
3 have been living here for
4 nicest food I have ever
5 sold my old bike to
6 sent me a
7 offered me a lift
8 you lend me

04 Things they don't teach you

Reading

Exercise 1
3

Exercise 2
2 True 3 False 4 True 5 Not given 6 True
7 Not given 8 False

Exercise 3
2 D 3 D 4 D 5 B 6 B

Vocabulary 1

Exercise 1

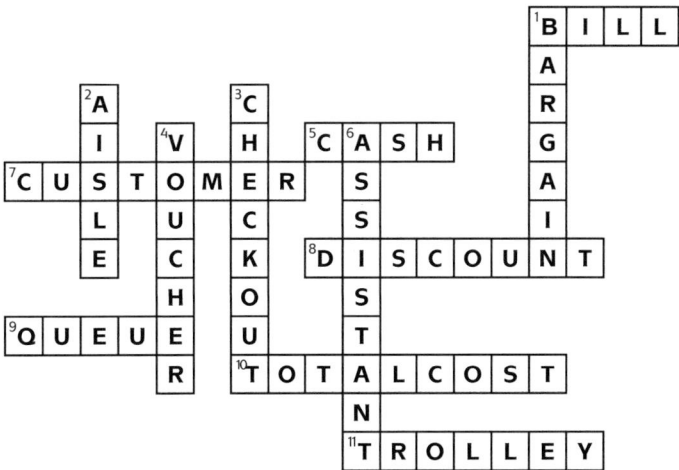

Exercise 2
2 spend 3 borrow 4 cost 5 are worth 6 economise
7 pay 8 save

Exercise 3
2 A 3 C 4 C

Exercise 4
2 personal 3 general 4 money 5 higher 6 practical

Grammar 1

Exercise 1
2 D 3 N 4 N 5 D

Exercise 2
2 which 3 where 4 when 5 whose 6 that 7 who
8 which

Exercise 3
2 B 3 B 4 C 5 C 6 C

Exercise 4
2 I have an aunt who loves hunting for bargains.
3 My friend, whose name is Tina, wants to start an online business.
4 I'll take you to the park where I usually meet my friends.
5 This old radio, which I bought for £20, is now worth £500!
6 This film, which cost $20 million, won three Oscars. / This film, which won three Oscars, cost $20 million.
7 The shoes that she bought yesterday are lovely.

Exercise 5
2 The girl who he met last week is very nice. / The girl he met last week is very nice.
3 Money management, which is a very useful subject, is not taught in schools.
4 That's the discount store which I told you about. / That's the discount store that I told you about. / That's the discount store I told you about.
5 This book, which I read last year, has lots of interesting information in it.
6 I met someone whose brother plays football for Manchester United!

Vocabulary 2

Exercise 1
2 with 3 for 4 to 5 by 6 on

Exercise 2
2 learning style 3 study methods 4 spider diagram

Exercise 3
2 look 3 with 4 down 5 set 6 out 7 give
8 through 9 ahead 10 keep

Exercise 4
2 B 3 C 4 A 5 B 6 B 7 A 8 B 9 C 10 C

Grammar 2

Exercise 1
2 sold 3 used 4 living 5 watched 6 taking
7 given 8 learning

Exercise 2
2 Students taking the exam should be at school by 8.45.
3 The law introduced last year has made no difference.
4 Students having breakfast before they come to school get better grades.
5 Confucius is a philosopher admired all over the world.
6 Supermarkets offering big discounts are becoming more popular.
7 The subject discussed in last week's programme was 'different learning styles'.
8 This is the latest film featuring James Bond.

Exercise 3
2 C 3 A 4 B 5 C 6 B 7 C 8 C

Listening

Exercise 1
2 January 3 Colombia 4 normal 5 keys 6 funny
7 sugar 8 stressed

Exercise 2
2 B 3 B 4 A 5 C 6 C

Speaking Skills

Exercise 1
2 e 3 a 4 g 5 b 6 d 7 f

Exercise 2
2 I can see your point but I'm afraid I don't agree.
3 I think so too but not everyone has enough money.
4 But what about people who can't use computers very well?
5 In my opinion, it depends on your situation.

Exercise 3
2 opinion 3 example 4 because 5 point 6 so

Writing

Exercise 1
2 one 3 this choice 4 some ideas 5 the headteacher
6 semi-formal

Exercise 2
2 e 3 f 4 a 5 d 6 c

Exercise 3
Model answer:
Dear Mr Peters,
In reply to your request I am writing to let you know my ideas for the charity event that you wrote about in your notice.

Firstly, I think the idea of a talent show is brilliant because everyone loves watching talent shows on TV. A fashion show and quiz show are good ideas too, but I think a talent show would be most popular.

Secondly, I have an idea about how to organise it. I think a show with teachers and students would be the best thing. The students can judge the teachers. It would be a lot of fun and I am sure we could get a lot of money from that.

People can pay to come into the show and then, they can pay to leave if they want to go before the end! The judges can give their opinions and everyone in the room can vote on the winner.

I hope you like my idea and I look forward to the show.
Best wishes
Anton

Revision Unit 4

Exercise 1
2 bill 3 customers 4 assistant 5 cash 6 discount
7 aisle 8 checkout 9 trolley 10 queue 11 voucher
12 total cost

Exercise 2
2 cost 3 saving 4 borrow 5 worth 6 lend

Exercise 3
2 by 3 to 4 with 5 on 6 for

Exercise 4
2 general knowledge 3 higher education
4 practical experience 5 learning style
6 spider diagram 7 study space 8 study methods

Exercise 5
2 through 3 up 4 on 5 about 6 on 7 out
8 down 9 with

Exercise 6
2 where / that 3 that / which 4 who 5 when / that
6 which 7 whose 8 who / that

ANSWER KEY: GOLD EXPERIENCE WORKBOOK B1+

Exercise 7
2 B   3 C   4 C   5 C   6 B   7 B

Exercise 8
2 watching   3 given   4 collected   5 known   6 written
7 waiting   8 teaching

Exercise 9
2 which I lent
3 who learn to read
4 who want to come
5 where you can buy
6 given on the website

05 Green world

Reading

Exercise 1
2 D   3 A   4 C

Exercise 2
2 A   3 –   4 B   5 C

Exercise 3
2 A   3 C   4 D   5 C   6 A   7 D   8 B

Exercise 4
2 endangered   3 waste   4 habitats   5 alternative
6 solar

Vocabulary 1

Exercise 1
2 organic   3 recycled   4 self-sufficient   5 rural
6 ecological   7 protected   8 urban

Exercise 2
2 report back   3 go towards   4 catch on   5 pick up
6 be into

Exercise 3
2 c   3 e   4 a   5 f   6 b

Exercise 4
2 B   3 D   4 C   5 B   6 A   7 C   8 D   9 A   10 C

Grammar 1

Exercise 1
2 going to   3 will   4 doing   5 are   6 as   7 the time
8 waiting

Exercise 2
2 A   3 C   4 C   5 C   6 A   7 C   8 B

Exercise 3
2 will be staying
3 will get
4 will be studying
5 will mend
6 won't be
7 won't be revising
8 will carry

Exercise 4
2 I'll probably be revising this evening.
3 It will certainly be an interesting experience.
4 She's possibly going to train as a nurse.
5 The meal probably won't be very expensive.

Exercise 5
2 won't buy
3 get
4 will probably be revising
5 am going to call
6 will probably do
7 Are you doing
8 are coming
9 leave
10 will probably be

Vocabulary 2

Exercise 1

p	r	i	s	t	w	b	u	n	t	e
e	r	t	i	w	h	e	a	t	g	e
s	d	o	f	l	o	v	l	e	t	s
t	b	r	l	h	r	d	e	l	j	u
i	m	p	o	r	t	y	e	x	e	b
c	s	f	o	u	e	w	i	m	x	e
i	n	f	d	r	g	e	l	t	p	s
d	t	r	a	p	o	h	r	e	o	v
e	r	a	i	n	w	a	t	e	r	e
s	a	e	w	p	i	w	l	k	t	t

Answers: import, flood, rainwater, wheat, well, export, drought

© 2016 PEARSON PHOTOCOPIABLE

Exercise 2
2 water shortage 3 floods 4 pesticides 5 desert
6 drought 7 rainwater 8 consumers

Exercise 3
2 without 3 do 4 Make 5 with 6 make

Exercise 4
2 B 3 A 4 A 5 B 6 C 7 A 8 B 9 A 10 B

Grammar 2

Exercise 1
2 There were so many people that you couldn't move.
3 It's such a good film that I want to see it again.
4 The box was so heavy that I couldn't carry it.
5 It's too cold to sit outside.
6 There's enough food for everyone to eat.
7 There were too many books for me to carry.
8 I've got too much homework to do.

Exercise 2
2 B 3 A 4 B 5 A 6 C

Exercise 3
2 enough 3 too 4 enough 5 such 6 enough
7 to 8 so 9 such

Exercise 4
2 wasn't warm enough to
3 so much rain that
4 too many birds to
5 such an expensive dress that
4 such a lot of

Listening

Exercise 1
a 6 b 3 c 5 d 2 f 4

Exercise 2
2 C 3 A 4 B 5 C 6 B

Speaking Skills

Exercise 1
Positive statements: So do I, So would I, I will too.
Negative statements: Neither have I, Nor did I, I'm not either.

Exercise 2
2 Neither have I 3 So was I 4 Neither do I 5 I did
6 I'm not 7 Neither am I

Exercise 3
2 d 3 a 4 e 5 c

Writing

Exercise 1
2 first 3 conclusion 4 start 5 final 6 Firstly
7 Secondly 8 lastly

Exercise 2
4

Exercise 3
2 B 3 A 4 B 5 A 6 B 7 B

Exercise 4
Model answer:
Everyone knows that we need to do something to help the environment. However, many people think it is only the government's responsibility to do this. It isn't. We can all do something ourselves.

Firstly, we need to change our habits. Today we throw away a lot of things like old food and old electrical gadgets and devices. This means there are enormous rubbish tips. We must recycle things more and perhaps get used to buying less in the first place.

Secondly, we use far too much electricity and waste electricity a lot, too. Everyone can be more careful turning off devices when we're not using them. We should also try to use more sources of energy such as solar or wind power. Finally, we can save water by collecting rainwater for our gardens. We will need to reduce the water we use in the house as well, although it won't be easy.

In conclusion, I must say that I am optimistic about the future. If people learn to change their habits, the world will still be a good place to live in for our children.

Revision Unit 5

Exercise 1
2 dependent 3 generations 4 endangered 5 pollution
6 recycling 7 neighbourhood 8 protected

Exercise 2
2 without 3 out 4 towards 5 with 6 on 7 up
8 back

Exercise 3
2 rooftop 3 botanical 4 concrete 5 shortage
6 fumes 7 natural 8 route

Exercise 4
2 self-sufficient 3 spaces 4 Toxic 5 Pedestrians
6 flooded 7 exports 8 desert 9 drought 10 well

Exercise 5
2 transport 3 paths 4 alternative 5 panels
6 organic 7 pesticides 8 habitats 9 species

ANSWER KEY: GOLD EXPERIENCE WORKBOOK B1+

Exercise 6
2 Where are we going to have lunch?
3 It's definitely going to rain later.
4 This time next year I'll be travelling.
5 The train will probably be late.
6 We definitely won't need an umbrella.

Exercise 7
2 will   3 won't   4 are   5 be   6 will   7 not   8 as
9 time   10 by

Exercise 8
2 enough
3 such
4 too
5 so
6 too much
7 big enough
8 such a lot
9 so much
10 too many

Exercise 9
2 am not old enough to
3 such a lot of clothes
4 work hard enough to pass
5 such a good book that
6 too many people to

06 Before time

Reading

Exercise 1
C

Exercise 2
2 False   3 False   4 False   5 True   6 False   7 True
8 False   9 False

Exercise 3
2 B   3 A   4 B   5 B   6 B

Vocabulary 1

Exercise 1
2 sigh   3 dry   4 breath   5 goose-bumps   6 heart
7 shivers   8 face   9 nerves   10 lump

Exercise 2
1 neck   2 shoulder   3 back   4 elbow   5 knee

Exercise 3
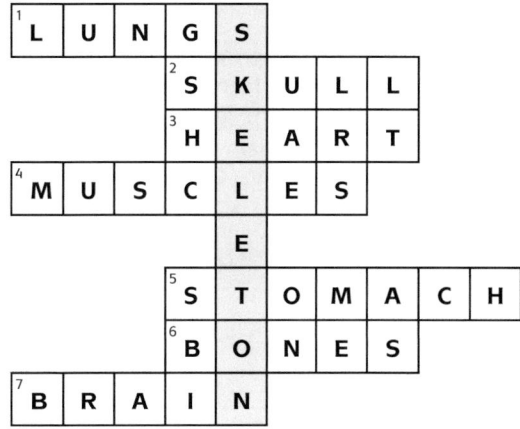

Mystery word: skeleton

Exercise 4
2 wings   3 fur   4 skin   5 tail   6 tusks

Grammar 1

Exercise 1
2 hadn't tidied   3 had given   4 had seen   5 had visited
6 hadn't organised   7 had forgotten

Exercise 2
2 A   3 A   4 B   5 B   6 B

Exercise 3
2 had lost   3 arrived   4 failed   5 had paid   6 asked
7 had found   8 had spent

Exercise 4
2 hit
3 had lived
4 caused
5 led
6 killed
7 had eaten
8 had already started
9 had already caused
10 was

Vocabulary 2

Exercise 1
2 B   3 C   4 B   5 C   6 A   7 D   8 C   9 A

Exercise 2
2 g   3 b   4 c   5 h   6 i   7 d   8 a   9 f

Exercise 3
2 giant   3 awesome   4 awful   5 terrible   6 horrible

Exercise 4
2 musical   3 ancient   4 historical   5 torrential

Exercise 5
2 mysterious   3 sophistication   4 decoration
5 colourful   6 complicated   7 fascinated   8 successful

Grammar 2

Exercise 1
2 Cara didn't work as quickly as me.
3 This exam was more difficult than the last one.
4 These are the oldest bones in the world.
5 The exhibition wasn't as popular as we had expected.
6 This is the most surprising thing about dinosaurs.
7 My sister is less interested in history than me.
8 Jack can't run as fast as me.

Exercise 2
2 was further than
3 do as well as
4 far more difficult than
5 the most important historical
6 learns much more quickly than
7 is slightly less ancient than / is a bit less ancient than
8 a bit earlier than

Exercise 3
2 C 3 C 4 A 5 B 6 C 7 C 8 B 9 C

Listening

Exercise 1
2 False 3 False 4 True 5 False 6 True
7 False 8 False

Exercise 2
2 Uluru
3 348 metres/348 m
4 boys
5 climbing
6 an hour/one hour/1 hour
7 4.30/four thirty/4:30/16.30/16:30
8 unlucky

Speaking Skills

Exercise 1
2 However 3 Both 4 whereas 5 main 6 Another
7 too

Exercise 2
2 In 3 wearing 4 though/if 5 There 6 shows/depicts
7 like 8 similarity 9 looks/seems 10 too
11 whereas/while 12 main/biggest/greatest

Writing

Exercise 1
2 b 3 d 4 a

Exercise 2
2 on my first day
3 The next day
4 Throughout the morning
5 After
6 At first
7 then
8 Suddenly
9 a few minutes later
10 Before

Exercise 3
2 a 3 e 4 d 5 b 6 c

Exercise 4
2 terrifying 3 massive 4 stared 5 sipped 6 silently

Exercise 5
Model answer:
The last day of the holidays was hot and sunny so Jack and I decided to go for a walk across the
fields near the site of an old Roman camp. Rory, our six-month old dog had a lot of energy and we
took him with us so that he could have a good run.

Jack knew a lot about the old Roman camp and during our walk across the fields he told me some
stories. Rory was having a great time, sniffing for rabbits and running around like a mad thing!

Suddenly he stopped and started digging. 'No Rory!' I shouted and we ran across to him. We were
trying to teach him not to dig holes because our garden was a mess. Rory sat down beside his hole
and when we reached him he was looking very pleased. Then I saw something shiny on the grass. I
reached down and picked it up. It was a gold coin.

'My heart started to beat quickly. Perhaps we had discovered something really valuable. 'Jack,' I said
excitedly. 'Do you think it's an old Roman coin?'

Jack looked at it carefully and turned in over in his hand. Then he laughed. 'No, not unless the
Romans had a Queen called Elizabeth 2 and were walking around here in 1985!' I felt extremely silly.

ANSWER KEY: GOLD EXPERIENCE WORKBOOK B1+

Revision Unit 6

Exercise 1
2 throat   3 shivers   4 thumping   5 gets   6 out
7 worked   8 came   9 up with   10 keep on

Exercise 2
2 skeletons   3 skull   4 neck   5 elbow   6 claws
7 muscles   8 bones   9 skin   10 brain

Exercise 3
1 dreadful   2 awful   3 terrible   4 wonderful   5 fantastic
6 marvellous   7 massive   8 giant   9 huge

Exercise 4
2 historical   3 baking   4 ancient   5 torrential

Exercise 5
2 amazed   3 success   4 entertainment   5 mysterious
6 decorations   7 fascinated   8 sophistication

Exercise 6
2 met; told
3 arrived; were
4 went; had seen
5 weren't; had eaten
6 showed; had taken
7 came; gave
8 discovered; had won

Exercise 7
2 just   3 already   4 just   5 for   6 had   7 already
8 already

Exercise 8
2 had already left
3 had just left
4 been to Paris before
5 had known Jack since

Exercise 9
2 the best   3 harder than   4 as clever
5 the most patient   6 the worst   7 more quickly
8 as good

Exercise 10
2 are not quite as valuable
3 much more expensive than
4 was far smaller than
5 is less competitive than
6 is a bit more popular

07 The feel-good factor

Reading

Exercise 1
2 D   3 A   4 B

Exercise 2
2 A   3 D   4 B   5 A   6 C   7 D   8 B

Exercise 3
2 True   3 False   4 False   5 True   6 True   7 False
8 False

Vocabulary 1

Exercise 1
2 opponents   3 coach   4 peer group   5 mates
6 council

Exercise 2
2 made   3 direction   4 set up   5 find   6 stand   7 trick

Exercise 3
2 up   3 away   4 back   5 in

Exercise 4
2 A   3 C   4 C   5 A   6 C

Exercise 5
2 away   3 to   4 in   5 about   6 own   7 at   8 about
9 about   10 up

Grammar 1

Exercise 1
2 couldn't   3 mustn't   4 can't   5 Would   6 had better
7 will be allowed   8 needn't   9 was able to   10 May

Exercise 2
2 to   3 don't   4 be   5 could   6 had   7 got

Exercise 3
2 C   3 A   4 C   5 A   6 C   7 C   8 B   9 C

Exercise 4
2 ought not to work
3 won't be able to
4 don't have to buy
5 had better not invite
6 have got to finish

Vocabulary 2

Exercise 1

(word search grid with circled words: confident, camera, ambitious, active, protective, etc.)

Exercise 2
2 decisive 3 ambitious 4 supportive 5 active
6 self-sufficient 7 competitive 8 protective
9 aggressive 10 creative

Exercise 3
2 suspect 3 destructive 4 furious 5 depend
6 fame 7 attractive 8 different

Exercise 4
2 active 3 supportive 4 dangerous 5 protective
6 confidence 7 cautious 8 suspicion

Grammar 2

Exercise 1
2 Talking about exams makes me nervous.
3 Mum won't let me get a part-time job.
4 Watching TV helps me to relax.
5 Our coach made us train for two hours.
6 I was made to apologise for my bad behaviour.

Exercise 2
2 C 3 C 4 A 5 C 6 B 7 C 8 B

Exercise 3
2 made 3 would let 4 helped 5 are made 6 makes
7 helped 8 be allowed

Exercise 4
2 won't let me stay
3 you allowed to use
4 were made to work
5 helped me sort / helped me to sort
6 makes me angry

Listening

Exercise 1
2, 5, 8

Exercise 2
1 A 2 C 3 C 4 B 5 A 6 B

Speaking Skills

Exercise 1
2 so 3 true 4 say 5 sure 6 that 7 right 8 idea

Exercise 2
Model answer:
Both pictures show people experiencing a very good moment. In the first picture the girl is celebrating something, perhaps it's her birthday. She looks really happy because all her friends are there and she has a lot of presents. In the second picture the man has won a competition. He's standing on the… what's the word… podium, I think. And someone is giving him a… it's the thing you can put round your neck. Yes, a medal. The other… you know, the people who take part in a race… the participants – are watching and they are cheering. In my opinion the swimmer needed to train a lot to win this competition whereas the girl just needed to arrange a few things.

Writing

Exercise 1
2 A 3 A 4 B 5 B 6 A

Exercise 2
2 should 3 about 4 might 5 don't 6 Try

Exercise 3
a 3 b 5 d 4 e 6 f 2

Exercise 4
1, 3, 4, 6, 7

Exercise 5
Model answer:
Hi Anna,
Thanks for your email. I'm sorry to hear things aren't that good at your new school. I know what it's like. When I changed school it took ages to get used to it.
Don't forget to keep in touch with your old friends – like me! And make arrangements to see them sometimes. Going to a new school doesn't mean that you have to lose all your old mates.

Why don't you join a sports club? That's a good way to meet new people. I know you like sports so you can make friends with people who like the same things. I'm sure there are lots of nice people there!

Work can be a big problem. I remember it well. The work at your new school is probably not more difficult – it's just different. You probably know lots of things that the class aren't doing. Perhaps you should tell the teacher about it. She may be able to suggest some extra reading.

Anyway, don't worry too much. Things will definitely get better soon.
Lots of luck and remember I'm thinking of you!
Speak soon
Helen x

Revision Unit 7

Exercise 1
2 part   3 direction   4 camp   5 opponent   6 coach
7 way   8 feet   9 mates   10 trick

Exercise 2
2 aggressive   3 decisive   4 imaginative   5 competitive
6 protective   7 anxious   8 supportive   9 ambitious
10 creative

Exercise 3
2 C   3 D   4 A   5 B   6 C   7 B   8 A

Exercise 4
2 persistent   3 attraction   4 famous   5 dependent
6 destruction   7 furious   8 active   9 suspicion
10 cautious

Exercise 5
2 A   3 C   4 B   5 A   6 B   7 C   8 A

Exercise 6
2 makes us train
3 am not allowed to stay
4 had better start training
5 ought to check
6 didn't let me go
7 don't need to be
8 were made to play

Exercise 7
2 When I was younger, I wasn't allowed to have a TV in my room.
3 We've got plenty of time. We don't need to hurry.
4 Do you think you will be able to help us tomorrow?
5 I must spend more time on maths this term!
6 We aren't allowed to have games consoles at school now.
7 Our teachers always make us turn off our phones in class.
8 The concert last night was free, so we didn't have to pay.

08 Magic numbers

Reading

Exercise 1
2 True   3 False   4 False   5 False   6 True   7 False
8 True   9 True   10 False

Exercise 2
2 C   3 A   4 D   5 B   6 C

Vocabulary 1

Exercise 1
2 multiplied   3 minus   4 plus   5 add   6 subtract

Exercise 2

Across:
3 CALCULATIONS
5 PATTERN
6 ZERO

Down:
1 MATHEMATICIAN
2 BASE
4 SERIES

Exercise 3
2 square   3 cone   4 cube   5 triangle; side   6 line
7 pyramid   8 rectangle   9 spiral

Exercise 4
2 height   3 deep   4 width   5 length   6 high   7 wide
8 depth

Grammar 1

Exercise 1
2 The Internet has been used for twenty-five years.
3 Calculators cannot be used in the exam.
4 All Tom's answers were copied from his classmate.
5 This textbook was chosen by our teacher.
6 The results will be uploaded to the website.

Exercise 2
2 C   3 A   4 B   5 C   6 A   7 B   8 B

Exercise 3
2 to a museum has been arranged for next week
3 was written on this subject
4 wasn't discovered by Galileo
5 can be found in the library
6 had already been solved
7 might be discovered in the future
8 was opened by a celebrity

Exercise 4
2 have been used
3 are moved
4 have
5 can be used
6 were taught
7 became
8 were told
9 have been replaced

Vocabulary 2

Exercise 1
2 research   3 news   4 experience   5 knowledge
6 advice   7 logic   8 imagination   9 intelligence
10 equipment

Exercise 2
2 U   3 C   4 C   5 U   6 U

Exercise 3
2 time   3 noises   4 lights   5 room   6 papers

Exercise 4
2 A   3 B   4 A   5 D   6 B   7 B   8 C   9 A   10 D

Grammar 2

Exercise 1
2 a few   3 little   4 few   5 little   6 a few   7 a little
8 few

Exercise 2
2 B   3 C   4 A   5 B   6 A   7 A   8 C   9 B   10 A

Exercise 3
2 nobody   3 everywhere   4 anything   5 nothing
6 everything   7 anywhere   8 something

Exercise 4
2 all   3 another   4 each   5 few   6 little   7 Neither
8 nobody   9 Everybody   10 anybody

Listening

Exercise 1
2 e   3 d   4 a   5 b   6 f

Exercise 2
2 A   3 A   4 B   5 C   6 B

Speaking Skills

Exercise 1
2 kind   3 it   4 special   5 remember   6 people
7 know   8 thing   9 place

Exercise 2
2 b   3 g   4 a   5 f   6 e   7 h   8 c

Writing

Exercise 1
2 Personally   3 recommend   4 ask   5 aim/score

Exercise 2
2 so   3 If   4 so   5 When   6 so

Exercise 3
2 False   3 True   4 True   5 False   6 False   7 True

Exercise 4
Model answer:
If you're looking for a fun game for several people I'd definitely recommend Monopoly! But don't play it if you've got plans because it can go on for hours!

Monopoly is all about buying property and in the UK version the buildings are in London. The rules are quite easy to follow. You throw a dice and move your piece around the board. When you land on a building you can choose if you want to buy it. Some of the buildings are cheap but others are very expensive.

When you've bought a property you can buy hotels to put on them and this increases the rent. However there are dangers. You might have to go to jail or you might have to pay things like some parking fines. If you lose a lot of money you can always sell your properties!

In my opinion Monopoly is a great game of chance but you also need to be quite clever when you choose what to buy and what not to buy. I would definitely recommend this game to anyone who wants a change from computer games. It's great entertainment.

Revision Unit 8

Exercise 1
2 cube – i   3 cone – f   4 square – g   5 rectangle – e
6 spiral – b   7 triangle – h   8 line – a   9 pyramid – d

Exercise 2
2 add   3 calculations   4 zero   5 sides   6 deep
7 mathematician   8 subtract   9 width   10 length

Exercise 3
2 light   3 noise   4 times   5 noises   6 lights   7 paper
8 time

Exercise 4
2 C   3 A   4 C   5 A   6 B   7 D   8 D

Exercise 5
2 was told
3 spent
4 can be used
5 haven't read
6 hasn't been reached
7 will be found
8 had been eaten
9 can earn
10 are employed

Exercise 6
2 new book has been published
3 portrait was painted by
4 results will be announced
5 windows are cleaned
6 can be bought
7 home had been destroyed by
8 two spies were arrested

Exercise 7
2 anything 3 Neither 4 nothing 5 both 6 anywhere
7 other 8 either 9 a little 10 none

Exercise 8
2 by 3 was 4 every 5 few 6 be 7 are 8 by
9 None 10 been 11 each

09 All change

Reading

Exercise 1
2 False 3 True 4 False 5 True 6 False 7 False
8 False

Exercise 2
2 d 3 a 4 f 5 b 6 h 7 c 8 g

Exercise 3
2 e 3 b 4 g 5 f 6 a 7 c

Vocabulary 1

Exercise 1
2 lighthouse 3 bungalow 4 log cabin 5 block of flats
6 caravan 7 igloo 8 tent 9 terraced house
10 cottage 11 semi-detached house 12 houseboat
13 detached house 14 mansion

Exercise 2
2 block (of) flats 3 log cabin 4 mansion 5 igloo
6 bungalow 7 tent 8 terraced 9 caravan
10 detached 11 houseboat 12 lighthouse 13 villa
14 semi-detached

Exercise 3
2 light switch 3 cushions 4 washing machine
5 lampshade 6 curtains 7 dishwasher 8 mattress

Exercise 4
2 cramped 3 messy 4 tiny 5 neat 6 roomy

Grammar 1

Exercise 1
2 g 3 c 4 f 5 a 6 b 7 h 8 e

Exercise 2
2 would live 3 gets 4 'd put 5 didn't 6 tidy 7 was
8 gets 9 could 10 don't like

Exercise 3
2 need 3 saw 4 won't let 5 wouldn't spend
6 apologises 7 is

Exercise 4
2 would spend
3 would get
4 did
5 could
6 would live
7 did
8 have
9 will never get
10 put
11 would work
12 manage
13 will be able to

Vocabulary 2

Exercise 1
2 departure 3 flight 4 pilot 5 platform
6 compartment 7 guard 8 track 9 passengers
10 dining car 11 port 12 cabin 13 deck 14 crew

Exercise 2
2 costs 3 take 4 for 5 heading 6 go through
7 on board 8 at 9 on the way 10 named after

Exercise 3
2 C 3 A 4 B 5 C 6 A 7 D 8 C 9 A

Grammar 2

Exercise 1
2 g 3 a 4 b 5 f 6 c 7 e

Exercise 2
2 C 3 B 4 A 5 A 6 C 7 A 8 B

Exercise 3
2 would have left
3 had left
4 wouldn't have arrived
5 hadn't been
6 would have remembered
7 hadn't happened
8 might not have been
9 had all been
10 wouldn't have made

Exercise 4
2 we could have got
3 would have been busy
4 I hadn't forgotten

Listening

Exercise 1
a 7   c 3   d 6   e 2   f 8   g 4   h 5

Exercise 2
2 computer
3 three/3
4 Manchester
5 a month/one month
6 park/beautiful park
7 English
8 friends
9 galleries/art galleries
10 the coast

Speaking Skills

Exercise 1
2 d   3 f   4 e   5 a   6 c

Exercise 2
2 c   3 f   4 b   5 a   6 d

Exercise 3
Students' own answers.

Exercise 4
Students' own answers.

Writing

Exercise 1
2 f   3 d   4 a   5 e   6 b

Exercise 2
2 giving advice
3 inviting
4 giving opinion
5 inviting
6 giving opinion
7 complaining
8 describing
9 complaining
10 giving advice

Exercise 3
Model answer:
Hi Belle,

Thanks for your letter and I'm sorry I haven't written recently. We've been really busy settling into the new house. I'm sure you understand!

I'm absolutely fine and I really love the new place. It's an old country cottage and it's just outside a very pretty little village. It's quite small but that's OK. I've got quite a big room with a view over the garden. The only problem is that I haven't got a lot of room for my clothes! So, I'm putting some in the spare room where there's another wardrobe.

There are a couple of houses near us, but then it's just open countryside with fields and trees. I took our dog Benny for a walk yesterday and we found a big lake with lots of fish in it!

Do you think you can come and stay for a few days in the holidays? It would be lovely to see you again and I know you'll love it here.

Write soon
Harry

Revision Unit 9

Exercise 1

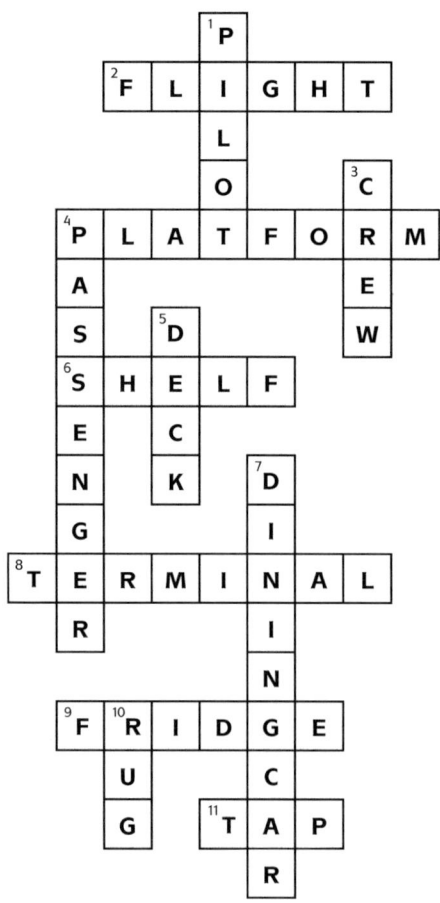

ANSWER KEY: GOLD EXPERIENCE WORKBOOK B1+

Exercise 2
2 light switch   3 duvet   4 curtains   5 drawer   6 stool
7 dishwasher   8 carpet

Exercise 3
2 igloo   3 lighthouse   4 houseboat   5 bungalow
6 caravan

Exercise 4
2 enormous   3 cramped   4 tidy   5 destination
6 on   7 track   8 into   9 keep   10 of

Exercise 5
2 would save up
3 leave
4 was
5 had travelled
6 don't have
7 knew
8 would have visited
9 will go
10 might have enjoyed

Exercise 6
2 were you, I would
3 was/were rich I would buy
4 might have gone on holiday
5 unless we leave
6 could have left on time
7 if it rains
8 will only call you

Exercise 7
2 The party won't be fun unless my friends come.
3 If we don't leave soon, we won't get there on time.
4 I might have been able to help you if you'd asked me earlier.
5 If I were you, I'd start saving up for your holiday now.
6 If the train had been less crowded, we would have enjoyed the journey more.
7 I'll text you if the train is delayed.
8 If I had a car, I would be able to drive you to the station.

10 Inspiration

Reading

Exercise 1
2 True   3 True   4 False   5 False   6 False   7 True
8 False

Exercise 2
a 5   b 2   c 4   d 7   e 6   f 3

Exercise 3
2 (an) inspiration   3 (a) challenge   4 transported
5 motivate   6 researching   7 circular   8 constructed

Vocabulary 1

Exercise 1

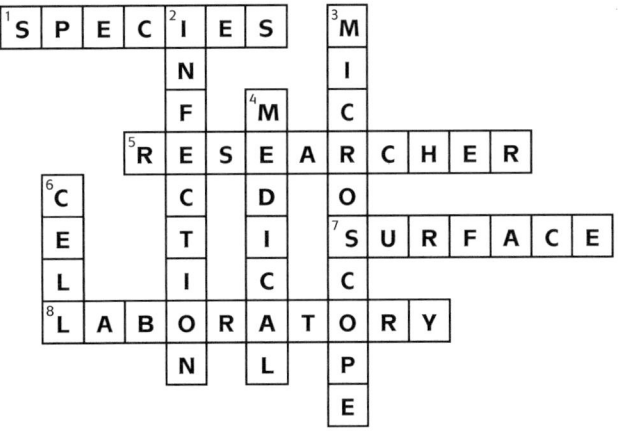

Exercise 2
2 sound   3 taste   4 sight   5 touch   6 vision   7 smell

Exercise 3
2 flexible   3 invisible   4 delicate   5 durable
6 waterproof   7 transparent

Exercise 4
2 B   3 A   4 D   5 B   6 C   7 A   8 D

Grammar 1

Exercise 1
2 to move   3 to become   4 go   5 to do   6 to help
7 working   8 living   9 applying   10 to ask

Exercise 2
2 to help   3 taking   4 to go   5 to be   6 to watch
7 to get   8 play   9 killing   10 Using

Exercise 3
2 involves working
3 love watching
4 hate being
5 had better take
6 is supposed to go
7 forgot to water
8 would rather study

Exercise 4
2 me   3 what   4 would   5 are   6 had   7 have

Vocabulary 2

Exercise 1
2 logical   3 practical   4 biology   5 inspirational
6 magic   7 magnetic

Exercise 2
2 microscopic   3 basic   4 panic   5 dramatic
6 scientific   7 electric

Exercise 3
2 metallic   3 magnetic   4 educational   5 electric
6 artistic

Exercise 4

ar-tis-tic	lo-gic-al
magnetic	magical
dramatic	practical
electric	biological
scientific	
microscopic	

Exercise 5
2 inspirational 3 musical 4 dramatic 5 biological
6 Scientific 7 magical

Grammar 2

Exercise 1
2 A 3 C 4 B 5 C 6 C

Exercise 2
2 have them mended
3 had his car taken
4 get it delivered
5 have the results checked
6 get it framed
7 have a tooth taken out
8 had new locks fitted

Exercise 3
2 have a TV fixed
3 have a mini science lab installed
4 have the walls painted
5 have your dream made

Exercise 4
2 had my microscope stolen
3 get your computer checked
4 would rather study
5 had better turn
6 what to do

Listening

Exercise 1
2 False 3 True 4 False 5 True 6 False
7 True 8 False

Exercise 2
2 heart
3 two/2
4 scientist
5 cat
6 dark
7 1934
8 fence
9 Trainers
10 seeds

Speaking Skills

Exercise 1
2 b 3 e 4 c 5 f 6 a

Exercise 2
2 C 3 B 4 A

Writing

Exercise 1
2 d 3 c 4 a

Exercise 2
2 d 3 c 4 a

Exercise 3
2 What a beautiful view!
3 What a difficult decision!
4 What an expensive shop!

Exercise 4
2 C 3 B 4 A

Exercise 5
Model answer:
If I had to choose one person who has given me real inspiration then I would have to say my cousin, Lucy.

I have always envied Lucy because of her apparent confidence. I used to wish that instead of being shy and timid I could be more like her. However Lucy had another gift that I didn't realise until last year. She can act.

When I was sixteen, my parents took me to see Lucy, who had just become a professional actress, in a play in London. It was an amazing experience! The auditorium was full and her performance made nearly everyone cry it was so good.

I realised that I wanted to be able to have that effect on people. Could I overcome my shyness to become an actor? I talked to Lucy about this later and she convinced me that I could follow my dream. She admitted that she hadn't always been full of confidence and that acting had helped her a lot.

I applied to drama school and now my first TV film is due to go out next week. Thank you Lucy for that inspiration

ANSWER KEY: GOLD EXPERIENCE WORKBOOK B1+

Revision Unit 10

Exercise 1
2 cells 3 microscope 4 durable 5 structure
6 transparent 7 surface 8 medical 9 flexible
10 invisible

Exercise 2
2 hearing 3 touch 4 sound 5 vision 6 taste
7 smell

Exercise 3
2 metallic 3 dramatic 4 magical 5 natural
6 inspirational

Exercise 4
2 D 3 A 4 B 5 A 6 C

Exercise 5
2 B 3 A 4 B 5 A 6 A 7 B 8 C

Exercise 6
2 better 3 to 4 rather 5 how 6 had

Exercise 7
2 The guide showed us where we to go.
3 My friend always wants to chat online, but I would to prefer to meet face-to-face.
4 I lent Mike £5 last week, so he had don't better not ask me for any more money!
5 Jack wants me to go out to the cinema with him, but I would rather to stay at home.
6 My parents want me to I become a scientist.
7 The exam is tomorrow, so you had better and revise this evening!
8 We're cutting up a mouse in our biology lesson tomorrow, but I would don't rather not watch!

Exercise 8
2 you had better phone
3 where to put
4 would rather not have
5 had her glasses broken
6 get the car checked
7 had better not be
8 is supposed to be

11 The art of make-believe

Reading

Exercise 1
2 False 3 True 4 True 5 False 6 False 7 False
8 True

Exercise 2
2 B 3 A 4 D 5 C 6 D 7 C 8 B 9 D 10 A

Vocabulary 1

Exercise 1
2 up 3 comes 4 away 5 for 6 have 7 rate
8 take 9 come 10 come

Exercise 2
2 fantasy world 3 vivid imagination
4 cartoon characters 5 artistic skill

Exercise 3
2 B 3 A 4 A 5 B 6 A 7 B 8 C 9 C 10 D

Grammar 1

Exercise 1
2 wouldn't
3 had never been
4 weren't selling
5 had to
6 should
7 had watched
8 ought to

Exercise 2
2 had already started
3 it would be difficult
4 we had to leave
5 had given
6 went / should go
7 I ought to practise
8 he wasn't going

Exercise 3
2 she had really wanted
3 hadn't accepted her
4 was a shame
5 could play
6 didn't matter
7 would probably get in
8 she ought to
9 knew
10 would cheer
11 there was
12 they went

Exercise 4
2 had 3 was 4 them 5 said 6 had 7 should
8 that

22

© 2016 PEARSON PHOTOCOPIABLE

Vocabulary 2

Exercise 1
2 première 3 acts 4 venue 5 show

Exercise 2
2 seat 3 row 4 stage 5 audience 6 interval
7 box office 8 sold out

Exercise 3
2 fan club 3 background 4 acoustics 5 fame
6 musicians 7 music-lover

Exercise 4
2 A 3 C 4 B 5 A 6 B 7 C 8 A 9 B 10 A

Grammar 2

Exercise 1
2 begged 3 ordered 4 advised 5 asked 6 allowed

Exercise 2
2 C 3 C 4 A 5 B

Exercise 3
2 not to be late home
3 to lend her some money
4 to hand our homework in on Monday
5 not to stay up so late
6 to stop making so much noise
7 to bring our sports clothes to school
8 not to give up playing the guitar

Exercise 4
2 asked her friends not to eat
3 reminded him to do
4 advised her not to accept
5 told the students to do
6 warned me not to spend

Listening

Exercise 1
2 priority 3 passion 4 challenge 5 calm

Exercise 2
E

Exercise 3
2 C 3 B 4 C 5 C 6 A 7 B

Speaking Skills

Exercise 1
2 What do you think about this one?
3 This would be interesting, wouldn't it?
4 Would you like to start?
5 Which do you think would be better?
6 Perhaps we should make a decision now.

Exercise 2
2 What do you think about this one?
3 Well, shall I start?
4 Perhaps we should make a decision now.
5 Which do you think would be better?
6 Would you like to start?

Exercise 3
2 C 3 E 4 A 5 B

Exercise 4
a 2 b 4 d 5 e 3

Writing

Exercise 1
2 end
3 sounded
4 going
5 a pity
6 on the whole
7 Although
8 with

Exercise 2
2 nervous
3 exciting
4 flat
5 impressed
6 professional
7 proud
8 influential

Exercise 3
2 It stars
3 It's a
4 I was
5 It's set in
6 It's about

Exercise 4
Model answer:
Did you enjoy the Inspector Morse TV series when it was first on TV? If you did, you'll love this new series, called *Endeavour*, which is about Inspector Morse when he was a young detective. It's like a prequel – it shows us Inspector Morse's first years as a policeman. And it's excellent.

There are four programmes in the series and they are about four different exciting adventures. Like Inspector Morse, they are all filmed in Oxford and they are about murders – of course! In the programmes we see how Morse developed as a clever detective and also how he loved classical music and cars, even when he was young and poor.

A lot of people thought that this series would be disappointing because it's difficult to write a good prequel. Also a new, young actor, Shaun Evans, plays Morse and people used to love the actor John Thaw. However, I was very impressed by Shaun Evans' performance and I think he's an excellent actor, too.

I can definitely recommend watching these programmes and I certainly hope that they film some more adventures for the young Endeavour Morse in the future.

Revision Unit 11

Exercise 1
2 row 3 exhibition 4 interval 5 audience
6 imagination

Exercise 2
2 musician 3 box office 4 seat 5 fan club
6 music-lover

Exercise 3
2 world 3 come 4 fame 5 away 6 learning
7 come true 8 go for

Exercise 4
2 A 3 C 4 C 5 B 6 A 7 B 8 D 9 C 10 D
11 A 12 B

Exercise 5
2 had already seen
3 weren't going
4 might be
5 had to see
6 would book
7 watched / should watch
8 ought to read

Exercise 6
2 B 3 C 4 A 5 C 6 B

Exercise 7
2 to 3 was 4 not 5 had 6 should 7 that
8 him

Exercise 8
2 advised me to become
3 suggested that we met / we should meet
4 encouraged her to go
5 think the show starts
6 us not to mess around

12 Find your voice

Reading

Exercise 1
B

Exercise 2
2, 7

Exercise 3
2 b 3 g 4 a 5 d 6 c

Exercise 4
2 issues 3 participate 4 raise awareness 5 launch
6 fixed

Vocabulary 1

Exercise 1
2 view 3 concluded 4 discuss 5 prepare 6 arguing
7 individual

Exercise 2
2 clarity 3 preparation 4 conclusion 5 discussions
6 speech

Exercise 3

		¹E	Q	U	A	L	I	T	Y
	²S	T	R	E	N	G	T	H	
³R	E	S	P	O	N	S	I	B	I	L	I	T	Y
	⁴R	E	S	P	E	C	T		
	⁵H	O	N	E	S	T	Y		

Mystery word: unity

Exercise 4
2 rights 3 difference 4 advice 5 truth 6 skills

Exercise 5
2 part 3 together 4 for 5 on 6 in 7 for 8 for
9 up 10 in

Grammar 1

Exercise 1
2 C 3 A 4 C 5 B 6 A

Exercise 2
2 can't 3 might not 4 must 5 should 6 Could
7 may not 8 could

Exercise 3
2 A 3 B 4 A 5 C 6 A 7 B

Exercise 4
2 might not like
3 Could Jem be
4 tickets can't cost
5 should have
6 you think she is

Vocabulary 2

Exercise 1
2 legible 3 invisible 4 immature 5 responsible
6 lucky 7 irrational 8 unplanned

Exercise 2
2 impolite 3 untidy 4 unreliable 5 incorrect
6 dishonest 7 illogical 8 dissatisfied

Exercise 3
2 informal 3 illegal 4 irresponsible 5 unnecessary
6 impossible 7 incorrect 8 invisible

Exercise 4
2 dishonest 3 unlucky 4 impossible 5 unfair
6 unnecessary 7 dissatisfied 8 unacceptable

Grammar 2

Exercise 1
2 Wasn't it?
3 Will you?
4 Haven't you?
5 Won't she?
6 Aren't you?

Exercise 2
2 Didn't she?
3 Won't it?
4 Could it?
5 Did they?
6 Aren't you?
7 Weren't they?

Exercise 3
2 don't you
3 did they
4 shall we
5 wasn't he
6 will we
7 hasn't he
8 have you

Exercise 4
2 aren't they
3 wouldn't it
4 Have they
5 don't they
6 Did he
7 Is he
8 shall we

Listening

Exercise 1
2 Speaker 2
3 Speaker 1
4 Speaker 5
5 Speaker 3

Exercise 2
2 h 3 a 4 e 5 d

Speaking Skills

Exercise 1
2 might 3 maybe 4 can't 5 need 6 must

Exercise 2
2 haven't we 3 isn't it 4 do we 5 is it 6 shall we

Exercise 3
2 fair/correct/right 3 say/think 4 point 5 forget
6 listening/coming

Exercise 4
Model answer:
I'm here today to talk to you about selfishness. I know a lot of people think that everyone today is becoming very selfish. But is it true? Do we really think too much about ourselves and the things we want instead of helping other people? I don't think it's fair to say that. I think it's true that people today can have a lot more things than our parents could. Perhaps we have more money, I'm not sure. But also, we are very busy and we don't have much time. Perhaps that's why people think we're selfish. However, even with only a little time I'm sure that we help our friends and our families just like other generations have. Maybe we do it in different ways. For example, we help each other by talking on the phone or online. Another point I'd like to make is that I think being selfish is about a person's character and not about society or the world today. There have always been selfish people and there will always be some! And finally we mustn't forget that we learn to be unselfish when we are children. So, when we become parents we must teach our children that lesson, too. That's all. Thank you for listening.

Writing

Exercise 1
2 on the other hand
3 Although
4 whereas
5 overall
6 conclusion

Exercise 2
2 A 3 D 4 A 5 B 6 C 7 C 8 B 9 C 10 B

Exercise 3
2 A 3 A 4 NA

Exercise 4
Model answer:
We are usually taught from an early age that it is important for us to tell the truth. But is this always the case?

To begin with I believe that people who should definitely always tell the truth are people in authority, or people who make big decisions about our lives, such as politicians. We need to trust them.

Next, let's consider the people who are close to us, our friends. On the one hand it's important to trust your friends to be honest but on the other hand there are times when a small lie might be better than saying something that will hurt them. For example if your friend has a new hairstyle, should you tell her that it looks awful? I don't think I would.

Thirdly I would like to say that parents should try to be honest with their children. If children later find out that their parents have lied to them, they will lie themselves.

In conclusion, I think that although people should generally be honest with each other, a little lie to prevent people getting hurt is sometimes acceptable.

Revision Unit 12

Exercise 1

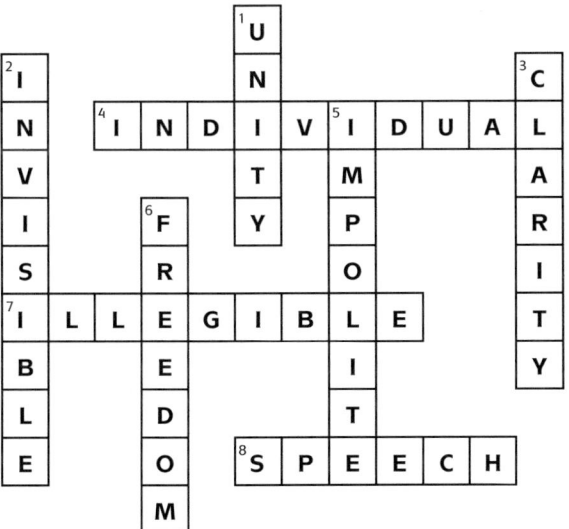

Exercise 2
2 conclusion 3 arguments 4 discussion 5 irrational
6 illegal 7 dishonest

Exercise 3
2 admit 3 responsibility 4 respect 5 equality
6 honesty 7 human rights

Exercise 4
2 in 3 in 4 tell 5 on 6 up 7 making 8 have

Exercise 5
2 C 3 A 4 C 5 B 6 A 7 C 8 B

Exercise 6
2 must be very scary
3 might not come
4 may have a bike
5 can't be
6 we should get there

Exercise 7
2 Does it?
3 Will you?
4 Wasn't he?
5 Can you?
6 Didn't they?

Exercise 8
2 do they
3 hasn't he
4 will it
5 didn't you
6 shall we

Exercise 9
2 haven't you
3 aren't you
4 Haven't you
5 Will you
6 won't you

Audioscripts

Track 1.1/1.2 Unit One Exercises 1 and 2

1

GIRL: Hi there! Did you apply for that summer job at the leisure centre? I know the money's not that good but it's probably going to be great fun.

BOY: I know, although I really need to earn as much as I can to go on holiday in September. I didn't apply in the end because they're looking for someone full-time and I can only do three days a week.

GIRL: That's a shame. Now there's a restaurant job I saw advertised yesterday – that's three days. Shall I give you the number?

2

BOY: You look a bit fed-up. What's the matter? Did Miss Davis get angry because you didn't hand in your essay on time? I saw you talking to her.

GIRL: Yes. And it's understandable – she gave me a week extra. But it really wasn't my fault.

BOY: So, whose fault was it?

GIRL: Well, I suppose it was mine really – just not directly. I wrote up the essay on the computer. I downloaded lots of interesting information to use and it looked great. I was really pleased with it. Then I clicked the wrong button and I deleted the whole thing.

BOY: Oh no! And you couldn't get it back?

GIRL: Nope. All gone. I've got to do it all again for tomorrow!

3

Hi Sally. I thought I would let you know – I went online this morning to look at the clothes sale at CoolClothing.com because I wanted to get some new jeans. They didn't have any suitable jeans but the prices on their coats are amazing. I know you're looking for a new winter coat so why don't you have a look? There are some lovely styles and you won't find anything cheaper. I ordered a necklace and some earrings from their accessories section but I'm going to have to try somewhere else for the jeans. Anyway, check it out! Let me know if you buy one!

4

GIRL: So, tomorrow we have to decide what subjects to study at college – it's a big decision, isn't it?

BOY: Yes, I just don't know what to do. I'd like to study drama ... but my parents say I should do sciences because I'm good at that.

GIRL: I think you should make your own decisions. Don't worry about what your parents want – it's your life, not theirs!

BOY: I know but perhaps I should do sciences. I'm more likely to get a job, aren't I?

GIRL: You should think about what you'll enjoy. And I think you'll be a brilliant actor!

5

S1: You're going to your brother's wedding this weekend, aren't you? What are you going to wear?

S2: I still haven't decided. I was thinking about my new blue dress with the short sleeves – you know the one. It's an expensive designer label.

S1: Yes, that is SO pretty. But I've heard it's going to be a bit cold on Saturday – will you be warm enough?

S2: Good point. But I don't mind being uncomfortable for a short time – it will be warm when we get to the reception. I spent a lot on that blue dress and I don't wear it very often.

S1: OK. I'm sure it will look great.

6

A lot of people think that the job of a writer is really easy. You just sit at a computer when you feel like it and write stories. However, it isn't quite like that! You can't just work when you want to – you have to get a routine and keep to it. You also need to be imaginative and have great ideas and not everyone can do that. There's a lot of advice around for new writers – some very good books you can get. Of course, going on a writing course can help a lot, too. But if you like telling stories, it may be the job for you. Good luck!

Track 2.1/2.2 Unit Two Exercises 1 and 2

Today it's very easy to communicate with our friends using new technology, isn't it?

Most of us don't think twice about sending an email, writing a text or talking on the phone. But it isn't that easy for everyone. Think about the many people who have disabilities. Maybe they can't speak very clearly or maybe they can't use their fingers accurately to type on a keyboard.

Semantography, which later became Blissymbols, was created by Charles Bliss in Shanghai, and later in Australia. It was meant to be an international written language that didn't use spoken words of any language: it used very simple pictures instead. Around 1970, it was discovered that people with a disability who could not speak, could learn to understand and use Blissymbols to communicate. They could point to the Blissymbols and another person translated the meaning of the 'picture words' into spoken language. It was a brilliant solution and it helped a lot to improve the lives of disabled people. But there was a problem. The disabled person always needed an assistant to do the translating for them. They couldn't communicate alone.

Then, in 1984 a young Canadian girl called Rachel Zimmerman invented something that solved this problem. Rachel was only twelve years old when she decided to enter a science competition. She was lucky to have a mum who was a very clever scientist – and Rachel thinks this helped her a lot. Rachel was looking for information to help with a school project when she read about Blissymbols. Rachel thought that she could help. She had found her idea for the science competition! Rachel carefully designed a special board with the symbols for the user to touch, not to point at. She also developed some new computer software to translate these pictures into written words on the computer screen. The disabled person now didn't need someone else to help – they could do it on their own. Now they could email their messages to other people or print them out. Rachel called this invention 'the Blissymbol printer' and it won lots of prizes all over the world. Today Rachel works for NASA, the Space agency. She tries to adapt new inventions to help disabled people. Rachel is one of the most famous young, female inventors of our time – and it all started with a science competition!

Track 3.1/3.2/3.3 Unit Three Exercises 1, 2 and 3

1

My parents both played instruments when I was growing up. My mum played the piano, but it was my dad who I really wanted to copy. He was great on the guitar. He only played at home, but while I was at primary school I told all my friends that he was in a band and that they had recorded some successful songs. They thought I was lucky to have a dad in a band! So, then I told them that he did concerts in London and New York. Everyone wanted to be my friend. It was cool.

2

I was very honest when I was young, probably because my parents were quite strict and I was scared to do anything wrong. But I remember once my mum had made a big chocolate cake for my brother's birthday and I ate some of the sugary chocolate cream from the top. There was a big hole in the cream, so I smoothed it with a knife, but it was very thin and my mum noticed immediately. She asked me if I'd done it and I said 'no'. But she knew because there was chocolate on my face!

3

It was my brother's birthday last month and Mum had arranged a surprise birthday party for him at home. She'd invited twenty people to our house for seven thirty and it was my job to keep him away until then. So, I said that I'd lost my laptop and asked him to take me to all the places I'd been to that afternoon. Poor Steve, he took me to school, to the library, the swimming pool and the supermarket. Of course, it was a great surprise when he got home.

4

One of the worst things I've ever done was a few years ago when my brother was irritating me. He kept borrowing my guitar and breaking the strings. And then he borrowed my phone and I couldn't find it. I decided to do something horrible. He really liked a girl in my class at school, but I knew she didn't like him very much. I told my brother that she liked him and wanted to go out on a date. So, he called her! Oh, he was so embarrassed. His face went bright red! He's never forgiven me.

5

One week last year I borrowed a box set of a crime series from a friend. It was brilliant and I watched it in my room every evening for a few hours. My parents thought I was doing my homework, but the series was much more interesting! So, when my teacher asked for my English essay, I told her that I'd left my school bag on the train. She was really nice and suggested we phoned the train company to check. I felt very bad about it and did my essay as soon as I got home!

Track 4.1/4.2 Unit Four Exercises 1 and 2

INTERVIEWER: So, how's your memory? If it's anything like mine, then you're going to love the advice our guest today can give. Elizabeth Small is a psychologist from the USA and for many years she's been studying what people remember and how they can improve their memories. Her book – *I remember it well!* – has been in the UK top ten non-fiction book charts since January. Elizabeth, it's a great pleasure to have you with us today.

ELIZABETH: Thanks for that great introduction. You got a couple of things wrong though – my name is actually Smallwood, not Small. You may well need some memory coaching yourself! But you're right, I live in the USA, although I originate here. I come from a small town on the south coast – Fawley. My parents moved to Colombia when I was two and then on to the States a couple of years later.

INTERVIEWER: I'm glad this is radio so you can't see how red my face is! Let's move on, shall we? Elizabeth, I imagine my memory problems are pretty typical. You know, I go into a room for something and forget why I've gone there. But that's not too bad. It's annoying but I just go back to where I was at first and then I remember. It's worse when I'm out and suddenly forget people's names. I go red then too!

ELIZABETH: What you're describing is perfectly normal. We all have things we remember easily and things we don't. Don't worry about it – that makes it worse.

INTERVIEWER: So, how can we make sure that doesn't happen? Is there a cure for a bad memory?

ELIZABETH: Sorry – I haven't got the perfect answer! But there are some things you can do to help. One trick is to make more effort at remembering things that we often tend to forget. You know, like if you often forget where you put important things like your keys – then take a mental picture when you put them down. Think about what's beside them. The more we think about something, the better we remember it.

INTERVIEWER: OK. That makes sense. Now, another thing I have problems remembering is – lists. I go into the supermarket to get three or four things and I come out without one of them. I remember as soon as I get in the car. Any suggestions?

ELIZABETH: There are several ways you can remember lists. Think about memory champions. Sometimes they remember fifty or more things in a competition! One way is to have a picture in your head of a place you know well, like your living room. Then you imagine the different things that you want to remember in places in this room. But the trick is to make them memorable – that is to make the pictures in your head funny or strange. We remember unusual things much better than boring ones.

INTERVIEWER: Right. I'm going to try to remember my shopping list for tonight. I need milk, eggs, cheese, a chicken, some potatoes, a bottle of lemonade and some flowers. So, in my picture of my living room I go in the door and on the left there's a table. I'm putting a book on the table and it's got a picture of a cow on the cover – cow-milk. Then on the wall I have a painting of a ballet dancer - I'm putting an egg on her head! Yes! Then there's the sofa and on the sofa now there's a chicken and it's singing. Am I doing this right?

ELIZABETH: Perfectly.

INTERVIEWER: This is very interesting. Can you tell us what we shouldn't do if we want to remember things, for example for an exam?

ELIZABETH: The important thing is that we are all different and we learn and remember things in different ways but generally speaking our memories work better if we're relaxed when we're learning. So, try not to get too stressed. A lot of students leave revising until the last moment and then stay up all night working. That is NOT a good idea. Before an exam you need a good sleep. It lets your brain remember the things you've learned.

INTERVIEWER: Thank you so much Elizabeth. Now, do you think you could note down some of those points again so that I don't forget??

Track 5.1/5.2 Unit Five Exercises 1 and 2

1

Hi, it's me. I'm phoning about swimming this evening. I'm really looking forward to it as I need the exercise! I haven't done any running or swimming for ages. I spoke to Mark earlier and he'd like to join us, but he's got art club until six. So could we make it an hour later than we said – about six thirty? Let me know if that's OK for you. And don't forget your towel this time! See you later.

2

BOY: Hey – I like your new bike. Are you going to ride it to school every day?

GIRL: That's the plan. It will be quicker than taking the bus and better for me.

BOY: I'd really like to ride to school, but I was in an accident a while back and my mum and dad won't let me.

GIRL: Oh no! The cycle paths on the roads are really very safe. And you're a great cyclist.

BOY: Thanks. I love cycling and go out in the country every weekend. Oh well, let's hope mum and dad change their minds soon. I'm fed up with taking the bus.

3

I'm pleased to tell you today that our series of talks about healthy eating and exercise is beginning next week. We have invited several experts, including some chefs and doctors, to come to talk to you and we are sure that you will find it interesting and useful. The talks will be on Tuesdays after school in the Hall at four thirty and please sign the list on the noticeboard if you would like to attend. The speakers need to have an idea of how many people to expect because there will be handouts and, when the chefs come, some food as well! So, if you can do that before Friday, we would be grateful.

4

S1: Have you seen the article in the magazine about the plans for a new road coming into town?

S2: Yes, it looks as if it will cut through the park. That's terrible.

S1: But we definitely need a new road. The traffic jams are really bad on the other one.

S2: It's true the traffic is heavy there, especially in the rush hour, but we should persuade people to leave their cars at home and use other transport.

S1: I don't think people would like that! It would take them too long. The new road might only cut through a short part of the park. The exact plans will be out next week.

5

S1: Have you done your essay on the environment yet for Mr Drake?

S2: Not yet. I've looked at the question but I haven't even started writing it.

S1: That's not like you! You always do yours before I do mine.

S2: That's because you worry too much about getting it perfect! You must write your essays at least three times! No, I'm not too sure about the question.

S1: Oh, it's easy. Shall I explain?

S2: Please do! Last time I wrote about completely the wrong topic.

6

The new book by Tina Summers is a must-read for anyone who is interested in or worried by climate change. Tina is an expert but the book isn't full of scientific words and statistics. It's easy to read and very clearly written. There are some very frightening pictures of areas affected by climate change in recent years and the book really makes us think about what could happen soon to the climate of our world. No one will be unaffected. But the book isn't intended to terrify people. Tina wants to give a clearer picture of what is happening and her book definitely does this.

Track 6.1/6.2 Unit Six Exercises 1 and 2

Hello everyone! My name's Ruth and I'll be your guide for today. Before we set off I'd like to tell you a bit about our excursion and what you can and can't do when we get there. I really think you'll love Ayer's Rock. I'm Australian and I've been all over Australia, but there's a real magic about this place!

Now, it's called 'Ayer's Rock' in your guide books but its traditional name is Uluru. The guy who first reported seeing this amazing place in 1873, William Goose, named it Ayer's Rock after a famous Australian politician. But the land has always belonged to an aboriginal tribe and Uluru is their old name for it. So today we use both names!

I'm sure you've all seen pictures and you'll know that Ayer's Rock is a very unusual rock formation made of sandstone. It looks very red in most pictures. Some people have called it a 'mountain island' and you will see why! It's very big, almost 348 metres high and it rises on its own out of the earth, just like an island – but there's no water! If you want to walk all the way round it, that's 9.4 kilometres! It's a long way!

Scientists have their ideas about how the rock was formed but the Aborigines have their own stories. One story says that when the earth was created, two boys played in the mud and they made this strange shape that grew bigger and bigger. Another story says that the rock grew out of the Earth after a big fight between two tribes. The leaders of both tribes died and the rock holds their spirits.

Now this amazing rock still belongs to the Aborigines and it's very important to them. They believe that it's the home of the spirits of their dead ancestors. So it's an important religious place for them. There used to be lots of hotels near the rock for tourists but they were closed down because of the bad effect of tourism on the area.

Obviously it's still a big tourist attraction but visitors have to travel to get there. Also visitors need to show respect for the old beliefs. So, there are a few things we'd like you to think about. One is climbing the rock. Lots of people want to go right to the top and it is possible. There's a special rail to help you up. But it depends on the weather. It can be very dangerous if it's windy. Also, the Aborigine tribe don't like people climbing up to the top because they have to cross some religious places. They ask visitors not to go up. But if you decide to go up anyway, it'll take about an hour. Please remember that the coach will be leaving at four thirty sharp.

Visitors are also asked not to take photographs in some places. This is because of the Aborigines' religious beliefs. Another request is that visitors should not take small rocks away with them as souvenirs. There are stories that people who have done this have had bad luck. You can believe this or not ... but I certainly wouldn't risk it! So, I hope you all have an excellent day and enjoy this magnificent sight. Let's ...

Track 7.1/7.2 Unit Seven Exercises 1 and 2

INTERVIEWER: If you're looking for a challenge, then you don't have to look much further than the Tough Mudder assault courses. Today we're talking to Ella Masters who completed one of the courses last weekend. Ella, how are you feeling?

ELLA: Well, I hurt all over! I've got cuts and bruises everywhere and my arms and legs ache a lot. But I feel absolutely fantastic!

INTERVIEWER: OK, I know a lot of our listeners are thinking – what are they talking about? What is Tough Mudder? So, can you explain please?

ELLA: Sure. It's a series of assault courses. These are designed by the military and they're part of a soldier's training. You have to run for 16–19 kilometres and climb walls, go through water, crawl through mud and things like that. Obviously, people like me who do these events aren't in the army – it's just the sort of thing that soldiers have to do. It tests your mental and physical fitness and it helps you overcome your fears. You know, fear of water, heights, electricity – things like that.

INTERVIEWER: It sounds horrific! So, the obvious question – why do people (who don't have to) choose to run this course?

ELLA: It's all about the challenge! We need to have challenges in our lives and this is one of the biggest! It's very, very hard physically. You have to run up and down hills and do really scary things. But you do it in teams and the idea is to use teamwork to get everybody to the end. Everyone who enters raises money for charity too – so there are lots of good reasons to do it.

INTERVIEWER: What was the most difficult part of the course for you Ella?

ELLA: Well, I was actually pretty good at the water challenges because I did a lot of competitive swimming when I was younger. At one point we had to swim underwater through ice water and I did that fine. Of course, then you're cold and wet for the next part ... but that wasn't too bad. For me, there was just one wall that I couldn't get up. My mates tried to help me, but I just couldn't make it. Oh yes, and I really hated running up the hills. I got so tired that I couldn't think straight.

INTERVIEWER:	Do you regret entering the event at all?
ELLA:	No way. It was brilliant, because you feel so good at the end. We all finished and every one felt so proud of themselves! I actually think it was the most difficult thing I've ever done in my life. But I'm going to do it again in three months' time.
INTERVIEWER:	Again? Are you crazy?
ELLA:	Perhaps a little! This time, I'm gonna do some more training and get a bit fitter for the hill running. I should spend some more time on my bike and down the gym. But I'm really looking forward to the experience.
INTERVIEWER:	How did people react when you told them that you were going to enter the event?
ELLA:	Well, my boyfriend thought I wouldn't do it. He thought that I would cancel at the last minute. But I couldn't do that, could I? I didn't want to let everyone else down! He also thought I wasn't fit enough. He's the one who goes running, plays football and works out every day in the gym. No, he thought I'd cancel. My mum was worried sick. She thought I would fall, hurt myself – end up in hospital. You know what mums are like!
INTERVIEWER:	So, I imagine you'd recommend the event to other people.
ELLA:	Yes. Even if you're not that fit. It gives you a goal to work towards and it shows you that you can do things that might seem impossible. Since it started in 2010 more than one point three million people have taken part in Tough Mudder events – in lots of different countries. Most of them were just normal people like me – they wanted a challenge and they succeeded. Why don't you try it?
INTERVIEWER:	Let's move on to another subject …!

Track 8.1/8.2 Unit Eight Exercises 1 and 2

1

GIRL:	I can't believe it. My computer's giving me problems again.
BOY:	Really? I thought Tommy solved that for you.
GIRL:	I know. He spent ages on it. But it's doing the same thing. It shuts down on its own. It's really annoying. Maybe I should call Tommy again. He is very good with computers.
BOY:	Maybe the answer is to get a new one!
GIRL:	That would be much more expensive than Tommy!

2

Molly Hadfield's newest book will definitely be a best seller. If you like a mystery, you'll love this one and in my opinion it's much cleverer than her previous books. Although the person who did the murder isn't a complete surprise – I guessed correctly half way through – the reasons for it are complicated and I guarantee you won't guess those! I also really like the setting for the story – the Scottish countryside. It's in the shops now in paperback – or you can download the e-book online.

3

I'm sure you've all heard the stories about this house. The Darcy family have lived here for hundreds of years and of course, many of them died here too. It would be surprising if there weren't any ghost stories! Lady Marcia Darcy was killed – according to the stories – in this bedroom, perhaps on the spot where you are standing now. Her husband discovered that she was in love with another man and he stabbed her with a knife. Local people have reported seeing strange lights in these windows at night. They say if you stand under the clock outside at midnight, you can hear her scream. I've never tried it.

4

S1:	Come on! Help me with this homework. Please!
S2:	I've only got one more answer to find … I won't be long.
S1:	You've been looking at that crossword puzzle for an hour. Perhaps I can help you with the last answer. Then you can help me.
S2:	No, it's OK. I can do it myself thanks. Let me think. It's something your teacher needs – and it starts with an H and ends with a K.
S1:	You're joking. Think about it! What did I ask you to help me with?
S2:	What? Oh – OK. Homework. Right. Thanks!

5

S1: You've got a twin sister, haven't you? I bet that's a lot of fun!

S2: Yeah, Evie. We look very similar and we can play jokes on people. Sometimes the teachers don't know whether they're talking to me or my sister when they ask us questions. It drives them mad! She's cleverer than me, so that's good!

S1: Do you ever know what your sister's thinking?

S2: Not really. We have the same ideas about things but I can't read her mind. But when we were young we had a secret language between us – that only we could understand. So, no one else knew what we were talking about. Our mum used to get very angry!

S1: Now, that's cool!

6

BOY: Hi – are you feeling better? I hope you went to the doctor yesterday. You didn't look very well.

GIRL: Yes, I did. I've felt bad since our holiday. I thought perhaps I'd eaten something bad but the doctor thinks it's a bit like flu and I probably caught it on the plane from another passenger. He gave me some horrible tablets, but now I feel much better.

BOY: I guess it's hard for doctors to find out what's exactly wrong with people. I wouldn't like their job. But I'm glad it wasn't anything serious.

Track 9.1/9.2 Unit Nine Exercises 1 and 2

MISS TURNER: Today Suzanne Baker is going to tell us about her recent experience of moving to live in another country. Over to you Suzanne.

SUZANNE BAKER: Hi everyone! So, as Miss Turner said, I'm talking today about something that happened to me and my family a few years ago. My dad works for an international computer company and three years ago they transferred him to Paris. This was a big shock for the family – as you can imagine. We'd lived in Manchester for ten years, after moving there from London when I was two, and our home and my school was there – as well as all of our friends. So, at first, dad decided to spend the week working in Paris and then come back to spend weekends with us. He did that for a month but then it just got too hectic. He spent all his time travelling and at the weekends he was too tired to do anything at home. We missed him loads and my two young brothers started to have problems at school.

Mum and dad decided we should be together as a family and move to Paris with dad. So, we did – and wow, was that a shock to the system! To begin with we were all very excited and we loved our new home in Paris. It was right beside a beautiful park and about ten minutes' walk from the River Seine.

We all loved the city. My brothers and I went to an international school where everyone spoke English, so our education wasn't a problem. My brothers liked the school a lot and immediately made loads of friends – at school and with the French children who lived near us. They're quite young and picked up the language very quickly. It was much harder for me, I think. I missed my friends and I found speaking French very hard. But one thing I did like was the shopping. Mum and I spent a lot of time in the markets and the clothes stores and when I came back to England I had a much better collection of clothes than when I went! People often ask me if we went to art galleries while we were in Paris – but we didn't very often. I think that's a shame now because it was a good opportunity. But we were always busy. We often went to the coast at the weekends because the weather was fantastic in the summer. Anyway, Dad's job continued for about three years and I was just beginning to enjoy life in France when he got transferred back to England again and we came home. I was very glad to be back. I love living here in England – but Paris was an interesting experience.

Track 10.1/10.2 Unit Ten Exercises 1 and 2

Good morning everyone. Our teacher asked us all to prepare a presentation about how some inventions were inspired by animals. I know we've looked at a lot of these during the last few lessons but we haven't looked at animals that are very close to us. I love dogs and I know a lot of families have cats too, so I thought I would see if there are any inventions that were inspired by our pets!

It's amazing but I found quite a few! One of the biggest inventions ever was electricity. Without it we wouldn't have lights, TVs or any of the gadgets that we use all the time these days! Apparently, in the beginning, there were two scientists who were working on developing electricity, Thomas Edison and Nikola Tesla. They were both looking for a safe way to provide electricity. They couldn't agree on how to do this but in the end Tesla won. But what interested him in electricity in the beginning? It was his cat! He loved animals and he was stroking his cat one day when he felt the electricity from its fur. You know, you can feel it sometimes when you brush your hair.

And there's another invention which was inspired by an animal. When you're driving down a road at night and it's completely dark, have you noticed the shiny things in the middle of many roads? They're called cat's eyes and they reflect the car's headlights so that drivers can see where they're going. In 1934 an English man called Percy Shaw was driving home along a road that was close to a cliff. It was very dangerous as you can imagine! Shaw was driving very slowly and trying to see the edge of the road when he saw a cat sitting on a fence at the side of the road. His car headlights shone in the cat's eyes. That made him think hard and soon he invented cat's eyes. People depend on them all over the world now. It's amazing that such a simple idea – inspired by a cat – has probably saved thousands of lives.

Dogs have done well too! I'm sure everyone here knows about Velcro. It's a material that sticks to itself and is used to stick things together instead of zips or buttons. You can find it on all sorts of things like coats and jackets – and today of course, on trainers. Well, the person who thought of the idea was a Swiss man called Mestral. He got home after going hunting with his dog and he noticed that lots of little seeds from flowers had stuck to the dog's fur. He thought he could copy this process to make other things stick together. Velcro has since been used by astronauts in space and even in the first artificial heart operations! Now, it would be hard to live without it!

Track 11.1/11.2 Unit Eleven Exercises 2 and 3

INTERVIEWER: Hi Adam! So, tell us what a stunt performer does.

ADAM: A stunt performer takes the place of an actor when they have to do something that could be dangerous – like driving a fast car. That's called a stunt. The job needs different skills, because you might have to do anything from jumping out of a plane to climbing a mountain. The director tells you what he wants and you're responsible for working out how to do it. Although safety is the top priority, it's also make-believe – the audience must think that the stunt is real.

INTERVIEWER: Claire, who's fourteen, has emailed a question asking why you became a stuntman.

ADAM: It wasn't my original plan! I've always been into films – my sister and I acted out scenes from our favourites when we were little. I would have loved to be an actor but I don't have the talent – I'm hopeless on stage! I love sport and might have tried to make that my career, but it was my drama teacher who told me about stunt work. I guess it combines all my passions, and luckily it's quite well-paid.

INTERVIEWER: Carlo, who's fifteen, wants to know what you find difficult about the job?

ADAM: You have to fit in with the filming schedule, and that can depend on things like the weather. You might spend ages in uncomfortable places – like underwater – while the cameraman gets perfect pictures. I don't mind that because I enjoy the challenge. Also you often need to wear protective clothes when you do a stunt – obviously – but you also have to look like the actor in the film, maybe in a smart business suit! So you have to be clever with your clothes. I don't find that easy – it can take hours to get the look right.

INTERVIEWER: Eleanor asks whether you have to keep fit.

ADAM: Definitely! Because I'm starting and I'm young, I realise I must build up my strength – I can't get tired on the film set. I watch what I eat – that's not nice because I love food, but it's OK. I work out in the gym every day – now that's boring! Jogging helps me to develop stamina and I love being out in the fresh air. You must be good at different sports, from tennis to boxing, and that's a challenge.

INTERVIEWER:	Your first stunt was on the film called *The Escape*, wasn't it?
ADAM:	Yes. On my very first day I had to work on a stunt which involved jumping from a bridge and landing on a moving train – I had to learn a lot very quickly! I didn't do the actual jumping – the experienced stunt person did that, which was a relief. Timing of the jump was really important and it took days to plan how to do it safely. Then of course it was over in seconds! Reviewers said the effect in the film was spectacular.
INTERVIEWER:	Any other stories or examples you can share with us?
ADAM:	On the second film I was involved with – called *The Big Robbery* – we were supposed to escape from some gangsters by running down a street and swimming across a river. There was this cute dog we were supposed to take with us, but the problem was he hated water and wouldn't go in! Every time we got to the river he just stopped. The director got very cross, and we ended up getting a stunt dog to take his place, which was crazy!
INTERVIEWER:	Finally, Joe asks what makes a good stunt performer and how he can become one.
ADAM:	There's no official training scheme, though some drama schools offer courses in things like fighting or working with fire. You need to stay calm under pressure – things happen quickly and you must be ready for anything. It comes down to being well-organised to be honest – and paying attention to detail. It's quite a hard job but I love it.
INTERVIEWER:	Thanks, Adam.

Track 12.1/12.2 Unit Twelve Exercises 1 and 2

S1: We had a really good class discussion today about climate change and lots of people had strong views. I've always thought that there isn't much we can do about it but my friend Mark pointed out a lot of ways we can help change things. He was very convincing and I think he's right. We shouldn't just accept that the future's going to be really terrible. We need to start doing things to slow down the effects.

S2: I like a good discussion – like today when we were talking about the effect of TV programmes on young people. It's important to know how other people feel. However, I think some people are easily persuaded by those who can argue well. OK, I know it's good to see both sides of the argument but you have to know how you feel and express your own opinion. It's not all about who can shout the loudest!

S3: There's a lot of talk at school at the moment about whether we should have a different start time for the school day – like 9.30 instead of 9.00 and there's an after school discussion about it today. A lot of my mates have strong opinions about this. They think teenagers like us work better if we get more sleep. Personally, I'm happy either way. I mean, I'd like a lie-in but on the other hand we'd finish later, wouldn't we? And I do a lot of stuff after school. I don't think it's a big problem though. It's up to the school to decide and I'm sure they'll make the right decision.

S4: We'll be able to vote in the general election next year. That's going to be interesting! Most people my age have no idea about politics and don't know who to vote for. I don't have that problem because we talk about it a lot at home. My dad's always been a supporter of the Green Party because they help the environment. So, because he knows a lot about it I think I'll vote for them too. We're having a debate at school about the different parties next week. I hope they ask me to speak.

S5: Most of my friends use e-books these days but you wouldn't catch me doing that! I love the feel of a book in my hands and you can look ahead and backwards so easily. I'm absolutely positive that paper books will never disappear. No one agrees with me and they say I'm old-fashioned. But I don't care – that's what I'll say in the debate tomorrow. That's what I believe! Scientists also say that we remember things much better if we read them in paper books and screens make our eyes tired and give us headaches – so … I'm right, aren't I?

Made in the USA
Monee, IL
28 April 2026